TO ALL APPEARANCES

TO ALL APPEARANCES

Ideology and Performance

Herbert Blau

New York and London

First published 1992
by Routledge
a division of Routledge, Chapman and Hall Inc.
29 West 35th Street, New York, NY 10001

Simultaneously published in Great Britain
by Routledge
11 New Fetter Lane, London EC4P 4EE

© 1992 Herbert Blau

Phototypeset in 10 on 12 point Baskerville by
Intype, London
Printed in Great Britain by
Clays Ltd, St Ives plc

Library of Congress Cataloging-in-Publication Data
Blau, Herbert.
To all appearances: ideology and performance / Herbert Blau.
p.   cm.
Includes bibliographical references and index.
1. Theater.   2. Dramatic criticism.   3. Drama—History and literature—
Theory, etc.   I. Title.
PN2039.B58   1992
792′.015—dc20   91–46688

British Library Cataloguing in Publication Data
Blau, Herbert
To all appearances: ideology and performance.
I. Title
792.01

ISBN 0–415–01364–X   ISBN 0–415–01365–8 (pbk)

There is no longer any doubt – the struggle against ideology has become a new ideology.

Bertolt Brecht,
quoted by Walter Benjamin, in Reflections

It has nothing to do with ideology. There is no ideology and never has been.

Gilles Deleuze and Félix Guattari,
A Thousand Plateaus

We split, we split, we split!

William Shakespeare, The Tempest

CONTENTS

CONTENTS

CONTENTS

FOREWORD

A book is always at hazard in the movements of history; even if theoretical, perhaps inevitably out of phase. Yet since I first wrote about the theater in the image of the Cold War, as if that alarming stalemate were the human condition itself, there's been an inclination to think about performance as the tremulous shadow of social and political history, even as the history was more or less in the making. The quite obvious liability is merely keeping up with it, despite the now conditioned reflex of the readiest sidelong glance. The problem was compounded in the current project by what I had chosen to write about – performance and ideology as shadows of each other – and the rather unexpected bearing upon the subject of the history breaking around it. While that was actually more *in* than out of phase with the drift of thought in the book, it was also breaking so fast that I had to absorb as I went along what the media, for the most part, were exulting about, and what, given my concerns, I couldn't just leave to peripheral vision: the apparent failure of ideology just about everywhere in the world. What it means for performance is still in the shadows, but it brought a certain urgency to my usual habit – carried over into theory from long practice in the theater – of keeping a wary eye on surrounding events. Now and again I've found myself revising passages to update something that happened the other night or, since the writing was started in Milwaukee and finished in Paris, that looked rather different in another country.

That *was* to be expected. We live in a stream of consciousness that is, to all appearances, incessantly subject to change. But the writing of this book, more and more as it approached an end, corresponded to a period in which the world was, in an especially precipitous way, going through radical transformation. Or that seemed at first like radical transformation. That changed, almost as precipitously, into widespread seizures of radical doubt. Although I've been making frequent revisions in order to give an immediacy to certain ideas, I've done so with an old (aesthetic) reserve about the blessings of immediacy. I also realize as I do it that there is more than a certain vanity in trying to equilibrate thought with the rapidity of events. This becomes a rather bizarre enterprise in the age of information, *en direct*, when everything seems to conspire with history in the form of rapidity itself, as if in reality too swift for a past. Or as if the mortifying infinity of tomorrow and tomorrow and tomorrow had become at last, through the rushing syllables of recorded time, the future in the instant. How much of a future that leaves us is up for grabs, but there were some obsessive weeks in Paris when I was watching avidly, between sentences, CNN accounts from Baghdad, and correspondents from Washington and London and Moscow and all over the Middle East, reporting a war in which the instantaneity of technology had the curious effect of *distancing* us from occurrences, so that while everything is accessible at once it seems precisely that warp in space when an accelerating body seems to be heading toward us and swerves away, leaving a bigger gulf in the *mise-en-abîme*.

Back to earth once more, before the ground war began, even the Pentagon was not sure, after the euphoria of the first strikes against Iraq, that it had obliterated either Saddam Hussein's air force – which was thought buried in impenetrable bunkers before it took off to Iran – or his command structure. But the smart bombs did their job, leaving the rest of us behind, dazzled by competencies we could hardly understand, including the Hail Mary! maneuver that abruptly ended the war. All of this was explained, to be sure, with charts and briefings and round-the-clock news, but there we were – never mind the Kurds or the Palestinians in the wings – with occurrences entering consciousness at very nearly the speed of light, in the only too familiar postmodern condition: a miracle of awareness psychically cut off, no better than Fabrice in *The Charterhouse of Parma*, removed on his little stage from the larger designs of history. That still assumes, of course, that history has a design, which has long been at issue with radical doubt. Meanwhile, though our wars are documented as Napoleon might have wished, our access to information has come to seem, even discounting what the briefings hold back, like a blight of excess. And as I tried to leave, or rectify, the traces of what was happening – a sort of filigree in the book of the swift trajectory of events that impelled, supported, or modified its ideas – I felt occasionally like a Patriot missile keeping up with the aleatory moment in the uncertain flight of a Scud, maybe on target, maybe not.

That uncertainty may be reflected in the text by a lapse of tense or slip of chronology, some overlooked discrepancy in the referential field. There are, however, other uncertainties that are more thematically in the grain. This is, it could be said, a book of appearances. When it appears to be about ideology, it is about performance; when it appears to be about performance, it is about ideology. What is it really about? It is, as it seems, about *appearances*, and at just about every appearance – of an idea, an event, an occasion for thought, in the theater, in the world, or the apparent suffusion of the world by theater – it is concerned with the threshold moment in perception or classification when one thing turns into another. Or seems to. While percentages were pretty good for the Patriot missile, it's hard to be accurate about appearances, probably *impossible*, which was the key word in the first book I ever wrote about the theater, and still a fundamental term in my thinking about performance.

Neither intimacy with the subject nor an impartial distance makes any reliable guarantee in dealing with appearance, though at a given historical moment either intimacy or distance may seem more reliable, or provisionally necessary. That depends on the nature of the appearances, and the point of view from which they are seen. The notion of point of view can be troublesome here, since it's attached to what in recent discourse is the theoretically discredited framework of perspectival thought. If we transpose it, however, to a more acceptable term, say, "subject position" – performative perhaps, but trying to extrude from its perspective the dominance of the specular, an excess of theater – we are thinking ideologically. Which is not to say we are thinking better, although we may have been thinking usefully, thus, for a limited period of time. It may be that this book inclines ideologically to that excess of theater, more or less as a habit of mind. Yet if its partial subject is ideology, it is a book without a thesis. It has, rather, a sense of things, derived (I think) from years of working in the theater, a form which more than any other is both nurtured and disturbed by, or subject to, the contingencies of appearance.

I wish I could say – to use the title of a poem by Wallace Stevens – that it is a plain sense of things. But then, the titles of Stevens' poems are likely to be misleading, a matter of appearance, or as if the intention were betrayed by what he is trying to be plain about. I think that's likely to be the case when you talk about performance. Even if it weren't entangled with ideology, which it may very well betray.

Paris
April 1991

ACKNOWLEDGMENTS

However it may be with performance, there is one place, at least, where reliability does seem to be guaranteed: the Center for 20th Century Studies at the University of Wisconsin – Milwaukee. While I have more than once attested to that, in this respect redundancy is a pleasure.

First of all, two dear friends: though she is no longer at the Center, I have some leftover reasons for gratitude to Jean Lile, a woman of unfailing grace who did, however, disappoint me once over the course of years, by scheduling her retirement party when I was away; as for Carol Tennessen, she does so many things so unobtrusively well that I'm sure there were occasions overlooked on which I should have thanked her before, no less those I trust will accumulate for years to come. Kim Novak, who came on the scene as a temporary replacement, made herself instantly indispensable, and should remain forever; so, too, with Barbara Obremski, who among other services rendered takes software codes in stride, in the case of this book permitting the text to travel on the right-sized disks. Among others at the Center who have been particularly helpful on this project were my former research assistant Brian Doherty; while she was at UWM, Laura Gray; and David Crane, who may regret reading another manuscript with such scruple to detail that it made him a natural to prepare the index for this. I won't say anything here about Kathleen Woodward, director of the Center, but my double good fortune is that I can thank her at home.

The idea for this book was picked up by Janice Price of Methuen, now with Routledge, after I had done a talk on ideology and performance that was later published by *Theater Journal*. I am grateful for her alertness and subsequent patience while the book was waiting its turn among other commitments in the long theoretical project with which I've been engaged for more than a decade. The material of the essay has either been dispersed or considerably expanded into chapter 2. A part of chapter 3 has been published (by MIT Press) in *The Drama Review*, edited again by Richard Schechner, whose vigorous thought I've enjoyed, in friendship, since he was about to launch that journal into the politics of the sixties. The

ACKNOWLEDGMENTS

opening sequence of chapter 1 appeared in *Critical Theory and Performance*, edited by Janelle Reinelt and Joseph Roach (University of Michigan Press).

1

STATUTES OF LIMITATIONS

TELLING IT LIKE IT IS

Many years ago I thought I could get a performance out of an actor by naming his or her blindness. I prided myself on a certain analytical power, not only in respect to the text but to the textuality of the psyche. What went with that was, to be sure, the necessity of a director: skill at reading signs, signs of behavior, what made a performance and also undid it, habits, tics, giveaway reflexes, the pathology of a surface, as well as the fantasy text of a subtext which was palpable self-evasion. As soon as I felt anything like that I would, as if with a Geiger counter on the originary trace, go right to the heart of the matter. It was like being a moral monitor at the level of the drives. If I could tell the actor precisely what was, in any appearance, being repressed, that ought to solve the problem.

Putting aside the onerous aspect of *getting* a performance out of anybody, there was reason to think I had misgauged the dimensions of an issue for which Brecht, defining it in other terms, had proposed another method. The subconscious has a bad memory, he had remarked, the actor's psyche so impaired by the production apparatus of a class-divided society that it is "not at all responsive to guidance."[1] Which doesn't mean that it is merely quiescent, nor quite reducible to ideology, whose relation to performance is the subject of this book. What I shall say about ideology is not meant to enter the proliferous debates on that matter among neo-Marxists ("a veritable deluge," as Stuart Hall has said of the early eighties[2]), but to deploy a term that may, with its risks of reification, bear upon the materialities of performance, particularly in their resemblance. If this makes for somewhat looser-minded thought than stricter theory would allow, I trust it will be loose with the rigor of performance – especially as it is engaged with what memory wants to forget. (I shall be referring in the book to various performance events outside the structure of institutional theater, but what I have in mind at the moment is best considered there, in relation to the precarious art of acting, which in the theater as we mostly know it has a long investment in psychological depth.) Damaged,

1

preempted, colonized as it may be, the subconscious can also be stubborn, with the ingenuity of amnesia. In the more or less Nietzschean form of an active forgetting, that may be making ideological claims of its own.

This is an obscure if generic aspect of performance that is perhaps best characterized by the apparent resistance of the finest, most dutiful of actors to what seems inviolable in a text. Or, more obscurely, to the undeniable logic of a director's best conception with which the actor seems to be, and believes s/he is, in complete accord. Yet there s/he is, conspicuously if unconsciously – or with the minimal measure of hypocrisy requisite to acting – doing it another way. "No cause, no cause," says the unspecious Cordelia (*Lear* 4.7.74) – who *did* object to the conception – when her own stubbornness was justified by the humiliated king, whose original *mise-en-scène* went so horribly wrong. If we tend to think of an Iago (depending on how we think) as the most (un)canny or subtle of actors, there are also actors in whom, like Cordelia, the line between acting and being may be far more subtle yet. So it appears to have been with Eleanora Duse who acted, we are told (by Rilke, among others), without any false rhetoric or rhetoric at all, no sign, no sign, in what seems to have been the pure unprotected semiosis of self-effacing performance. Or what's even more perplexing, the materialization of performance in its emptying out, the nothing which comes of nothing: in the mirror without an image, the apotheosis of absence. This would appear to be as far from ideology as performance can imagine itself.

Or as deep into ideology as it can be without knowing it. For there is a sense in which "ideology curves back upon itself, creating outside of itself a void that cannot be explained because it is, precisely, nothing."[3] This is the space without boundaries in which ideology seems to merge with the structure of the unconscious, from whose (unimaginable) coign of vantage there is no frontier to cross because there is no geography, nor any existence but its own. A null, a nothingness, it is an existence without a history, which is what Freud appeared to have had in mind when he proposed that "the unconscious is eternal." And it is precisely this metapsychological notion of Freud's that Althusser had in mind, "word for word," when he thought of history without a subject and ideology as eternal, that is, not transcendent or without temporality, "but omnipresent, trans-historical and therefore immutable in form throughout the extent of history . . . exactly like the unconscious."[4]

If there were times when the habits of an actor also seemed immutable in form, exactly like the unconscious (and nothing in its emptiness as lustrous as that of Duse), one of the things I had to learn is that repression in the actor has remarkable versatility or resources of displacement. Adept as I was at reading a text, what I'd missed at the outset was the sticking point in, say, the plays of Ibsen or O'Neill, the paradox of enlightenment, whose dubious brilliance not only informs and darkens the entire history

2

of the canonical drama but is, in the avid ritual of exposure and self-discovery, the nervous threshold of every rehearsal. What I found myself discovering through countless rehearsals – and with every rehearsal, the recessive economy of revelation – is what should have been self-evident to begin with: telling it like it is can be a disaster. That seems inarguable enough after the exhaustive intimacies and calamitous truths of a Hickey or Gregers Werle. But even with Brechtian distance, honesty is by no means the best policy. So the perverse pragmatics of the Brechtian text suggests, no less the perversity of a form which is – in either minimizing or emphasizing its own presence, letting you know it's theater or pretending that it's not – verified by or verifying illusion.

Over and over we learn, as it is in life so it is in theater, which in its reflexive mirror doubles the inadequacy of any truth. Regarded thus, theater is the instrumental virtue that gives the lie to life – in the doubly unjudgeable sense of *giving*: refusing it as a lie and endowing it with falsehood at once. So it was with my own truthtelling about the inadequacy of the actor's truth; it merely doubled the bind. It was particularly chastening to discover that, far from being the solution to this conundrum, I had with the blindness of insight in naming the blindness become an instrumental part of the actor's problem. Perhaps the most grievous part. Such is the aesthetics of candor. About which, and the illusions of demystification, I shall have more to say in other contexts.

CREDIBILITY AND COMMODIFICATION

No matter that I wanted to maintain credibility with the actor. Aside from the risk that the desire for credibility is an effect of vanity, what accounts for it in performance remains elusive in method. Credible in respect to what? for whom? where? when? who speaks? it is hard to say, though most of us instinctively say it even while, theoretically, denying we can speak for others or while dismantling the ideological frameworks within which judgments are made. Meanwhile the actor, constrained to accept the fiction that it is the audience "in the last instance" that determines any truth, goes about establishing credibility in performance – at least within the structure of our theater – by duplicities of which even s/he is unaware. This meets its match (or *méconnaissance*) in the complicity of the audience. (In the mutual admiration society of certain forms of alternative theater – where alienation, camp, and ideology embrace – the acting may be broader and, in a masquerade of awareness, the complicity even thicker.) The history of the drama provides us with prototypes of the actor who, resisting the entire process, refuses to play the actor, making matters worse. So it is in the conception of Alceste by Molière, an actor himself with the acutest mastery of the idea of acting, and a sense of its duplicity that goes much deeper yet, since it directs itself at the end of all honesty to the desperation of duplicitous *need*. "Pretend, pretend that you are just and true,/And I will do my best to believe in you."[5] Thus Alceste to Célimène, who has no trouble pretending, but can't quite guarantee anything like that, even if Alceste, giving audience to her pretense, could keep his part of the bargain.

There is in any case a critical gap between repression and pretense, the construction of an appearance and, more or less overdetermined, the appearance of indeterminacy. If the character of Célimène moves through the play something like the principle of indeterminacy, submitting herself to the world's gaze, it is the actress who performs Célimène who is in this regard (the consistency of her caprice) more indeterminable yet. (Let me not complicate this with the possibility that she might be, in a disengendered theater, played by a man, and not only in the Theater of the Ridiculous, where the candor of the aesthetic, its *jouissance*, includes playing it in drag.) From the evidence of his texts, what Molière understood is that, for all the display, the actor is accountable to the rites of repression. The crucial issue is *concealment*, as it is in ideology, linked as it has been, crucially, to the fetishism of commodities, with its grounding in appearances as seductive as Célimène, the factitious or phantasmic character of commodity form.

That the image of the woman has itself been linked, through the entire history of the theater, to the status of a commodity has been, we know, the ideological burden of much recent theory, as of all kinds of feminist performance, whether in compensatory drama on a conventional stage or in the more experimental hybrids of the gallery scene. So far as the theater, however, has perpetuated the image of woman as absence or empty signifier it has also revealed in its concealment the historical, if not generic, reality of the actor: that there is, irrespective of gender, *no way of escaping the commodity form*. If that does much to explain, at least in the profession today, the psychopathology of the actor, the other side of the coin is that there are actors not blind to this at all, who never thought otherwise, and with the inarguable aura of expensive commodities turn that knowledge into a stage presence that is, with the acquiescence of the audience, something more than a facsimile of power. Between such actors and the recessiveness of a Duse there is the very difficult question of what constitutes power in acting, as well as an entire spectrum of attitudes about what the theater is and what it should be, with more or less conviction about the (ir)relevance of ideology or with more or less utopian vision of going, like Artaud's actor signaling through the flames, beyond ideology.

THE CAMERA OBSCURA

Compared by Marx in its operations to a camera obscura, ideology has developed over the years an always questionable and erratic reputation –

all the more so after events in Eastern Europe, its apparent exhaustion there. (If usage of the term is also erratic, Marx himself is partly to blame. For while it could be said that it was with *The German Ideology* that the concept came of age, it by no means arrived with any strict definition.[6] As for the subsequent sparse or uneven commentary in Marx's later writings, it had nothing like the analytical rigor brought to labor, capital, surplus value, and the concept of fetishism as well.) Subsumed as it has been in the dimension of the imaginary, we tend to think of ideology with a certain wariness or instinctive melodrama, if not as mere dogma,[7] as an inverted image of life that can only be distrusted, and distrusted all the more if we accept Marx's proposition that the reality inverted has already been inverted by the relations of production, leaving us doubly deceived.[8] As there are also actors, however, aware of their status as commodities, who struggle against the realities of the profession, so there is ideology that knows itself as such, and which is, as we say, ideologically committed. It is, nevertheless, the habit of mind cultivated by our sense of reality *as theater* that makes us distrust all commitments as merely effects of partial knowledge. And so it is that with self-reflexive attention to the politics of the unconscious and the theatricality of psychoanalysis, with its dramaturgy of the transference, that we have come to distrust most the one who is presumed to know: the analyst, the director, those heuristic or specular figures expert at exposure while (at least in traditional practice) remaining concealed themselves.

What we learn, however, from the archetypal figures of the drama, Oedipus, Hamlet, who lent their names to psychoanalysis, is that the more the actor shows the more might be in hiding. And the more I named it in the name of truth the more it seemed that I had become a crucial element in the "given circumstances" (Stanislavski's term for what, in the play, grounds the rehearsal, repression's agency or double, the parlous ground of inhibition). Here one begins to feel more than a little like Alceste. *Must one see it and not say it?* As I put my unerring finger on the actor's secret drive, naming it for what it was, I had not thought much about the insidious power of naming.

Nor could I make anything like the distinctions involved in Freud's reading of signs, a conception of interpretation so discerning and bold that, as Lacan remarked in his seminar on "The Direction of the Treatment and the Principles of Its Power," it has been robbed by popularization "of its full mantic significance." What I hadn't quite caught on to in the exposure of a drive, is that the drive in its appearance implies "the advent of the signifier," with "the great compulsive scenario" or slippery slope of the symbolic and its "cryptographical tracing off" into the impasses of the imaginary, where judgments are being made that are profoundly ideological but, like the interpretation going out of sight at the dream's navel, escape all ideological vigilance. Of course, we didn't think then, and directors are

5

unlikely to think now, in either ideological terms or Lacanian language. But Lacan moves the issue into familiar territory when he remarks that what Freud has recovered in the exposure of a drive is "the subject's lines of fate," and adds that "it is the face of Tiresias that we question before the ambiguity in which his verdict operates."[9]

THE FARTHEST EDGE OF LIMIT

I actually staged a production of *Oedipus* quite early in my career, but like those who think they resolve the complex by merely repeating its terms (which is, all told, what most productions do), it may have taken a while before the ambiguity registered. Or the ineluctable lesson about the illusions of exposure: that in attentiveness to the transparency of the symptoms there may be a failure to read the equivocating signs. For whatever the verdict was, I also thought at the time, with something like oedipal presumption, that there was not an actor living that I couldn't make respond to the force of an *idea*. Or an image. Or some powerfully developed concept of what was, if he, or she, only *saw* it, possible in the role, though s/he not only didn't see it but couldn't even imagine it – or gave up believing years ago, if the truth were known, that such a thing was possible for her or him at all. I blush to think of the number of actors – actors who admired and even loved me – that I tried to get to do things they could never do because *I* wanted them done (the prospect exhilarating! the conception brilliant!), and what's more that they tried to do, against their self-conceptions, *because* they loved or admired me or – as I did acquire the authority of a director (with all its job-giving power) – because they were simply afraid. I believe that I learned over the years that what *is* possible for a given actor has to be determined by the actor's own sense of what in the most suggestive circumstances remains within range, so that possibility may be released at the farthest edge of limit. No idea will survive the unnamable stage fright of an actor who knows – with whatever desire, idealism, faith, determination, or self-surrender – that s/he is simply not up to it. Not now, here, under the circumstances materially given (and with *you* present), perhaps never.

There is also the chastening point when ideas are not up to it either. Or pushing too hard, overplaying or growing rigid, like the "unperfect actor" of Shakespeare's sonnet, "Who with his fear is put besides his part" (23.1–2). Assuming to begin with a certain quality of mind, a seriousness about ideas, an engagement in a "community of the question"[10] with the fact that there *is* a question, one can expect from ideas only certain limited possibilities under particular historical conditions. There is much talk about transgression in theory, but one sees very little of it in performance, either with actors or with ideas. Even the most audacious of actors needs the most auspicious of circumstances to leap boundaries. What we look

6

for is the propitious meeting between history and desire, or as Artaud perceived the site of "essential theater," between dream and events. No more is possible to any given idea under constraints of time and objective conditions than is possible for a particular actor under constraints of training, psychological makeup, the director's presence, the other actors, the production scheme, the means and relations of production, the staging, the opening date, the deadline, and in the United States the still-marginalized profession itself, including the material conditions of (mostly) unemployment. As for the submerged ideas, half ideas, half-baked ideas, mere guesswork, fantasies, ghosts of thought and fragments of apprehension, the phantom objectivity that (in one of its definitions) makes up ideology, one hardly knows what is possible to that – though Althusser suggests that just because such ideas are taken for granted, or "govern us without our consent,"[11] they are not necessarily invalidated, aesthetically or politically useless.

Any idea, fertile as it may have been, wears out its welcome, and some ideologies have been liberating for their little moment and lethal the next. We all know that. It is the one truth that should be self-evident as we come to the end of the twentieth century, with its repertoire of ideological slaughter. I suppose, however, that if it *were* self-evident, then the very notion of revolution with its promise of living truth – the belief that it could really happen, *must* happen – would not be possible. The necessity of this blindness – the discrepancy between what we know and what we may choose to forget – accounts in large measure for the ideological nausea in the mordancies of Heiner Müller, as in the bloodbath of *The Task* or the grotesquerie of his *Macbeth*. The mordancies were given another twist in the version I saw by the Stadttheater of Hanover at Experimenta 6 in Frankfurt, where the grisly joke for a mostly young and already jaded audience, absorbing with mixed delight and derision the collapse of ideology along with the onerous Wall, was upon the "velvet" lining of the idea of revolution itself. It's as if they were taking for granted, even before the accelerated unification of East and West, the spontaneous reproduction of the Same.

This is not quite the same, however, as the subliminal accretions of ideology or ideology that like the common cold merely sneaks up on us, occluding the origin of value in the relative innocence of "false consciousness," which Althusser was trying to rescue, in his notion of an ideology "spontaneously lived" (*For Marx* 150), from mere self-deceit. There are, to be sure, elements of false consciousness wherever in language we turn our thought. Yet as we think of ideology in any committed sense, as a body of thought to which we give our bodies, it's well to remember another thing that memory tries to forget: if there is something mortifying in thought itself that is particularly deadened when institutionalized, that is all the more so when it turns, in the guise of a critical practice, into

7

the great compulsive scenario of rectitude. As Müller obsessively shows, sometimes with a jaundice to the point of self-revulsion, there is no exemption in all this for revolutionary thought, and in the art of this century we have seen – out of the most admirable idealism *or* rigorous critique – liberating affinities with totalitarianism.

WHAT REMAINS TO BE DONE?

"In the destructive element, immerse," said Conrad, enunciating the principle which gave subversive energy to high modernism. Immersed itself in a correct politics, the same principle seemed to congeal the thought of certain heroic figures who, in disjunct and fractured, exemplary forms of art, taught us to hold contradictory ideas in the mind at the same time. For some now engaged in the critique of modernism, that was the problem to begin with: not the correct politics, but the wrong politics, marked by contradictions. There are any number of variants on the theme, but the lamentable binarism or schizoid split in the case of Ezra Pound may be read as a cautionary tale of an alienated culture virtually consumed by contradictions. "In Pound," wrote Charles Olson after his visit to St Elizabeth's, "I am confronted by the tragic double of our day. He is the demonstration of our duality. In language and form, he is forward, as much the revolutionary as Lenin. But in social, economic, and political action he is as retrogressive as the Czar."[12]

But if Olson's view of the revolutionary in Pound seems a little hyperbolic, consider Gramsci on the futurists, who were sufficiently distressing to a socialist politics even before, like Pound, their affiliation with fascism. "What remains to be done?" Gramsci wrote in 1921 – one of the landmark years of the modern – echoing Lenin. The answer is still being echoed by certain of the more schizoanalytical voices and radical practices of the postmodern: "Nothing other than to destroy the present form of civilization . . . . It means not to be afraid of innovations and audacities, not to be afraid of monsters." Pointing out that the futurists grasped the necessity for new forms, philosophy, behavior, and language, Gramsci identified this as a "sharply revolutionary and absolutely *Marxist* idea," in which socialists were not even vaguely interested, though they had, according to Gramsci, no idea of their own, not even political or economic. If the socialists were frightened at the prospect of having to shatter the machine of bourgeois power, the working class, which could hardly imagine it, would take a long time before it could do "anything more creative than the futurists [had] done."[13]

If this evaluation of the foresight of futurism was, at the time, not absolutely accurate, it was sufficiently on the mark. As we think of it now, however, what seems to me important in the sharply revolutionary and absolutely Marxist *idea* is the degree to which it turned by innovations

8

and audacities into something else. Whereupon we might conclude, retro-spectively, that it was not so sharp and absolute to begin with. Or too much so. And that the contradictions had always soiled or invalidated whatever truth there was in the idea, as with Marxism itself almost every-where in the world. Particularly where it released the monsters. Which are always more tolerable in theory and fiction than they are in human form. Or for that matter, in the human form of theater, as we may see on the edge of taboo in certain excesses of rehearsal, or in actual performance when something of that excess, the uncontrollable mystery, breaks the frame of pretense and is about to spill over the stage.

Yet if there is in all its diminished (or monstrous) truth one Marxist imperative which seems inarguable, that is the necessity to *historicize*. No doubt that process will be moving through habitual categories, the concep-tual sediments in the dynamics of interpretation. With all due vigilance about our own reflexes, and the "intangible historicity"[14] with which, designating a context, we may confound it with origins, we must also remember that contradictions, too, are a matter of context. What appears to be systemic may only be so by hindsight. Or it may be more ambiguous than that, adventitiously subject to the course of events, a latency in the system released by history, though it mightn't have been released if it weren't *that* system. Thus it might be said that certain ideas can give rise to certain pernicious effects in history while it's hard to imagine others taking the same course.

But taking a cue from Ronald Reagan, let's "stay the course" for a moment by moving back in history, to one of the great periods in which politics and the image of statecraft were at the heart of theater and vice versa: the early seventeenth century. There we can see another factor that is, in its analysis of power, at the anguished faultline of Jacobean drama. So it is in the cracked brain of Lear when he is weighing contradictions in the extremities of the sky, but with a material base in the body and economics as the last instance: "No eyes in your head, nor no money in your purse? Your eyes are in a heavy case, your purse in a light, yet you see how this world goes" (4.6.145–8). Maybe we do, maybe we don't. If it remains the task of ideological analysis to look for contradictions, we must also expect that contradictions will have, depending on "who's in, who's out" (5.3.15) and the predisposition of analysis (not quite the same as its intangible historicity), a more or less benign or inimical face.

Our eyes are in a heavy case, however, in Matthias Langhoff's production (Paris, 1991) of John Webster's *The Duchess of Malfi*, a sort of post-punk roundelay of cadavers or ebullient literalization of an economy of death, with "good" and "bad" characters coming out of the grave. Picking up cues from the compositional habits of Webster's texts, the collaged performance is enormously inventive, with the immense enthusi-asm of its heterogeneity (Caravaggio and walkie-talkies, Pergolese on the

9

sax, luminous tulips and *coups de théâtre* of pure gadgetry and kitsch) as a mad facsimile of liberating power, as if the cemetery at Père Lachaise (with Jim Morrison's grave near Héloise and Abelard, not far from Proust) were the necrophilic site of an optimistic aesthetic. But as the living and the dead – or all indifferently, the living dead – confirm what amounts to a Bedlam of value, the wiping out of distinctions may have gone too far. It is a view of history, and the operations of power, as nothing but pernicious effects, not the least of which is that, as we try to sort out the contradictions, what is true of statecraft is also true of its critique – which is, I suppose, what Webster saw in a character like Bosola, or Flamineo in *The White Devil*, despite the unerring trenchancy of the critique.

Returning to our own century, we may not want to accept the extremity of this view, but Lear's measure of who's in, who's out is no less germane, as we try to assess the analysis of power, even by theorists we might respect. For example: despite contradictions and, like Adorno, an indisposition to certain new forms (non-hegemonic, like black music[15]), Gramsci himself is *in* with American intellectuals looking for ideas to justify a political function in the academy; but he came in just as he was going *out* with Italian intellectuals, who felt his ideas exhausted by their having become scripture in the Italian Communist Party, which was even before the events in Eastern Europe thinking of changing its name. The name has now been changed to the Democratic Party of the Left, but before that the loose gathering of its uncertain constituency was, through the ideological transition, temporarily called The Thing. Which was not, I gather, the thing itself.

Thus, some of the intellectuals, whether "organic" (Gramsci) here or by "weak thought" (Viattimo) there, are also looking for ways ("non-totalizable") of thinking past contradictions, or without contradictions. What makes things more complicated, however, is an unpurged sense of permanent crisis that was the constituting agency and legacy of modernism. Sustaining itself with more or less advanced paranoia, this crisis-addiction of modernism certifies for its critics (Marxist, psychoanalytical, poststructuralist, feminist) that it is the symptomatic mirror image of advanced capitalism, divided to begin with in the apparent rationality of its logic of domination, tearing itself apart with contradiction. The most radical ambition, perhaps, of postmodernism is to shatter the mirror itself, or in a kind of homeopathy of hemorrhaging image to void it like the Taoist mirror that is a reflective surface without an image. Meanwhile, the hemorrhage is unabating, and in the "society of the spectacle" – *capital* accumulating to such a degree that it becomes an image[16] – we seem to be dealing with a hemophiliac. Or, for those who see the spectacle congealing in its dispersion, the arterial possibility of a massive clot.

AN IMMENSE REALITY

Without laboring the mixed medicine or a diagnosis in the mirror, there was certainly good reason for the critique of modernism, and for searching out a counterlogic or alternative forms of thought. Nor is there any reason I can think of for art to remain the same, even if that may threaten, as it periodically has threatened, to dissolve the categories, collapse genres, and abolish the idea of art. One of the claims made over the last generation, in the debates over minimalism, is that it was not only the anesthetic global spectacle but, more locally, the dematerialization of art into theatricality that threatened the death of art.[17] What has been, however, doubly perplexing to critique is, for all its contradictions, the durability of advancing capitalism and, for all the collapsing of genres, the recurrence of categories and the stubbornness of art.

Yet if the art object is returning, it is returning with a high quotient or consciousness of theatricality, and performance itself as a somewhat autonomous phenomenon is in various mutations still on the scene, the (im)materiality of its passing strangeness having passed over into a theater of images (and from thence to MTV) which had very mixed feelings about escaping the hegemony of art. It was during this period of innovation and audacities, with its valorization of body language, that performance was for a time dissociated in experimental theater, and still in critical theory, from the (allegedly) repressive dramaturgy of the oedipal tradition. There are residual contradictions here that could be examined, but the idea of performance has become in theory, and in all the humanistic disciplines, an exemplary model or heuristic principle: a form of inquiry which is materialized in the bodily succession of signifiers that is emptied into thought, consuming itself thus and, so the theory goes, escaping commodification.

It is curious, however, that this seems to describe (in much the same words I used earlier) the acting of Eleanora Duse, whose destiny it apparently was in forsaking rhetoric to become a fetish. That's surely what she was to Rilke when he described the "unutterably touching" quality of a performance in which, "so slight, so bare, without pretext of a role," she virtually disappeared from the eyes of the audience as if, in a premonitory instance of recent film theory, she had read its specularity as an appropriative gaze. The power of theater has always been in the mystery of its vanishings; yet what are we to make of her hiding there, "as children hide," with her hair, her hands, or a spray of roses before the face "on which they preyed," or her fingers crossed in a sign to ward off the evil eye? Sublimely, subliminally, is it an escape or a seduction? For, in Rilke's evocation, as her performance moved toward an "immense reality," still recoiling from (or with?) the "long gossamer threads" of the gaze, the spectators were "already breaking into applause: as though at the last

11

moment to ward off something that would compel them to change their life."[18] Someone like Chekov would say the odds are against it: except for appearances nothing would change, or maybe a hundred years or a thousand years in the future, despite the sublimity of the performance or, in a peculiar inversion of the pure natural exposure of a self, its *alienation*. Whatever this memorable performance may have been – and we can only guess at a distance, or fantasize – it does suggest in a sort of tripled paradox of the mirror of production the suture between the image of woman as consummate absence, the idea of acting itself, as most accomplished when wholly consumed, and the empty or occulted nature of the commodity.

This immense reality has, of course, been the subject of severe distrust, while the notion of woman as absence has been, if not strategically adopted as the ironic virtue of an imposed defect, severely rejected as a historical burden. There is more to be said, however, about the variable manifestations of acting that appears, by method or mystique, other than acting, and about the body that (dis)appears in the ghostly procession of signifiers. (Or in a kind of parody of this spectral phenomenon, as when Laurie Anderson clones herself on PBS, enfolding the self's identity into the mediatized image, as if giving itself over not to the procession of signifiers but to "the precession of simulacra" (Baudrillard).) For this is an ideological problem of some consequence in the ontology of theater, as one might expect it to be as well in "the postmodern condition," in so far as that is inseparable – through the crudest public display of the *bruitism* of heavy metal or the myriad gossamer threads of alluring image – from the commodified spectacle itself, or the spectacle as the pure venereal "nature" of commodification.

SUBTEXT OF THE SPECTACLE

But we came to reflect upon that condition by way of the modernist obsession with crisis, which remains the ruptured and dismembered subtext of the spectacle. And while we continue to seek theoretical alternatives to a thwarting binarism or a phallic formalism or the sovereign reach of modernist desire – its collusion with the principle of sovereignty itself – we are no further along, in the massive commodification of culture, in responding massively to the last of Marx's theses on Feuerbach: so much for interpretation, let's get on with change – unless it be, as in the immediate aftermath of revolution in Eastern Europe, the massive desire for commodities. I am not saying this ironically. In a recent colloquy at the Festival of Avignon (summer 1990), Ewa Walch, dramaturg of the Deutsches Theater in East Berlin, spoke discerningly and compassionately about precisely this development in relation to the future of the theater in what was the DDR. After years of unquestioned subvention and reliable audiences, there is now confusion in the repertoire and vast insecurity in the work force. "Today," she said, "our theaters are half empty. Since last October, the public has left the theater for the street. Very few of them have returned. The large majority have rather made the trip to the supermarkets of the West. It is unthinkable to condemn this attitude, but it is a true problem for the theater."[19]

Meanwhile, if there has been some change, revolutionary or otherwise, since the (somewhat indeterminate) advent of modernism, nothing recent in our given circumstances – from deconstruction to *perestroika* to the incursion on the economy of Japanese microchips – suggests that the situation of crisis has in any way abated, except as wish fulfillment. If there is something more than wish fulfillment in the emancipation of Eastern Europe, the euphoria has already abated into a host of new problems, from the economy and governance to ethnic minorities, tribal vendettas, latent fascism, and the perils of uneven development – not to mention the deflection of worldwide attention, weapons, and financing to the Middle East, when suddenly, unexpectedly, Iraq invaded Kuwait, providing a geopolitical cover for new repression in the Soviet Union. At best we might be able to say – in the rhetoric of the postmodern, as in newer modes of performance or $L=A=N=G=U=A=G=E$ poetry – that the situation of crisis has been put into the subjunctive. Nor has there been any appreciable change in the existential sense of impermanence itself, with pollution everywhere and ozone depletion threatening, and the cataclysmic irony (fortunately, of course, in remote parts of the world) of exploding populations imperiled by AIDS. Such things fall, sometimes unnamably, into what American-Soviet negotiators have called "the fifth basket" (beyond the usual agenda of arms control, human rights, bilateral relations, and regional conflicts). Aside from oil spills and radioactive waste, it's the collocation of the uncontrollable, what even in contemplation can make a basket case of us all, in ways that weren't even imagined in the most paranoid days of the Age of Anxiety: drugs and terror at every level, not only systemic but insidiously viral, and with bootleg missiles and poison gas a vengeful fundamentalism besides that may soon have, beyond its faithful masses and human waves, the technological resources to match its rage.

I'm not concerned at the moment with what's historically justifiable, what not, nor the sum of former depredations for which bourgeois imperialism will be held accountable by history, only the cumulative animosities staring us in the face, some of them, for whatever good historical reasons, almost demented. At the same time, what may be a saving grace or last-ditch defense against all this – aside from "the forces of moderation" everywhere – is not anything so spaced out or conjectural as Star Wars (though the Scuds over Israel and Patriot missiles have given some encouragement to that). It is, rather, the multinationalization of capitalism itself,

13

and the fact that with the unsteady dollar we nevertheless still own, with exponential growth, much of the fantasy life of the world. What I am referring to here has been the major focus of recent critique: the coloniz- ation of the unconscious on an international scale by American forms of desire, attached as they are to the supposedly defunct values of the bour- geois Enlightenment (a virtual litany of which we heard in the inaugural speech of Vaclev Havel as president of Czechoslovakia). That, and the blade-running impetus of cultural diffusion – most important of which is the deterrent presence on American soil of heavy investment from else- where, real estate holdings by Arabs and Japanese, with bankers-in- residence and other personnel – this may keep us, against the actuarial tables or ressentiment or the unburied curses of the Ayatollah, from the devastation we never experienced through two world wars, not to mention, before the bombardment of Baghdad, the defoliation of the jungles. Which is not to say that the pacifying effect of diffusion will not find more immediate and local reasons – including the unimaginable poverty no longer unimaginable, since if it's not on television it's right there on the streets – for further rage and murderous division.

Whatever the disinformation on the six o'clock news – or as a postmod- ern manifestation, the dispersive effect of its spastic, incongruous, fragmented images – one thing would seem to have been documented conclusively: we still live in an age which seems to have been struck from history in the form of contradiction. And to return on that "wobbling pivot" of a palpable truth (if I may use a Confucian phrase from Ezra Pound) to the issue about the durability of ideas under particular historical conditions: it would seem that contradiction has been absorbed as some- thing more than myth (or mythology in Barthes' sense) into the ideology that is spontaneously lived, where it is, if politically or culturally useful at all (in Althusser's sense) more like the condition of its spontaneity. As for the instrumental promise of anything more consciously programmed, the formulation of models or "subject positions," no less doctrine, the datum would seem to be that no idea can be stable for very long, without contradiction, no less ideologically certified with an extended life expect- ancy. What remains to be done is still the major issue, but it hardly takes a commitment to modernist obscurantism to believe that Freud was as close as we're likely to come to the truth of thought when he said we must learn to live in uncertainty and doubt.

THE IDEOLOGICAL MOMENT/SHADOW OF A MAGNITUDE

If that doesn't mean there should be no ideological analysis, we are still left with the question of who is doing it? to what end? with what *predis- position?* and the degree to which the end assumes priority over the unrestricted movement of thought. True, there are times when, like

14

the breaking of clocks for the renewal of history, it seems that the free flow of consciousness must have a stop. And there may be an ideological moment, a moment where thought is arrested, as in the ideographic fix of a Brechtian *gestus* or the emblematic still of an Eisenstein film or the temporal pulsation, the closing up of the unconscious, which is the "Gordian knot" of the transference.[20] But the knot is a sort of vortex or, with the obstructed torsive momentum of Hamlet's "mortal coil," a gathering of thought at its limit, where the thought which empowers thought is always escaping itself. What is sometimes forgotten, it seems, is that there is no guarantee in the autonomous movement of thought that it will escape in the right ideological direction.

Ideas may strike us with the force of the absolute, but in history they are of necessity provisional. " . . . all is a – (*he yawns*) – bsolute," says Hamm, in the *mise-en-abîme* that sets the scene for the aporias of Beckett's *Endgame*.[21] Speaking of contradictions, it is Beckett's drama more than any other which, while positing the question of what's to be done as a recursive non sequitur, turns the appearance of paralysis, the ubiquity of its exhaustion, into a sort of reversing warp of entropy that is a reflexive form of energy. Or it's as if, in the hapless labor of diminution, its "exhaustive enumeration," desire were drawing sustenance not from the growth but from the impoverishment of capitalist accumulation. (As a dividend in the process, the *work*, the "impossible heap" – what must be "finished, nearly finished" (*Endgame* 1), the surplus value of the *remainder* – keeps alive, with whatever nostalgia, the modernist question of the power of the aesthetic. Or is it a question, ideologically, of the power of nostalgia? In discussing the problem of affectivity within the provenance of alienation, that is an issue to which we'll return.) However mordantly fractured in Hamm's yawn, the idea of the absolute is still there in Beckett, not merely as conceptual *bricolage* or residues in the text, but in his insistence as well, in his own directing, on the *absoluteness of the music* in the discontinuities of the text.[22] From Plato through Artaud the imagination (imagination dead imagine[23]) has been moved by the vast abstraction of this transcendent idea, the shadow of a magnitude, the Absolute itself. But to all appearances – and this is the aleatoric substance of the Beckettian music – we live in a universe where transformation is the only law, and that appears to contain, however unfortunately, an immemorial statute of limitation on the salutary life of any thought. This does not preclude the possibility that the recession of any thought may undergo a historical rebirth in the return of the repressed. It is hard to think of anything worth thinking – including things that seem at a given time too absurd to think – that does not thus return, though like the materials of the unconscious refigured in thought.

As it emerges from the unconscious, with which, in the bottoming out of intention, it remains forever merged, ideology is itself a temporal pulsation. It is not only a function of time but, as an activating source, *timing* as well. As the actor learns, timing may be acquired as a matter of technique, but it veers in practice back toward the metaphysical, if not in accession to an absolute (though one speaks of absolute timing like absolute pitch), shadowing the magnitude of the eternity of the unconscious. (I have written of this elsewhere, while examining the "origins" or ideological grounds of my own theaterwork, whose metaphysics, I should add, was by no means theological.[24] Thus:) *Take time*, says the director, working against time, in what is for the actor (*take* time or take *time?*) his/her customary double jeopardy or, professionally and ideologically, another version of the double bind. Here we have, perhaps, the unassuageable contradiction, the contradiction of/in time, which escapes analysis in the name of history. This is at the level of praxis, the *making* of theater, what the drama has always known since it articulated in its emergent form – which Aristotle placed between philosophy and history – the appearance of a reality that *looked* like theater.

The forms of theater in turn depend on their attitude toward this appearance. With the ideological consciousness of postmodern theater – extending beyond the proscenium into performance art – we have seen various attempts to minimize the look by exaggerating it or playing with it, if not insisting on its extrusion on behalf of demystification: *this* being theater and *that* being reality. But the reality *is* immense, and like the slippage of the signifiers, not this, *that*, not that, *this*, the trouble with appearance is that it always gets in the way.

BRUSHING HISTORY AGAINST THE GRAIN

As we move, thus, between philosophy and history, whatever it is that appears to be real is what we have to explain, not reality itself, which we can never. At worst, that realization occurs with the anguished iteration of King Lear's never, as if it were the depth charge of appearance itself – "Never, never, never, never, never" (5.3.309) – to which (though better forgotten) it seems we shall ever return. Yet if it is only appearances we are talking about, then we must ask, as the theater does over and over – out of the unnerving implication that appearances are a deceit – why does reality, whatever it is, choose to play false? Which is, in its interrogative substance, as close as we may come to a definition of theater. This may also be, through the camera obscura, as close as we may come to the appearance of ideology.

What appears to be may or may not be, but it has been, in all its seeming substance, a perceptual complication in the dramaturgy of historical materialism. The historical materialist, says Walter Benjamin, in his "Theses on the Philosophy of History," "regards it as his task to brush history against the grain."[25] But like the "secret heliotropism" of the past, "this most inconspicuous of all transformations" (*Illuminations* 255), or like

16

the conception "of the present as 'the time of the now' which is shot through with chips of Messianic time" (263), it seems that something like appearance is doing the brushing. How Marxist is it? – if so suspiciously mystical – has been a question about Benjamin that I won't belabor here. For him, however, those chips irradiate the transformations and, like the talismanic petals on a wet black bough (the charismatic image of imagism), seem to be changing the grain of history. Even crystallized into a monad like the configuration of a *gestus*, they also determine any discrepancy between Benjamin's view of performance and that of Brecht. Where appearance begins to resemble revelation, we are in theory, at least, a considerable way from either Brecht or Marx, though even a Brechtian image in the theater – laminated by perception, or some inalienable glamour in the gaze – is always susceptible to being felt as auratic or epiphanic.

So long as there is in the idea of performance the remotest contingency of *theater*, with its play of appearance, this liability won't disappear. There are various strategies of new performance by which it has been disrupted, but as if the auratic thing itself were merely in abeyance. Thus we have seen – as in an arc of enchantment from Brechtian estrangement – attempts to undermine the supremacy of the specular, or to break up the materiality of the look, displacing the authority of the visual into the supposed immediacy of the other senses, or into the levelling proclivities of other body parts. There have also been events conceived around the actual invisibility of the performer, a disappearance announced (Chris Burden) or unannounced, but later documented (Jochen Gerz). Or we have had, with the somnambulant operas of Robert Wilson, the incantatory extension of the duration of the performance, with a gradual and soporific wearing down of the gaze, allowing the spectators to eat, sleep, converse, doze again, withdraw, as they do in other cultures. Or, with vast distantiation over the actual terrain of another culture, the magnificent sleepwalking project in which Ulay and Abramović approached each other in cosmic meditation over the whole length of the Great Wall of China. Or, no less arduous on an intimate scale, another protracted performance in which duration is an endurance: Linda Montano and Tehching Hsieh attached to each other with an eight-foot rope, living like that for a year.

Yet even on those antiscopic occasions where performance passes out of sight the specular desire is a semantic function of the event. All the more without seeing it, as with a taboo against seeing it, while in the absence of appearance the aura is restored. (Some of these events are now legendary.) It's as if the very imagining of the "*human sensuous activity*" that Marx identified with *practice*[26] could issue in nothing else. This was throughout his career a problem for Brecht, who at one point designated Marx as his ideal spectator. Committed to the idea of theater as a *sensuous materialism* – where "man must prove the truth, that is, the reality and power, the this-sidedness of his thinking in practice" (*Marx–Engels* 144) – Brecht was

17

(in life, in art) attracted if troubled by the turpitude of the senses and the many-sidedness of appearance, whose truth proved itself while escaping into the figuration of Baal. The sensuous activity was already manifest there, but maybe too much so, not only because of its nihilism or affinities with expressionism, but because there seemed to be no way to distinguish, in the libidinal image of the Canaanite god, regeneration from representation. Or, in his ravenously metamorphic appearances, one representation from another. It's as if they were without distinction folded into his nature or, as Baal dies into his appetite, merely accumulating on the bloated body as another layer of flesh.

At the time of *The Threepenny Opera* lawsuit, Brecht wrote: "Practice is always young while ideologies age and are never more than their weakest link: the isolated representation .... Practice watches at the bed of all ideologies, at the foot of their cradle and at their coffin."[27] He would always resist the singular representation of a unitary character as an ideological fix, but as he watched the multiply swollen body of the forever dying god it turned out to be an ideological embarrassment, all the more so in the radiance of its rot. That was, it could be said, sensuous materialism with a vengeance – what we might have expected rather in the plague of Artaud, who like Nietzsche with illusion had no use for appearance if it wasn't epiphanic. In his own delirious labors Artaud was as concerned as any Marxist with material existence or – in his physiology of the theater or "affective athleticism" – the objectification of the subject in a sensuous materialism. As for his view of bourgeois culture, the preface to *The Theater and Its Double* might have been published under the title of one of Marx's essays: "A Ruthless Criticism of Everything in Existence" – including, however, the binaries of western thought that are still operative in the dialectic of Marx. The problem for Artaud was that, with metaphysics coming in through the skin, he saw the division as ontological, and except in his madness irreversible. And it was the desire for an anteriority before separation – or the dream of appearance as *pure manifestation* – that made him want to bring the whole system of reproduction down with him into the abyss.

Within the history of Marxism that apocalypse has been imagined and perilously approached, and in the extremities of deconstruction it has been imagined once again. But in the this-sidedness of his thinking, we are brought by Marx himself to a certain impasse in the concept of praxis, which first appears as labor, whose transformative energy produces material existence. The trouble, we've come to know, is the distribution of labor. As soon as that "comes into being, each man has a particular, exclusive sphere of activity, which is forced upon him and from which he cannot escape" – even, we might add from recent experience, through forms of collective creation or participatory methods or by summoning up holistic energies from other cultures, whether in avant-garde performance with body disciplines from the East or postmodern factories with Japanese warmups. If human beings produce the condition of their freedom, they also fix the conditions of social activity into forms of entrapment, we ourselves producing "an objective power above us, growing out of our control, thwarting our expectations,"[28] as if what happened to Artaud happens to us all and metaphysics were coming in through the skin.

Both theory and performance have struggled through practice to dispel this overbearing power, but what Marx and Engels are describing above would appear to be both the subject matter and the source of subjectivity in the theater. It is certainly imbedded in the canonical drama, which is particularly sensitive to the forms of entrapment, with which the world, subject to division (perhaps of division born), seems only too ready to cooperate. Freud conjectured that the world might have been formed in accordance with the structure of the mind, but it's as if it were constructed as a mockery of consciousness, all of it false, with the senses as a refuge that – whether intersected by history or hermetically sealed or exhausted by *jouissance* – proves unbearable too. This is, of course, the worst possible case. But as we go on brushing history against the grain, it is here we may encounter the vanities of critique, that heightened form of consciousness which will, at the right judicial distance, keep not only the theater but the world from playing false. This is by no means to devalue the necessity of critique, but there are circumstances where critique guarantees neither clarification nor social change. What we fear, I suppose, is that the most ideologically acute, scrupulous critique may, in fact, alter nothing, since the possibility of transcendence is attached to concrete needs of time and place, and in some places the needs are so egregious as to be as much a deterrent as an incitement to action. Sometimes we have the impression that while they are being absorbed into consciousness as commodified images, critique itself is merely keeping up appearances.

O reason not the need! says Lear on his own behalf, before he becomes attentive to the poor naked wretches whereso'er they are. Yet the truth is that needs are so overwhelming in their concreteness, so repetitive, like drought and famine in Ethiopia, that consciousness is only too ready to have its attention deflected, if only to other more assimilable disasters. (Relief agencies attested to this phenomenon when attention shifted from the undifferentiated misery of Africa to Poland or Rumania, or even the Soviet Union.) Here we are dealing with something more than an ideological moment or the shadow of a magnitude, but the real undeniable magnitude itself, as if confirmed on the Richter scale. Here we see the evidence of human failing with the status of a natural catastrophe that, repeating itself as it does, almost seems ontological, like a fault in nature itself. We know better, to be sure, but to deconstruct that fatalistic thought amidst the shifting pressures of geopolitical realities hardly reduces the scale, nor the proportions of our inadequacy to what is likely to persist as

19

a running sore, a wound, of inadmissable dimensions, amidst the brighter indeterminacies of the postmodern condition.

Then there is another kind of problem which is a function of the culture of information. As we confront today the linkage between astonishing misery and disruptions all over the world, what becomes increasingly apparent is that the geopolitical realities are not exactly accessible to perception because, whatever the needs may be (like those of Arabs focused by Saddam Hussein) they are functions of appearance doubly confounded by a complex of representations (including, as I write, the collapse of Saddam Hussein's). What do we make of it? In the processes of demystification, there is the tendency to think of appearance as the private property of capitalism, and its dynamic of reproduction. It may very well be, as Marx thought, that the essence of capitalism is a mask, but there is still cause to wonder if any alternative social order will be able to do without it. Other tribes, other scribes, remarks the anthropologist James Boon, and the same may be true of the mask. What seems to be truer than true – the deepest perception, perhaps, of darkest modernism – is that the mask itself is no illusion. No doubt, the appearances that distort and mystify awareness of the reality of capitalism are also real, but what is it that we know, or can even imagine, that doesn't present itself in disguise? – including, to be sure, the imagining of utopia, which perhaps imagines the end of disguise. So, as a coda or counterpoint to the Hegelian pantomime, there is the old signature mime of Marcel Marceau (maybe borrowed from Rilke), the incessant tearing off of mask upon mask until – is this the end of it, the final disguise? – the torn flesh of the face is the tragic mask itself.

This is a possibility that has been, as in Derrida's essays on Artaud, very disturbing to postmodern thought, as it has been in the historical marrow of theater, no more so than within the reproductive structure of tragedy, which has always been – as promised end, or "image of that horror" (*Lear* 5.3.264–5) – a horror to itself. It could be, as it has always seemed to me, that Marceau's mime was, if beautifully executed, sentimental, only pathetic, though I shall have more to say later about the issue of pathos. The surprising thing about tragedy is that it can still be somehow – with its sadomasochistic pleasure, its perverse sense of proportions and limits, and its conclusive image of the failure of power – empowering, though there has been, since Brecht, an ideological problem in believing that.

PROTOCOLS OF EXPERIENCE AND POLITICAL PRACTICE

While my ideas about the theater are drawn from more than thirty-five years of working them through in rehearsal, they have moved considerably, since I stopped the theaterwork, toward the theoretical, where I have been working them over again. I am not claiming, however, as some theory does, that theory is a praxis at anything like the same level of concreteness. Or if it should happen to be (and I have claimed something like that before as a heuristic fiction), then I want to make the distinction made by Althusser in his preface to the English reader of *For Marx*, where he criticizes himself for not giving in those early essays "precise indications as to the function, place and role of Marxist theory in . . . concrete forms of existence" – and where he does make a precise distinction between "theoretical practice" and "the union of theory and practice within *political practice*" (15). I want to work, however, a reversal into the first distinction, without quite, as Marx did to Hegel, turning Althusser on his head, nor confining the issue to Marxist theory:

I started out by focusing questions of ideology and performance around my own experience with actors. There was in that, as in all the theory derived from my work in the theater, the liability of claiming a phenomeno-logical advantage in Whitmanian terms: I was there, I saw it, I did it. (With affect getting short shrift in theory, I must even admit to a certain affinity with, say, Yeats' truth of the heart, fortified by experience. I shall try, in the last two chapters, to give longer shrift to affect, and maybe the truth of the heart, though prompted to that by Meyerhold, who is normally thought of as a constructivist attached to the truths of science.) This subjectivist impulse of "concrete experience" has been suspect or repudiated from structuralism on, leading eventually to Althusser's own conception of history without a subject. In recent years, however, this anonymous history has also been questioned, as we've become more aware of the geopolitical diaspora of "subject-effects" and the emergence of "authentic" subjects who, rather than being interpellated, want to define their own "positions" while constructing their own histories. If I have, in previous writing, done some of that for myself, it's not been from anything like the same anxiety of dispossession, nor the threat that somebody would do it for me.

At the same time, I have not been inclined, through the new legitimation of authenticity, to overvalue the claims of experience, though I base that upon experience, including, where grievances are concerned, my own capacities for self-deception. One of the areas in which we may be self-deceived has to do with our capacities for identification, which would seem to be one of the prerogatives of experience. As there are some things, however, we cannot know, the implication of the most extreme forms of tragic experience is that there are, though it would seem to be soliciting empathy, limits to projective feeling as well. I will be saying more about empathy in a later chapter, but it's as if in its critique we forgot to think, first, of the sort of experience in which alienation would be required only because it's impossible to feel enough. That's what Oedipus suggests, at Colonus, when in gratitude for the rescue of Antigone and Ismene he refuses to let himself kiss Theseus, whom he urges to keep his distance,

21

though it's another sort of distance than we think of with Brecht: "The only ones/Fit to be fellow sufferers of mine/Are those with such experience as I have."[29]

Is this another case of oedipal excess? Maybe so. In any case, the question of experience, where it matters and where it gets in the way, has been at the heart of almost all disputes about acting method, from the use of "emotional memory" or the "private moment" to the various stylizations of distance, the rites of estrangement, and historicization. Which is why I shall try, in approaching such issues, to give more or less precise indications of the function, place, and role of concrete forms of existence, so far as differences can be perceived, in the formulation of theory. Or, since it's hardly systematic theory, in the sort of thinking that I do, which at the selvedge of speculation, pursuing the kind of thought that is likely to escape itself, insists upon its subjectivity. The insistence is by now, I suppose, somewhere between an unavoidable reflex and an ideological commitment, with a certain accountability not only to the protocols of experience, but to the relative degrees, where and when and on what scale, of any kind of experience.

That is an issue of some consequence, I think, in the relation between ideology and politics. For example: of the years I've spent in the theater, some of them have been quite controversial on political grounds, both in much-publicized institutional theater and in the relative obscurity or ingrown circuit of experimental work (which has its ideological factions and politics too). The political repercussions were as often as not fallout from other motives, but the result was that for many years the work I did, even when formally experimental or sometimes rather hermetic, was associated with the idea of political theater (or anti-political theater). Since there are those I respect deeply, however, whose practice was/is *specifically* political, sometimes so laboriously, sacrificially, or dangerously so – that is, in the concrete form of existence – I do not want to make any excessive claims about theater and/or performance as a political practice. I will survey in the next chapter the unrelieved sweep of ideology over the forms of theater, but if Marx was right about history being measured in its effects, one encounters in our part of the world very little practice with a measurable politics. Here common sense comes into play, and not in the form of mere mythology, ideas so absorbed into the spontaneous ideology that they remain, as if ordained by nature, forever unexamined. I am speaking rather of that other quite conscious domain of ideology, not theoretical or philosophical ideology, though both are, as Gramsci understood, governed by politics.

"It is very hard to know what is political and what isn't," said Grotowski in an interview a few years back. Amidst the cult following he developed in the sixties, and the occultation of his method, it was not at all widely known that he had been, as a theater student in Cracow, an anti-Stalinist member of the Provisional Central Committee of the Union of Socialist Youth. "When I worked in Poland," he pointed out, "it was very useful to say 'I am not making politics.' But I was."[30] There was, in Poland itself, considerable question on the dissident Left of the formalist aesthetic of the Laboratory Theater, and there was to come, at a sometimes exclusivist distance, the mystifying secrecy of his later paratheater (which he pursued, with a characteristic American irony, in Orange County near Disneyland, and later in Italy). Whatever the questionable politics of this work, we have also seen theater people claiming to be making politics in contexts where it couldn't conceivably be making any political difference at all.

AT RISK: THE PRIVILEGE OF REPRESSION

While I shall make some reference to theaters and modes of performance with specific political agendas, the ones about which there is little argument as to what constitutes the politics are usually in countries where to work in the theater, or to perform at all, is to put yourself in jeopardy. Thus it was until very recently in Chile, under the Pinochet government (he still controls the armed forces), when even some of the most distinguished actors and directors, as well as officials of the actors' union, received threats from a right-wing death squad, "Commando 135, Cultural Section, Trizano action for people movement, for a culture and art free of foreign contamination . . . ." In this country, not even Marketta Kimbrell, a really sacrificial figure (relatively unknown, but the Mother Teresa of our theater) with an absolutely committed left-wing politics, is at similar risk, though her Caravan Theater has performed with some danger in *barrios*, jails, on Indian reservations, in the muck of Resurrection City and, in the backyards of tenements, amidst the garbage of the South Bronx.

When I was, however, in Israel several years ago, I spent time with the young directors of a Palestinian group who would (though they didn't *say* it) rather have been doing Beckett and Genet, but who saw their mission in strictly ideological terms and, moreover, could not have survived for a moment among the Arabs of East Jerusalem, where they were based, if they weren't doing political plays. (They would, by the way, discuss almost any issue I raised, about their repertoire or working methods, or the dual prospect of censorship, by the Israelis or their own people – everything but where they got the money to support the theater. My guess at the time was the PLO, but I've since heard they are getting money from the Ford Foundation. I'm not sure, however, from their reticence and evasions that it was true then. If so, their discretion may have been due to their not wanting, by any circuitous route, to make that known among the Palestinians.) Ngugi Wa Thiongo, in his book *Detained*, about his detention in a maximum security prison, has described the perils of a playwright who was critical of the authorities in Kenya, a situation which has not, according to latest report, much changed. And there was the conspicuous case, amidst the uproar of Eastern Europe, of the recurring incarcerations of Vaclev Havel, whose plays could only, until the revolution, be performed abroad.

This can now be approached with the accomplished irony long nurtured in middle Europe, and which manifested itself in the colloquy at Avignon that I mentioned before: "I am truly sorry," said Jovan Cirilov, artistic director of the Belgrade festival, "that Marshal Tito did not imprison our playwrights." He was obviously talking of that dynamic you can only wish for when you don't have it, that which several other participants also spoke of: the sense that art acquires a power under censorship that, however admirable it may be otherwise, it simply won't have elsewhere. With this in mind, Andrzef Ziebinski, director of theater in the Polish ministry, described a virtual *Samizdat* of theater strategies, like performers in churches and private homes, and open rehearsals in which even Havel was performed. Then he went on to say – with fraternal regret for the good old days, the reigning humor of the occasion – that "with the seizure of power by Solidarity, theater artists lost their privileged situation" (*Libération* 15).

The situation was differently privileged in East Berlin, and perhaps more subtle yet, since the theater there had international status and, so far as the censorship was concerned, the duplicitous model of Brecht. Addressing her colleagues in the West, Ewa Walch said she understood why they had always envied, for all *their* privileges, what she described as the especially clairvoyant relation, under the censorship, between the actors and the audience, which had to learn to read between the lines. My own experience in the East has been that sometimes, even at the Berliner Ensemble, there wasn't all that much to read, but there may have been things that escaped me, and at its repressive best, as she said, "the censor gave birth to a new form of art." It was a paradox, however, that – with her considerable discretion in this encounter – Walch didn't "want to make into a desirable thing" (16). Still, we may continue to desire it when our most fervent political impulses in the theater seem to be stillborn in a society where nobody except Jesse Helms takes them seriously enough to be vigilant about them at all. Between that and the censorship that Walch does not find – whatever the privilege – desirable, there is a spectrum of other ironies and paradoxes.

There are, for instance, other performances which are decidedly political where they first happen, on home ground, like the plays of Athol Fugard in South Africa, but which are questionably so when transplanted, depending on where. In the case of Fugard's plays on Broadway, or off-Broadway, they may serve the liberal fiction of high seriousness with next to no political efficacy at all. Joseph Papp has always had good social and political intentions (like integrated casting), but the same is true of the dissidence of Havel when performed in Soho at the Public Theater, no less the transplantation, some years ago, of the Teatro Campesino in zoot suits from the *barrios* of Los Angeles to the Winter Garden in New York. Here the question arises, too, as to what happens to a theater with a political agenda when, for whatever motives, it goes for the big money or national recognition, as a means, perhaps, of acquiring power. (To avoid any piety here, I should add that quite a few years before, in the political turmoil of the sixties, I was responsible for a similar decision when, despite my own polemic on behalf of decentralization,[31] we took most of The Actor's Workshop of San Francisco to Lincoln Center in New York. There is an extensive commentary on that in *Take Up the Bodies*, where I may indirectly suggest that much of my own strategy in the theater was to intensify the stakes, perhaps unconsciously and even self-destructively, so that something like a censorship would come into play.[32]) Actually, the complex and often ambiguous relation between power and scale may be illustrated by the career of Fugard, for whom home ground to begin with was almost underground, but whose international celebrity has given him access to the commercial stage, not only in New York but in South Africa as well. At the Market Theater in Johannesburg, his latest play, *My Children, My Africa*, may still seem to be merely liberal, compromising, even retrograde, especially in its attacks on the African National Congress.[33] Yet on that stage, at this time, it's hard to say that Fugard's play is either a copout or a redundancy. It's very unlikely that many blacks in Soweto even know it exists, but given Fugard's public status now, it may add significantly to the pressure, even by sympathizers, that will cause the more militant black leaders to alter an adamant policy of recourse to violence as the stranglehold of apartheid is released by the gradual but accelerating measures of de Klerk. (As we shall see in a moment – no more, perhaps, than a footnote to this prospect – the policies of the ANC were at least in a single instance not wholly irrelevant to theater in the United States.) As for Joe Papp, his liberal reputation was under siege when, more recently, he scheduled the Palestinian theater I mentioned above, the El-Hakawati of East Jerusalem, at the Public Theater, and then cancelled the production with the explanation that it would be offensive to the Jews who make up a high percentage of the theater audience in New York. Given Papp's record on political issues, the reversal seemed unfortunate, the shakiness of the decision no more stabilized when he said, as further justification, that he had never produced an Israeli play.

The given circumstances may provide us with ideological ironies some-what less familiar, like the version of Molière's *Don Juan* that I saw in Paris (in 1989), performed by the company of Mikhail Tumanishvili, from Georgia in the Soviet Union, the first time this theater had ever gone abroad. While there were any number of political resonances that went by even in simultaneous translation, what was apparently, in Georgia, the most inflammatory gesture in the production required no translation at all, though it took a moment of conceptual rollback to register, in Paris, that anybody might have been offended by the fact that all the music was western jazz, or induced to cheer when, suddenly in the action, the first blaring sounds of it were heard. On the other hand, it was a fear of offense – perhaps premature and, given the play, more than ironic – that caused Marcel Marechal to cancel the production of Genet's *The Screens*, scheduled by la Criée, the national theater in Marseilles, at the outbreak of hostilities in the Gulf. It would seem that few dramas of this century have as much relevance to the cultural dynamics of that war, but Marechal defended the replacement of *The Screens* with Aristophanes' *Peace*, by stating for the company of la Criée that the decision had been taken to avert "partisan uses of the thought of the author, and above all the risks of a bad reception of the work itself so far as it found itself diverted from its meaning [!], badly heard if not badly understood, even if it happens to be an essential masterpiece of the contemporary theater."[34]

Essential to what? one may ask. I say this with a disinclination to urge risks upon others at some safe distance from what may, indeed, be dangerous circumstances. (In the case of la Criée, they work in a city that has a large Arab population, along with a racist bias from Le Pen and the National Front.) As it happens, I was on the scene when, under remarkably similar pressures, the first of the nervous decisions had to be made about *The Screens*. At the time (1966) I was meeting with Roger Blin, who was directing the play for its première at the Odéon, which was then under the administration of Jean-Louis Barrault. This was a few years after the Algerian War, with considerable rancor aroused over the (still unabsorbed) realities of a postcolonial France. Threats to the production had taken various forms: anonymous letters, incendiary articles in the right-wing press, and phone calls from extremist commandos who eventually showed up in the theater, in the audience at every performance. Barrault and his wife, Madeleine Renaud, were in the production, already confused about the play, which they didn't particularly like, partly because its meaning was apparently not so clear. So far as they were concerned, it was hardly to be diverted because circuitous at every level. One thing was clear, however: the threats were sufficiently virulent that they'd rather not have been on stage, and certain meanings that showed up in the acting confirmed not that they were political but almost scared to death. Yet Barrault and Blin refused to withdraw the production, and because Genet did not quite agree with Artaud about masterpieces, one can well imagine what he might have thought if they had withdrawn it. As for putting his thought to partisan uses, he did that in America for the Black Panthers, and then for the Palestinians, leaving before he died the powerful "witness" to the massacres at Chatila and Sabra, in which he said he was defending the

Palestinians because he loved them, but then wondered whether he would have loved them if the injustice they suffered had not made them a vagabond people. It is a testament that, perhaps, only Genet could have written, with an idiosyncratic delicacy, in which we are reminded nevertheless of both the absoluteness and fragility, the deeply capricious bearing, of any allegiance to a cause.

There have been, of course, great figures in the theater with a certain contempt for partisan uses. If we were to summon up the folklore on this issue, there would surely be Yeats at the Abbey Theater, shaming the mob (as he saw it) at the opening of *Playboy of the Western World*, and later producing O'Casey whose politics, for Yeats, was still another world apart. If repressive forces provide the occasion, such heroics in the theater, rare as anywhere else, are more than balanced by acquiescence, compromise, and a normal quotient of cowardice. Or, sometimes with intimidation from where it's unexpected, ugly incidents besides. To stay with contemporary history and coming again closer to home: a few years ago there was another production from South Africa, not a native play, but *Waiting for Godot*, with a cast of black actors, which came to a festival in Baltimore, where it was threatened by black activists if they performed. The local blacks were hostile to the festival because their own groups hadn't been asked to perform, and to Beckett's play because even the South African blacks couldn't disguise its "elitism." There were apparently more than hints of dire connections between the black groups in Baltimore and the African National Congress, and the actors – including one whose face had been slashed before as a political punishment – felt in sufficient jeopardy at a distance that the production was withdrawn from the festival, and they didn't perform elsewhere either.

THE FUTURE OF ILLUSION

For most of us, however, the degree to which performance is political is itself an ideological question. If that remains an open question which, for all the demystifications of recent theory, remains embarrassingly inseparable from aesthetic questions, it also intersects the theoretical discourse on issues of power: who has it? under what circumstances? in what institutional forms? and what are the alternative possibilities? Or are we dealing, in Foucauldian terms, only with "effects of power" which in the random access of their dispersion return us to the harrowing prospect of a reality which is nothing but spectacle whose principle is illusion, but illusion so exhausted by history that it can barely reproduce itself? If this is the world with which we have become theoretically familiar in the later writing of Jean Baudrillard, we came to it earlier, along with questions of power, in the theater of Genet, who wrote in *The Screens* what is perhaps the greatest political play of our century – certainly if we follow the implications of poststructuralist theory, though we may think of Brecht's later drama as ideologically sounder.

If we reflect, however, as Genet causes us to do, upon the fantasy of power in the midst of which and out of which we make theater, what can that possibly mean: *ideologically sounder*? I won't say *correct* at the moment (but more of that later). Nor will I rehearse right now Brecht's critique of the bourgeois theater and its incapacitating practices, to which we'll inevitably return, since it was Brecht who virtually initiated the discourse on ideology and performance. As we think, however, at the still conjectural edge of the questions he raised, we may recall that he had to concede from the last revision of *Galileo* that, with the atom bomb, we were dealing with issues of incomparable dimensions, something utterly anonymous or vastly impersonal. He had once written about the petroleum complex that broke up the five-act play, but he had seen nothing at the time like the oil spill in Alaska, not to mention the release, as a deterrent to an amphibious landing, of a huge black slick in the Gulf. That actually seemed to have an old-fashioned human component to it in the unpredictable behavior of Saddam Hussein. But if, even with such provocation, the nuclear terror has been contained, why is it that the prospect of historical change seems, in the magnitudes of a postindustrial society, more impersonal than ever before? if not out of control, beyond our control?

It's as if the belief in anything more than the efficacy of the most incremental social practice goes against the evidence of history. It's hard to believe otherwise, even when history seems to be giving evidence that a turbulence is moving through the world and, even if radical change is only in backward countries, that there is no way for advanced societies to escape the repercussions. The prospects are surely there, but so is the principle of displacement, a sort of ecology of geopolitics in which, as the proportions of human misery are maintained, the repercussions may include at least a partial recovery, elsewhere, of what we thought was surely past. While it's no doubt important to ask, and to *show* in the theater, as Brecht wanted it shown, how something became that way, so that it might not happen again, it would seem equally important to show that things are the way they are, however impossibly so, but precisely for that reason (as Chekov thought) not in the foreseeable future very likely to be changed. If Brecht's argument was to submit illusion to the deflationary effects of alienation, this would seem to be in the grain, though by no means without illusion which, even if we wanted to, we can hardly do without.

It's possible to say, of course, that it was Brecht's illusions which produced a theater whose mission would now seem to be "ideologically in ruins."[35] But that certainly doesn't invalidate the questions he left to the theater (some of which we'll rehearse in the next chapter). The urgency of those questions may have been just as strong for those who didn't share

28

his politics as for those who did, the politics being an impediment only when the questions cease. This is not quite the same as the arresting moment in epic theater when, ideally, time must have a stop. To refer to Benjamin again, on the temporal index of a materialist history:

> A historical materialist cannot do without the notion of a present which is not a transition, but in which time stands still and has come to a stop. For this notion defines the present in which he himself is writing [or making] history .... The historical materialist leaves it to others to be drained by the whore called "once upon a time" in historicism's bordello. He remains in control of his powers, man enough to blast open the continuum of history.

(*Illuminations* 262)

If that sounds a little hyperbolic, what I've been saying – with a cautionary glance at the resistant forces in the continuum, and the historical evidence of its recuperative powers – is not without its own propensity (as the record shows) for encouraging that blast. There were times during my experience in the theater when the better part of materialism was to believe, as I have believed, that power is only fantasy. And there were times when I felt that history was corroborating that, as it sometimes confirms idealism as the toughest realism. (This seems to me to give a little resilience to history, and the way its evidence works.) It is not, in any event, what Brecht resisted: a matter of attributing it all to unalterable destiny, though destiny – even as an ideological force or formulation – continues to work in mysterious ways. It would seem to be a question, rather, of returning the impelling power of illusion (with its utopian dreams, or "horizon," coordinating the ideological with the utopian[36]) to life as we mostly live it, amidst the *impossible* – the full indomitability of which, painfully felt, can arouse an efficacious outrage and the passion for change.

In making illusion admissible, I am not draining it out of ideology nor, if we think of illusion as perceptual aberration, the ideology out of it. What I am trying to suggest is that there may be a productive latency in ideology that is compact of illusion, not merely complicit with it (as there may be more to dream, with its compacted imagination, than a dramaturgy of repression). That's part of the appeal, for me, of Gramsci's notion of an "organic ideology," in which – suffused with illusion, desire, and contradiction – there are the decantations and traces of prior systems of thought, the alluvium of former fictions (some of them passing as current truths), and in its complex stratification (a virtual genealogy of fracture and dispersion) the circuitry of conflicting truths, as if the organism were a template of the nervous system itself. In this "structure" there is no perfect hegemony, nor a mere incessant displacement of inaccessible power, or at least a displacement toward that other illusion or enabling fiction of power.

29

What moves the structure is the struggle to sustain it, parsing out illusions, whether as mere appearance or promising appearance or the form of defective value, that is, the appearance of mere illusion, though the merest illusion tomorrow may, through the altered necessities of ideological formations, resemble another promise. That may still be the merest resemblance, but to acknowledge it as a prospect in the system is something other than a utopian horizon. It is, instead, the realistic addition of an important element missing, I think, from Foucault's analysis of the layered discursivity or rhizomatic energies, the cybernetic repertoire of the microphysics of power.

The ideological struggle itself has always been a struggle over nothing less than the future of illusion. This is the mostly unacknowledged subtext of the struggle over signifying practices, though in thinking about performance it's a little harder to ignore. We may think of ideology in its various stratifications, as a consciously articulated force or as a social formation or as an inverted genealogy of culture, but the thing at issue, as they intersect each other in the taxonomy of the idea, is the degree to which it is also and always a manifestation of the imaginary. That is the avatar of ideology of which recent theory has been particularly suspicious, though it may at some intersection of history with the eternity of the unconscious move against impossibility with extraordinary power. Which doesn't mean that it overcomes the impossible, which never changes.

PROMISSORY NOTES

What I have been trying to suggest, by acknowledging the imaginary in the movement of altered necessities, is a margin of difference in the disposition of the system. And that is why, ideologically, though I have been in theory and theater practice long indebted to Brecht, I have never been quite convinced by his argument that tragedy is disempowering. It remains, however, a complicated question that activates the subtext of this book, along with the critique of representation, the ideological status of mimesis, and the now orthodox view of realism as the theatrical form of a reactionary politics.

Aspects of these issues will surface here and there, but the ensuing chapters of the book will consist, first, of a detailed account (with a defense of theory in a resistant theater) of what I call "The Theatrical Fact," that is, the ideological saturation of performance; then, its focus today in the ubiquitous body, and its relation to the ideology of desire, which has developed, curiously enough, out of theories of demystification. Since this proceeds by techniques of alienation, or a bracketing of affect in favor of structure, or the "structurality of structure,"[37] we have found ourselves talking of questions of subjectivity, desire, a signifying body, while leaving emotion somewhat in the dark. The last two chapters will deal with that distressing problem, or what may be thought of as "Distressed Emotion," which is not quite the same as the indeterminacies of desire. In the last chapter, the question of emotion will attach itself, with an intensification of equivocal feelings, to the ethos of surface or, out of the myth of persisting depth, "The Struggle to Appear."

If affect has been displaced from structuralism to deconstruction, it has come up again, but in an omnibus way, in reflections on the fusion of postmodernism with the energies of mass culture. Among younger cultural theorists there is the belief, for instance, that the "empowering nihilism" of popular sensibility is a function of postmodernism's reduction of reality to "a question of affect."[38] If so, it would seem hard – especially in view of the resurgent humanism of Eastern Europe – to avoid reassessment of the empowering prospect of empathy, dependent on mimesis, and with it other properties of that presumably bankrupt dramaturgy that was borne along by, and privileged, the bourgeois democratic tradition. The paradox of this dramaturgy has always been, by the way, that it was also a devastating critique of that tradition, with a process of inquisition that was, if mystifying, based on demystification. What emerged, then, in modernist drama was a relentless form of *exposure* at the sociological and political levels that seemed, from the Button Molder in *Peer Gynt* to the pipe dreams of O'Neill, to bottom out in an ontological mystery. We may remain uneasy with the secreted metaphysics in the liberal values of this tradition, as with the (eventual) solipsistic enclosure of its theatrical forms, but there is a discomfiting politics, too, in the random egalitarianism of mass, popular, or subcultural forms. Whatever the will of Baudrillard's "silent majority," or its noisier avatars, what is equally hard for ideological criticism to live with is the full range of the pluralism it seems to desire, including the often repressive implications of popular emotion and the uglier sentiments of emarginated dissidence. Putting aside the religious fundamentalism in country music, or the aggressive residues in rap, hiphop, and Rastaferianism, think of Bruce Springsteen, Michael Jackson, even Madonna, not to mention the New Kids on the Block: it doesn't take a discourse on appropriation within the recording industry to see that in such a domain of affect things do not remain very long, if they ever were, in the phase of an empowering nihilism. Or at least we might ask: empowering what?

It may be that we want to think of it as a continuum of affect in which as the power recedes here it is passed along there. Havel has spoken of how the lifestyle and rhythms of the American counterculture were, even as it subsided in the United States, an inspiriting force to a younger generation in Czechoslovakia who were, as he said, "growing up 'outside.' "[39] The phrase echoes Paul Goodman's description of another generation, "growing up absurd," and Havel himself was still being influenced by the theater of the absurd as it was beginning to lose its impact on our theater. With its strategies of dissent and guerrilla instincts, the Movement of the sixties did have the effect in Eastern Europe of an

31

empowering nihilism, the old image of which surfaced again before the entire world in the music and dancing, the joyous revelries, on the Berlin Wall. Yet what should be self-evident from events that followed the celebration is that *after* the revolution, *if* there was to be anything but an authoritarian government, the nihilistic principle had to accept, along with an electoral politics, the paradoxical repression of a compromising form. When the decibel count goes down on the dissidence, how one thinks about it ideologically becomes a matter of finer tuning.

In rehearsing these issues, at any rate, as they affect theatrical practice, I would hope to avoid the sort of ideological analysis that turns out to be, once you've named the subject position, a foregone conclusion. If I've stopped naming the actor's blindness, I'm not inclined to name my own, which will no doubt be sufficient without giving it a name.

Studies of ideology usually come from Marxists or, in the wake of a *mea culpa*, from the renunciation of Marxism. While there was a fair amount of socialism where I came from, I am not now and never have been a Marxist. But if I see no grounds whatever, in my given circumstances, for calling myself a Marxist, I have nevertheless been stimulated by the revisionist discourse – anomalous as it is under pretty much the same circumstances – of some of those who do. Similarly with feminism, not at all anomalous under the circumstances. As almost everybody now agrees, feminist criticism has been one of the more threatening discourses of recent years to those with any investment in the inherited systems and conventions, habits and reflexes, that are in art and culture – even in the most revisionist performance – still very much alive. Some men doing theory today are calling themselves feminists. Granting this man's opportunism and that man's queasy deference, I see no reason why they shouldn't, so long as they're prepared for the scornful attacks by feminists wary of appropriation. (In this I adhere to the principle that nobody owns an idea.) Yet I simply don't feel the need – rather it seems to me inconceivable that I would call myself a feminist. What I have admired in feminist theory as in the new academic Marxism – allowing for affinities and differences with the overall substance of a sometimes merging critique – is the high intelligence of some of the practitioners. Which is precisely the criterion that operates for me, across ideology and with whatever subjectivities, when assessing what I see in performance.

As we move across class, race, culture, and other categories, there are certainly significant differences in the forms and measures of intelligence, to which I am quite susceptible, though it may still be an impediment in my capacity for collectivity that, in theory as in theater, I find it hard to adjust the measure or make identifications on ideological grounds. I don't see this as being, however, without ideology, since that seems to me next to impossible. That should be even more apparent in the next chapter, along with the possibility that all of this is a matter of indifference to most of those working (or not working) in the American theater. Yet increasingly there – in the remnants and continued promise of an alternative theater – and surely elsewhere, some would object strenuously to the absence of a stated position. The objection was, perhaps, most forcibly put by a practitioner widely respected, the radical playwright/performer Dario Fo, when he was asked to comment on certain practices of postmodernism: "Fashion . . . is what results," he said, "when there is not a fundamental, real reason, ideology or morality behind a discourse. In other words, when discourse doesn't make an argument."[40]

In the past – when I was working in the theater – it was said that I was being ideological or political when I thought I was being moral, which is for me discerning a path of action through the making of distinctions, without, today, the prospect of a clear morality or the certainties for a decisive politics. For some, the bringing of any complexity to a political issue is still a sign of a needlessly dilatory or delinquent politics. (That view can come from the Right or the Left, though in the shifting coordinates of politics today it may also come from the center: so it was that both sides were fumbling attitudes while George Bush marshalled world opinion and a coalition of power against the invasion of Kuwait. What was extraordinary, moreover, in the precipitous certitudes of his decisions, based on the old puritan morality of good and bad, is that they nevertheless dispelled among European intellectuals, especially on the Left, old tenacious platitudes about America's political innocence.) There is always, I suppose, the risk of hesitancy or of piety in bringing the moral to the ideological, but so far as I understand it there is the potential virtue of another risk: that of a certain ambiguity which, if it doesn't preclude an argument, does raise the question of *how* an argument is made. In any case, I've never had any reason to worry about being fashionable, and given the rather correct politics (the opposition is crude, but not entirely wrong) in the subject positions of recent discourse, it seems unlikely here. There will probably be more as I go along on the appearances or absences of my own position – as well as the appearances and absences of which I'm unaware.

Meanwhile, as I have said about performance, there is also the question of *where* an argument is made. That can be demonstrated by the altered situation of Dario Fo himself, whose politics was pronounced enough to have kept him at one time from getting a visa to enter the United States when a play of his was being produced. He has not exactly been an establishment figure anywhere, except on the margins, but it's hard to say what sort of argument he is making now, or able to make, as the raunchy slapstick that may have carried a message in the ghettoes has moved onto the stage at the Comédie-Française, where his productions of two plays by Molière seem, for all the high-energy caustic of their lowdown types, like the merest, and crudest, bourgeois entertainment. It hardly requires any extensive ideological analysis to make that distinction, for the context has already made it, or at least been a powerful determinant, which few have been able to overcome. The recurring question that attaches itself to this is the degree to which, in an institutional framework, anything like subversive work can be done. I'm not saying that it can't, only that it takes a subtler and more persuasive, or more shocking mode of argument, though as with the landmines on the borders of Kuwait our culture has managed to defuse almost any shock.

Actually, it will not, for the most part, be ideological analysis that I am doing, but rather a kind of speculative double take on aspects of performance, with attention to the particular circumstances or variable conditions that put them into question. What I want to do is to approach any element of performance as it is in potential an ideological question, while observing the theatrical features of various ideological practices. History has already designed or designated certain aspects of performance – for instance, the performative nature of the audience – as more or less problematic or urgent today, and that was rather extensively the subject of my previous book, where the idea of the audience was something more than the gathered body of spectators before the rise of the curtain in an established theater. Here too, as I've suggested, the scope will be wider and more speculative, though I shall now and again return to the practices of institutional forms of theater, with acting method as a crucial figure. In any event I shall be throwing the emphasis upon those nuances, alterations, ruptures of appearance when something thought productive or taken for granted is destabilized by history or seems to subvert itself, turning in another direction, or merely wasting away; or with undiminished possibility, it seems, is once again up for grabs. Thus, mimesis or realism or the A-effect of Brecht or, after the theatricality of the sixties, the hegemony of performance itself – which in its dispersive effect opened a debate on the vice of theatricality, and in its recessiveness or (dis)appearance awakened another on surface and depth.

Any of these notions may become the object/subject of critique, as it was the fate of Oedipus to be. But I shall refuse to take for granted that this form of theater or that is ever conclusively either the repressive or liberating thing it appears to be. "I don't deny history," says Musset's Lorenzaccio, "but I was not there."[41] Actually, I have been there through a considerable portion of the major changes in the theater since the end of World War II, watching the emergence and recession of formal values and emotional needs, things once up front now in the wings, or the other way around. I spoke of the issue of concealment before. "Once I saw the proscenium, that was it, you know?" said the young *cinéaste*/theater director John Jesurun, " . . . I know there were people hiding behind there, and I can't help thinking that. I always want to see what's behind the curtain."[42] It may seem as if he's rediscovering Brecht, but that's hardly necessary. For he's among those of his generation who appear to have been endowed

34

at birth with an instinct for *alethia* (unconcealment), while bypassing the old embittered arguments about the hegemony of realism in the obfuscating perspective of the Cartesian frame. Positioned as he was on the side of realism, Lukács was also censuring concealment, of course, when he defined reification as the process by means of which social relations are disguised in the appearance of objecthood or objectification. On the face of it, as we may see through the history of the canonical drama itself, concealment seems undesirable, but as we can also see through the same history, there is – shadowing the illusions of unconcealment – the ubiquitous question: *is it?*

"And that's true too," says the blinded Gloucester to the line (so often quoted as ineffably right) about ripeness being all (*Lear* 5.2.11–12), simply calling attention to what we all know about what follows ripeness.

Yet there is, though sometimes hard to discern, the brief truth of ripeness too. And it is in that regard that I shall be concerned with the shifts of expectancy in history that may put a convention or technique, or idea of performance, which once seemed ideologically bankrupt, back into currency as an energizing force, an audacity, or a virtual innovation. Think in this respect of the history of the mask in western theater; or after centuries of recession the insurgence of the thrust stage; or of various "naïve" techniques familiar to the futurists, or Aristophanes, that came of age again with the theater of the absurd; or, theorized by Walter Benjamin, elements of the baroque; or, in the sumptuous spectacles of Robert Wilson, the Italianate pageant and the masques of Inigo Jones.

CULTURAL DIFFUSION AND CATASTROPHE THEORY

Then there's the relation of ripeness and cultural difference. What may have to wait for the recycling of history in our own modes of performance may already be ideologically liberating to other cultures, which are disenchanted with their own conventions as they pass into our avant-garde. Or not quite disenchanted but accepting diffusion, or adulteration, as the Kutiyattam temple dancers have had to do in Kerala since that south Indian state elected a Marxist government and they were driven from the temple into the streets. What seems to be happening there is analogous to what happened in the "evolution" of medieval drama when it went from the altar up the nave and out into the open air, where it was susceptible to repressed theatrical elements from the subcultures of the time. Some years ago in a project in which we were exchanging performance techniques (a further adulteration?) I asked the leader of the Kutiyattam dancers, a gentle scholarly man, how he felt about what was happening to the form now that it is no longer in the sanctuary of the temple. "It is very sad," he said, "but then, you know, I am a Marxist too."

While there are ritual performers elsewhere without the quiet blessing of a new politics, it's obvious that neither acquiescence nor resistance is of any great concern to the good fortune of our acquisitive secularity. What with the Aborigines from Australia performing in Central Park, it would appear that resistance anywhere, in the remotest savannahs or desolate bush, is a rather hopeless cause. In what, despite managerial prowess and silicon chips, we still think of as the most obdurately traditional of countries, Japan, I talked to students in the only theater program in the multitudinous universities of Tokyo, trying to make distinctions between American acting and that of the Noh and Kabuki. I had barely started when I stopped in mid-sentence to ask – since I had been taking it for granted that they had – how many had ever seen the Noh or Kabuki. Not one. And moreover they couldn't care less, though they roared with appreciation (and without translation!) when a microphone handed to me flopped over my wrist and I made a reference to Mick Jagger. While I was there the major attraction for hip young people who were at all interested in the theater was *Comet Messenger – Siegfried*, an event staged by the multi-talented Hideki Noda, a postmodern pastiche of American cartoons, Wagner, Tolkien, Mark Twain, the proliferous Japanese comics called *manga*, with historical figures from Galileo to Nancy Reagan, and elements of what was really the going thing, cyberpunk.

Mediating between the avant-garde and popular culture, this was the production that in the commodification of the world was brought over to the Brooklyn Academy of Music while, in the mainstream theater of Tokyo (whose lights and giant billboards make Times Square look like a relic from *Gulliver's Travels*), the big draws that week were Andrew Lloyd Webber's *Cats* and Peter Brook's *Mahabharata*. I don't know whether many of the students showed up at either one (the prices were equally out of sight), but I did see a host of young people a couple of days later at a theater in the more venerable city of Kyoto, where a famous Japanese actor was appearing in what was billed in immense red letters above the marquee as: SUPER-KABUKI! The normal-sized Kabuki and the Noh continue to be performed, of course, if increasingly as tourist attractions (in that regard no different than, say, the Shakespearean productions at Stratford-on-Avon). Yet efforts are also being made to keep the heritage alive by making it more accessible, and one of my loveliest evenings in Japan was spent in a park where, from dusk to nightfall, with fires lit in front of the stage, a large crowd of mainly elderly people sat on the ground, eating, dozing, some with fine old parchment texts open on their laps (since the language of the Noh is as arcane as classical modernism, and in the estranged singsong of performance not immediately accessible), to watch a medley of different styles in the older form. What pleasured me, I must confess, was the resemblance of the evening to what I remember in Prospect Park in Brooklyn when the Goldman Band used to perform or, with cultured

36

immigrants following the musical scores, the concerts at Lewisohn Stadium in New York.

Still, if various older forms and rituals are severely threatened by social revolution, cultural forgetfulness, foreign elements, tourism, the ceaseless abrasions of alien eyes, their own avid tours and dissemination, there are also performers everywhere that look upon the wonders of cultural diffusion and think of it – whether as the source of new ideas or relief from the oppressive tedium of archaic forms – as an emancipating prospect. What is absorbed or refused in this prospect is inseparable from the more or less geologic shifts or tectonic slips in the subsoil of ideologies, while new social formations are consolidating themselves on an international scale. At the time it was not at all of this magnitude, but it is this process of diffusion or diverse currents or foundations in a field of ideologies (where there are even differential ideological formations within the dominant class or the working class, crosscut by interests, merging classes) that Gramsci tried to discern, and the reasons for transfer, fracture, coexistence, or movement of ideology along certain faultlines of differentiation and change. In a new historical phase, a new relative weight may be given to dispossessed or discredited elements of older ideological formations: "What was previously secondary and subordinate, or even incidental, is now taken to be primary – becomes the nucleus of a new ideological or theoretical complex."[43]

As the subordinate develops socially, the old formations dissolve into their contradictory elements. I would put this in a somewhat different way, or with the emphasis upon the imperceptible moment at which the rupture appears, the sort of occurrence that has been taken up in the mathematics of incipience, or the precipitous: catastrophe theory. What I have always been concerned with is the instance of emergence or transformative moment at which any practice, in the theater or elsewhere, becomes like ideology itself, something other than what it appeared to be, like theater itself before it identified itself; that is, before it could be distinguished for better or worse from whatever it is it was not. It is here, I suppose, that theater blends with ideology at the most disturbing level of demystifying thought, for when we think twice about the question of priority, whatever it *was* appears to be theater. While at a certain ideological level, or on ideological grounds, performance was over the last generation differentiated from theater, even the artists now doing performance have had to deal with *what appears to be theater*. ("What, has this thing appeared again tonight?" (*Ham.* 1.1.21).) That will be, as in my previous writing, the crucial issue in this book, for if it doesn't appear there is no performance, though that may be desirable on ideological grounds.

2

THE THEATRICAL FACT

IMPASSE OF THE DREAM

Over the course of history there has been more or less anxiety, more or less philosophical, about the possibility that life might be a dream or all the world a stage. That has been the curious substance at the troubled heart of the drama, its essential distrust of the appearances of theater. What complicates the matter is that the theater, which always needs to be watched, appears never to have trusted itself. Or at least that appears to have been the case since Apollo, invisible perhaps but near at hand, was enshrined in the rites of Dionysus as its principle of surveillance. There have been audacious experiments through the history of the theater to restore the pure festival by banishing Apollo from the scene, but even Nietzsche had to concede, as if pronouncing Freud's final verdict on civilization and its discontents, that there was no avoiding this specular presence, as in the dramaturgy of the unconscious. If it now appears that theater is the delirious symptom of the postmodern condition, anxiety more or less dispersed in the plenitude of appearance, what was engrailed in history by the canonical drama is an image of theater fearful of its own presence: the vertiginous truth of the inexhaustible Dionysus, what for all the plenitude is *essentially imageless*, and can't endure itself. We still think of the theater as the site of otherness, but there is the periodic evidence (in this anthropomorphic view) that it has always wanted to be something other than theater, if not in the symbolist spirit of music, then specifically more like life, though even in the spirit of realism it encounters life as a dream.

Now and again strategies are developed to throw off the dream or, by putting the phantasmic substance at a distance, to keep the theater *looking* like theater, that is, an artifice or construction that is only socially produced. But the fact of the matter appears to be, so long as we're thinking of theater, that there is no way out of the tautological impasse, which remains, from Strindberg to Pirandello and almost exultantly in Genet, the material obsession of modern drama. What's more, it reflects itself through the trickle-down economy of the psyche in every aspect of theater

38

practice. This carryover into practice of the long heritage of paranoia in the drama – what seems indelibly to mark the form – may be more or less diffused by method, but there are repercussions in any staging of a potential betrayal. Revisionist performance – that is, radical versions of the classics – simply makes the issue more conspicuous, but no matter what the approach, however conventional, somebody is always worrying that the drama is not being realized, as the textbooks say, but rather subverted by performance. The issue arises in any rehearsal, with the most superficial disagreements about interpretation of character or the meaning of the text. Or whether this or that, from a piece of stage business to the fabric of a costume, is what the playwright intended. Or whether or not the actor is expected to be, in respect to the text, "line perfect." Or for that matter, who cares? This attitude was theorized and, no doubt, exacerbated when Brecht came on the scene, but it was surely there before him, as a maybe surreptitious, more or less outspoken constituent of the scene – and even before, long before, with the recuperation of appearance that is the inception of the drama as theatrical fact. You can see the traces of it, and the vast metaphysical implications, such as questions of Real Presence or Symbolic Presence, in the molecular instance of the *Quem Quaeritis* trope, which carries along with it as well (in relation to a sacred text) the still-disputed possibility of the vice of representation.

Later on we'll be concerned with varieties of performance that, in their inception, couldn't care less not only about the drama but also the theater as we commonly know it (although there were events with a certain resemblance to the *Quem Quaeritis* trope). Some of this work was, as an offshoot of minimalism and conceptual art, more or less knowledgeable about the major issues of theory, including the critique of representation, with its assault on theatrical perspective, Oedipus, the family romance, the master narratives of domination and power. What is interesting, however, about the arguments and running discourse *in* the theater, on representation, meaning, intention, interpretation, and the hegemony of the text is that they still occur among practitioners, actors, directors, designers, who never read a word of literary theory or never heard of the death of the author, and who – though they may swear by the audience as a collaborator in performance, endowed by nature with last judgment on the play – would be hard pressed to buy the radical idea of textuality that, in its reception of the play, the audience is the author. As metaphor perhaps, but not much more, even if the author *is* dead.

What may appear in performance, however, as something more than metaphor is the impasse of the dream in the theater's escape from theater. Reality may seem to float through this impasse in the theater forms of the East, but in the West it's as if there were, in the desperate negotiations of the play within the play, an elision of the dream with false consciousness itself – as if, however, the falsehood were ingrained, not a matter of ideology but of the nature of consciousness. Some of the actors can tear you apart as they are caught up in this condition, the perceptual torments of hallucinatory being, the dreamlike opacity of performance itself. It can be harrowing, but easier said than done. When powerfully done, though, in the eloquence of interior acting, you may turn with a certain relief from the anguished dazzle of its narcissistic display or the manic dumb show of the wild and whirling words to "the dreamlike executioner's axe which," as Brecht wrote in the *Short Organum*, "cuts short such crescendos as so many excesses." (We may have a more accurate grasp of what troubled Brecht – aside from the inflated eloquence that still haunts German actors – if we remember that he might have been troubled more by what most of us, given the inturned bias of psychological theater, would consider great acting.) We shall come back to Brecht and his critique of a life that has become obscene in illusion, and of actors who are virtually pornographic for their unthinking implication in a catastrophe beyond criticism: "Human sacrifices all around! Barbaric delights!" (*Brecht* 189). If this at its worst suggests Marlon Brando in Coppola's heart of darkness, it is also a correlative of the barbarism which, according to Walter Benjamin, comes with every masterpiece in the history of culture.

Without minimizing that charge, I want to suggest in a quite different way than some have done before (usually to undercut the critique) that there may be a misprision or polemical exaggeration in Brecht's concern about the susceptibility of the actor to the enchantment he describes. For if life is a dream on stage, it quickly dissipates as such through performance, and – to use an extreme vision of barbaric delights that seem to be beyond criticism – there aren't many actors who take seriously, once the play is over, Irma's charge to the audience at the end of Genet's *The Balcony*, when she suggests that the play *isn't* over, and that they are returning to a reality as theatrical and factitious as anything in the brothel. (If any of us took it too seriously, we would probably never go home.) My guess is that not only the actors but most of those working in the theater would be, off stage, less distressed by the thought that all the world's a stage, than by the prospect of thinking about the stage as a generic space of contradiction suffused with ideological questions.

RESISTANCE TO THEORY/REHEARSAL PROCESS

There are degrees of thoughtlessness in this resistance, but it occurs as well in practitioners of considerable intelligence and distinction. I am thinking mostly of the American theater, but thus it was with Harold Pinter when, still early in his career, he was awarded the German Shakespeare Prize, for those elliptical and occulted plays in which the datum, the pure gratuitousness, of the dreamlike opacity of performance does, indeed, raise ideological questions. (In pursuing some of those questions through the chapter, I'll be returning now and again to Pinter, as a sort of exemplary figure whose seductive disavowals suggest what they can't evade, though over the last few years, or more, what he has been trying to evade, it seems, is more like the irrelevance than the gratuitousness of theater itself.) In a speech he gave at the time he received the award, Pinter distanced himself not only from ideology, but from theory as well. While he seems more recently, as in the play *Mountain Language*, to have become intensely engaged with politics or at least political injustice, Pinter said in the talk what I assume he still feels, that he distrusts theory and has never found it helpful in his own work, and rarely among his colleagues. As we know, this aversion to theory is customary in the English theater, where it is considered a bore, and in the American theater, where it has been until very recently – and then mostly among academics – next to non-existent.

That accounts, I should add, for any split focus in what I am writing here, or rather on whom I'm writing it for, since it has to be doubly addressed: to those in the theater, some of whom may be indifferent, even hostile to theory (though not if they're reading it beyond repair) and to those already involved with the theoretical issues (though mostly without, in practice, very much knowledge of theater). If theory was never exactly hostile to theater, there were certainly paradoxical feelings at the extremities of deconstruction, which wanted to banish representation and, as Gramsci said of the futurists, utterly destroy the system. To the extent that these feelings were derived from the sixties there might even have been an alternative view of the theater, which has had to move in the eighties, along with the accent on signifying practice, back to representation and, inevitably with it, conventional elements and aspects (if not forms) of theater.[1] The same has happened in performance art, which among other things – so far as anything like narrative is involved, and especially live performers – has had to improve its acting, thus shaping up its act, making it more professional.[2] Through all this the idea of performance has survived both as a critical principle and speculative procedure, presumably breaking down the formalistic methods and expected logic of inquiry, taking on and putting off ideas, trying them over and over, something like the actor in a rehearsal.

My own view of it is that it is for the most part more talked about than done. (In this there is a certain overlap with those who write with a disposition toward the discontinuities and aporias and autistic circuitry of postmodernism, as the register of "oppositional practice" and transgression, while the writing itself remains as academic as ever.) At the same time I suspect that very few who talk about it have ever been at a rehearsal, particularly the kind of rehearsal that approximates the more radical implications of theory. Here I am thinking of notions of limitless difference, undecidability, structures of "unmotivatedness," the agile slants and

41

breakings off of thought, the "teleology of an impulse,"[3] overing and dilatoriness, the unnerving dyslogistics that can, at its best, go with the incommensurable and look for more, including contradictions, without merely succumbing in any simple-minded way to the fallacy of imitative form. (For the fallacy will be there if you want to think of it that way, as a vice of poetry possessed by theater.) The fact of the matter is that a fair number of actors have never been at such a rehearsal.

Despite the featuring, then, of performance in a sweeping indictment of the logocentric power structure of theater, its metaphysics of the Word, what seems to me largely unreflected in theory is a more intimate knowledge of the complexly (un)encumbered praxis and apparatus of theater (conventional *or* experimental). This extends to the time-serving "materialities" of performance, its *refractoriness*, its temporal zones and urgencies, its deadlines, and along with the free play of the signifiers in the libidinal economy of the body, what I have called elsewhere the amortization of play, its deadliness, and the sometimes inspiring, sometimes deleterious presence of real people with turbulent emotions and stubborn wills. Immersed as they are in ideology (details about to come) they can't quite be summed up or put down as ideological subjects. Moreover, as a variation on a theme of the previous chapter, they are likely to look the finest theory in the face and say, at some critical juncture of rehearsal, I'm a *feeling* actor not a thinking actor, or, it's a terrific idea, but how do you *do* it?

If that simple question may on occasion both chasten and quicken thought, it is in my experience also likely to be evasive. If theorizing by the director can also be diversionary (not in the Derridean sense), it still doesn't justify the resistance to the theory. Nor is it entirely justified by the experience of Pinter, though any practitioner will have some doubts, as I do, about thinking too much. Unfortunately, this problem may be, as the self-conscious tradition of the oedipal drama knows, in the bloodstream of theater. I am well aware that what happens in the theater is, for all our thought, intuitive and adventitious, chance having the last featuring blow at events. (It was chance, by the way, that I happened to be in London just when *The Birthday Party* was first performed and given a bad time. I asked Pinter for the play and we did it at The Actor's Workshop of San Francisco, which introduced him to the United States, over thirty years ago, when he was something of an ideological cause, along with Beckett and the absurdists.) The crucial difference between practice and theory is well expressed by Pinter, or would appear to be, when he describes a working process that consists of "a kind of stumbling erratic shorthand, through which facts are lost, collided with, found again."[4] I happen to think that is also the way with theory, as one sees in the shifting certitudes and ideological nuances of Brecht and in the enfevered slippages, concussions, and cardiac arrests in the nervous system

42

of Artaud's thought. That thought is corporeal, carnal, as Grotowski used to say the theater should be in the theory he largely borrowed from Artaud.

About the corporeality of theater, its intentionality of the body – a factitious body as theatrical fact – I shall have more to say in the next chapter. When Pinter fetishizes the body, as he appears to do in *The Homecoming*, it is half a cunning put-on or, with the body losing control, the exhilarating pretext for a litany of abuse. While his drama approaches the uncanny with the motiveless appearance of malignant craft, deliberately inflicting pain, in the talk I am referring to Pinter speaks of his own pain, which occurs when he distorts or falsifies his characters, or jolts them into being by finding the right word. For Artaud, it is thought that does the jolting, self-inflicted, cutting to the brain. The pain is legendary, running like a lesion of impossible promise through whatever there is in our theater that remains innovative and proleptic. Admittedly, the theory of Artaud exceeds in desire anything he could ever realize, or any of us, refusing as it does in its unremitting meticulousness "every insufficiently fine, insufficiently matured form."[5] Yet the imaginative body of that insufficiency, its failed realization, seems to me more powerful, and *immediate*, in its decisive theatricality than most of what we see materially, or rather immaterially, on the stage. What is perceived by Artaud at the theater's remembered origins is not merely the sound and fury that once turned us on – the apocalyptic clamor of our love affair with myth, lights, noise, spurts of image, incantation – but the rigor and acuteness of a *conceptual power*. That's what we were also reminded of by some of the performance which left the conventional stage or came from sources other than the theater, certain kinds of performance art where if you put your body on the line it is put there theoretically whether or not, to save our theater, it is signaling through the flames.

But to stay, through the erratic motion of theory, with the fine line of dissent from Pinter's thought: when he does talk *about* theater, he tends to be laconic, dispassionate. The acceptance speech is like that, though he says at the outset that he is startled, bewildered, even frightened by the award. The bewilderment is a courtesy, however, a cue for the distinction he makes between the Pinter summoned up for the occasion and the private person, indifferent to praise or blame, who lives in an almost illicit intimacy with his plays.

Despite the intimacy, their meanings escape him. The words stare him down, he says, become stubborn, take control, as if he and not the characters were being worked over in the riddling double binds of his punishing rooms. I know what he means when he avoids speaking about what his plays mean. We all do, I suppose, and have come to expect it, the warding off of discussion. It is the recurring posture of high modernism that has become second nature, like Eliot's "It's impossible to say just what I mean" or Beckett's remark that if he knew who Godot was he would have said so. I have done my own share of putting off clumsy inquiries about clear meanings or the "message" – people still use the word – of a difficult play by some who think it virtually a criminal offense if there isn't one. "Make sense who may," says the inquisitorial voice of one of Beckett's last plays, *What Where*. "I switch off."[6] Yet his plays are an analytic continuum of the switching process, with a belated inflection of the overtly political (dedicated to Havel), and it is hardly a semantic reduction to feel that Beckett's remark is also a posture, an ideological posture, worked out theoretically as far back as his essay on Proust, a theoretical (un)grounding from which he's never departed. The only trouble with the remark about Godot is that, when overquoted, it does a certain amount of brain damage to people in the theater of somewhat lesser mind. For there are those who are only too relieved to think that if Beckett doesn't know and Pinter is unwilling it discharges them from the task of thinking at all or struggling with meaning, as Beckett does unceasingly from one impasse to another until he teases us out of thought.

Not so with Pinter, who is also teasing, and seductive, with a fine gift of *intimations*, though it is possible to ask about him, as Spooner does of Hirst in *No Man's Land*, whether a "truly accurate poetic definition means anything to [him] at all" or whether he is a mere virtuoso of insidiously unexamined propositions that remain unquestioned, *unthought*, and in the end "threadbare" (*Works* 93). There is the insistent question of Hirst before the curtain that worries the question for Pinter, "But what does it *mean*? what does it *mean*?" (150). This, however, seems a pretext for another rehearsal, a verbal round on a relatively closed subject, changed or unchanging, which seems a predicate of the plays.

LEAKING METAPHYSICS: THE ALCHEMICAL STATE AND THE SUSPENDED QUESTION

Nothing has significance. Everything has significance. Between these two extremes, one sweats. But, thinking it over, "Why this refusal to discuss?" as Brecht asked in an early essay. It is one of those questions that has to be asked, it appears, in every generation, as Eric Bentley once said of another question: what is theater? Brecht explains in the essay, "Modern Theater Is Epic Theater," how the refusal conspires with the ideological apparatus of cultural reproduction, including the established theater, to impose its views without our knowing it, "as it were incognito" (Brecht 34). Brecht and others, from Lukács to Foucault, have variously described the process of reification that produces mythologies, causing things to seem present and accounted for, natural, matter of fact, the way things are, when they are actually disguising and exuding at the same time traces of an origin that is no more than a theory – a theory so reflexive it does not recognize itself as such – or a process designed to cover up a theory or to make any signs of the process, which is an ideological process, seem spontaneous, innocent, invisible, or blank. Artaud speaks of metaphysics coming in through the skin; Freud speaks of our betraying ourselves at every pore. When we look again at what we have taken for granted, sometimes so subtly there it seems granted by nature or God, the metaphysics that went in will also leak out. It may be the metaphysics you prefer in your heart, but some of us do not know it is there. Which was the reason for Brecht's theory of estrangement, with its double take on the familiar and its misleading appearance of self-evident truth.

When Brecht was rediscovered in the United States in the late fifties, and in Western Europe as well, there was a tendency to discount his theory along with his politics, as if there were something fortunately schizoid about his art that extruded the ideology. Roland Barthes, who fashioned his own early thought around "The Tasks of Brechtian Criticism," pointed out then what *should* have been self-evident, though it still is not, that "there is no official decree or supernatural intervention which graciously dispenses the theater from the demands of theoretical reflection." Barthes makes short shrift of what, in the theater, is the anti-intellectual prejudice. Even in France, apparently, it was "no matter of indifference to encounter a man of the theater who is intelligent."[7] Brecht is not great despite the ideological Brecht – the agenda explicit if not exactly orthodox – but because of him. (Although I have expressed my own aversion to being named ideologically, what artistic work requires is anybody's guess.) Even now, when it may seem but a dream derided by events, to minimize the politics is like saying that Tolstoy's *War and Peace* is a great novel except for its theory of history or that *Moby Dick* would be better without the chapters on the whale, or for that matter, that Yeats and Strindberg would have made it if they had never messed with the occult, or Shaw if he had given up Jaeger suits and vegetarianism. (Benjamin quotes Meyerhold, who was asked on visiting Berlin, about 1930, what distinguished his actors from those of Western Europe: "Two things. First, they think; second, they do not think idealistically but materialistically."[8]) There is, moreover, a certain repression involved, a censorship, in the effort to separate the artist who suffers from the man who thinks, or woman, stripping the intuition from the theory. It is a repressive force that follows, as Barthes sees it, from "one of the basic theorems of *petit-bourgeois* culture," the romantic disjuncture between heart and head, keeping the ineffable in its anointed place while the rational tends to facts, ultimately masking "a magical conception of art" (*CE* 72).

Which is not quite the one that Yeats and Strindberg had in mind. Nor that other occultist, Artaud, in his conception of an alchemical theater. Remembering there the Great Mysteries – not from which the drama came, but which are rooted themselves in the *essential drama* – he opposes to the "excessive logical intellectualism" of bourgeois culture the stringency

45

of other mental operations, such as Freud imagined when he spoke of the unconscious as our oldest *mental* faculty (also attached to an essential drama). To achieve thence the alchemical state, in all its acuity and absoluteness, beyond the current trembling or false organicism of ideological forms, what Artaud required is a "rigorous intellectuality" of which "the mind must first prove that it [is] capable" before meriting, in a labor redoubled at "the incandescent edges of the future," the irreducible rarity of "material gold" (*T&D* 50–1). As this may be too mentally exhausting for any of us, we are back again to the organic currency of the ideological world, although there are times when Brecht addresses it so that, beyond the intellectual requirements, his theory intersects with Artaud's.

Quite well aware that Brecht's theater is constituted only by performance, Barthes nevertheless argues that the theoretical texts, "of a great ideological lucidity," are no mere intellectual appendages. They are, rather, generically functional, generative. We can see that clearly in the recorded (and no doubt edited) discussions of *Coriolanus*, the ideological labor through which Brecht leads his collaborators, into and out of the text, amending Shakespeare where, as he says, Shakespeare can be amended. To that extent they are changing the unchangeable, into the body of performance, in the case of *Coriolanus* one of the great productions of our age, not least because – as with Günter Grass' *The Plebeians Rehearsing the Uprising*, written specifically in opposition to Brecht – it was a production to be argued about. I referred earlier to Brecht's image of practice watching over the bed of ideologies, attentive to their birth and death. It is a vigilance, however, that is not unguided, so far as it involves a working method. "Practice demands that one step should follow another," Brecht wrote in another early essay, on "Form and Subject Matter"; "theory has to embrace the entire sequence" (29).

The demand persists even when, as Galileo says in his experiment with the sunspots, we cannot take steps but crawl by inches. That is, of course, a methodological principle, as it also is when he says with passion that he believes in the brain. What the brain believes is, at the extremity of meaning in Brecht, roughly Marxist. At the moment of materialization, however, *as meaning*, the solidification into a rhetoric, the Marxism is *suspended as a question*. The answer is imminent but arrested, as in the gestation of a *gestus*, which is never an answer nor even a pure question, for "a question is never," as Barthes observes, "anything but its own scattered answer, dispersed in fragments among which meaning erupts and escapes at the same time" (*CE* 264). So, between the conception and the act, the ideological shadow, which is as it were an implosive force.

THE ALLURE OF OPACITY

Whatever the resemblance between the scattered answer and the erratic shorthand where facts are lost, collide, are found again, theory may slip in without your noticing, as Pinter acknowledges. So far as he does theorize in the speech, it is about a more magical conception of art, though he wants to be pragmatic about "theatrical facts [which] do not easily disclose their secrets." It is very easy, he adds, "when they prove stubborn to distort them and to make them into something else, or to pretend they never existed" (*Works* xi). One senses that at the level of praxis Pinter knows what he is talking about; it has the feel of having been there, of concrete work, that Brecht would appreciate. Yet he might look askance at another aspect of the statement, as he does in his ambivalence about the Chinese actor, whose signifying detachment he admires while distrusting the fact that the A-effect is achieved "by association with magic." What he was appraising at the time was a "primitive technology" or "rudimentary science" whose secrets remain hidden and transferred among a privileged few in an otherwise rigid and stratified society (*Brecht* 96). While he is ready to appropriate the effect as a "transportable piece of technique" (95), what we always see in Brecht, ideologically, is a reflex for assessing the human cost of any technique. He extrapolates from the stubborn fact, whether technology or its object, to the social system it requires. He is always attentive to the possibility that there is a sediment of abuse in the anonymous process of labor that produces suspect objects and establishes the theatrical fact which does not easily disclose its secrets.

Still, it is a good theoretical statement, Pinter's, and I respond to it myself because it pays a certain tribute to the opacity of experience that has been the obsession of my own work in the theater, almost congenitally shadowed by ideological doubt (including various personal manifestations of the anti-theatrical prejudice, more or less absorbed into the work). It also pays its respects to the unconscious, which is for me if not for Brecht the alpha and omega of all process, the originary *mise-en-scène*, where the action really is, however we manage to bring it to the surface, and in whatever dubious or suspect forms. Unless we really believe that the solipsism of Baal was utterly purged from the more rationalized body of the later work, we can easily see that Brecht is always quite ready to exploit the economic resources of the unconscious as a political instrument. He tried, however, to rein in the libidinal energy at some limit, or even denounced it, as with the gluttony of Galileo that made him recant or the anarchy of Azdak when it threatened to disturb the equilibrium of restored order, or the incurable pathos of his wife's Mother Courage.

Having survived a historical evil that remains a scandal because inexplicable, Brecht refuses the opacity in principle. As remarked earlier, he distrusts the unconscious because it has been so politicized by the

47

ideological apparatus, the information systems, that our actors have the most unreliable access to it. Pinter doesn't analyze what it is that makes for the liability of distortion, but he might have been on to something similar were he to have thought it through. Despite the obfuscating strategies of his plays, he is not – in speaking of the theatrical facts that do not easily disclose their secrets – encouraging a needless mystification of process. A passage that follows may seem to be doing that, but it is insisting, rather, on an exactitude that is a kind of aesthetic morality. When the actors and directors, he says, arrive in rehearsal "at a given moment on stage, there is only one proper thing that can take place at that moment on stage, and . . . that thing, that gesture, that word on the page, must alone be found, and once found, scrupulously protected" (ix).

I suppose most theater people, scrupulous or not, would concur with that, favoring as we do a sticky organicism. I concur myself, but with rather mixed feelings in the present context. For there *is* an ideological difference at stake, as there surely is with Brecht who tells us over and over, as in "The Street Scene," that there are innumerable ways of looking at any event, the materiality of a historical instance, even on the stage, the material moment which reflects it. All of these ways of looking and reporting may intersect and leave their traces on what you finally *choose* to perform. As he says in the essay on Chinese acting, "Among all the possible signs certain particular ones are picked out, with careful and visible consideration" (93). They share the aesthetics of exactitude, but between Pinter and Brecht there is obviously a considerable difference in theory, mediated by ideology, which will determine *what* you choose. There are other things you *could* perform at that moment, though we may prefer not to believe it in our mythologizing of *discovery* in the acting process. There is nothing either natural or inevitable in performed behavior, although the scrupulous protection may be designed to make it ideologically correct or, like the artlessness of Duse through the spray of roses, disguised to make the ideology disappear. In the absence of her legendary inspiration, we have developed other means, in those acting techniques that, enseamed in the process they conceal, are meant to keep acting from looking like acting.

One may speak of an ideology of naturalness in acting which is the mask of ideology. As Nietzsche remarked, it is the truth of an illusion which we have forgotten is an illusion. There is a certain mystique about acting in the strangeness of a Pinter play, or about being, as they say, a "Beckett actor," but it is a very rare production of either dramatist that is not still working, with variant stylizations, in the naturalistic tradition. Meanwhile, as cultures cross in the narrowing economy of the multinational, all techniques, sacred and profane, are pretty much out there, available, circulating, in the marketplace of signs. When we buy into one or another, however, it is more likely than not to be in the condition of that forgetfulness. We move in our desires between the image of the natural and the image of the hieratic, sometimes pathetically, or transparently, like the cross-dressed hero(ine) of David Hwang's *M. Butterfly*; or more alarmingly so in the allure of opacity, like Genet's missing Queen who is either picking her nose or embroidering an invisible handkerchief, an insoluble problem, embroidering or not embroidering, more or less.

IDEOLOGY ENGRAILED: THE ACTOR'S SWEAT AND THE WINE-DARK SEA

The actor who acts more is no more ideological than the actor who acts less, and more or less may only be decided on some ideological ground. It is ideology which determines the answer to any question that any technique gives to whatever question, whether unconscious or suspended, and which determines *who* believes it *where*. It is the theatrical equivalent of what in international affairs Henry Kissinger once named the Doctrine of Credibility, whose operations (the since-documented scenarios, games and simulations, the unavoidably scandalous dramaturgy of foreign policy) were modeled after the theater, where credibility occurs as a politics of form (and the scandal in its primal scene). Credible in respect to what? we must always ask, although there are certain techniques, depending on *where* and *when*, that beguile us into forgetting, with which our natural weakness concurs. Amnesia, it seems, is the most adaptative state of mind, alternately known as selective inattention.

For the most part what we still take for naturalness in acting moves ideologically through a whole spectrum of computable appearances that synchronize the acceptable behavior of an actor with the price inscribed on a ticket or, in certain experimental quarters at certain times, the seeming absence of a price. But for any technique there is always a price, though it may seem to be working off a discount, which is a theoretical delusion. Before you even look at the stage, everything in the material reality of theater practice is ideological: not only the price of a ticket, but the conditions of the gathering, the attitudes of the ushers, the advertising or want of it in the playbill, program notes or their absence (on the grounds, as they say, that a play ought to speak for itself, which it never does because it ideologically can't), air conditioning in the theater, the size of the candy bar, the distance from the stage, and when you look, the thickness of the makeup or its absence, whether or not you can see the actor's sweat and whether or not they want you to see the sweat; the fact of a division from the stage, audience here, actors there (a figure of almost all ideological controversy, carrying through revolution and into religious wars), or the opening of the stage into a "thrust" or its displacement into an "environment" which, however dispersed or scattered, may be ideologically the same old frame, since ideology is a mental set, arising

49

it almost seems from the deep structure of theater and determining among its elements, seen or unseen, the economy of performance: the weight of the platforms that a specific quantity of labor has to move, even with two boards and a passion (in the large "plants" of our educational theater considerably more than two boards, an ideological ripoff on false educational grounds), the use and exposure of lights and the weird phenomenon of the curtain (emblematic fabric of an irreparable division, now you see it now you don't, even when the curtain is not there), the "teasers" and "tormentors" that conceal and seduce and suggest an invisible truth in their very names; the casting of a play, the number, gender, and age of the actors or, ageold, the very presence of an actor who, before he disrupted the ideological unity of the Chorus, once was *not* there, nor the second actor, nor the third, with their agonistic voices and competing claims: the space of desire in which a performance occurs, from the brightness of the landscape on a wine-dark sea to the motes in the air around a single lightbulb on a stanchion when the rehearsal ends, signifying as it were the forlorn economy of the theater we commonly know, with its producers and agents and reviewers and, with more or less paranoia, the authority of the director who, like Oedipus, may be blind, but sets the rehearsal schedule within that mental set in ideologically determined time; and of course the choice of the text to be performed, and to which we once thought we could be faithful, and so on through the habits and reflexes of our theater, its ideological consciousness, or absence, *in* the interpretation that, as it now appears, is ideological to its core, by the nature of interpretation itself, even when there is no text – to which we *could* be faithful if the text, unlike the teasers, were *transparent* and not concealing *something else*. That is why it has to be interpreted. For it is the locus of fetishism and exchange in the politics of the unconscious, with its network of repression, which is itself a symbolic production.

In this sense I am not speaking of ideology as something that comes *before* performance, but as something engrailed, invested, credentialed within, and charged with the fantasy of more or less formal solutions to unresolvable social contradictions, even if the performance is autistic. As an ideological act in its own right, any performance involves questions of property ownership, hierarchy, authority, force, and what may be the source of ideology according to Nietzsche: the will to power.

 ## WITH GAZING FED: THE IMAGINARY SOCIAL

What we take to be credible in acting is, within the ideological structure, a system of quite classifiable effects of which, in realistic or psychological acting, what we call *indication* with disapproval is, when you think of it, the least disguised. Later on I will discuss the taboo on indication in Method acting, but a developed capacity for indication might very well be acceptable or encouraged in another system, as it was apparently in the gestural repertoire of Le Brun or the realism of Garrick or the Delsarte method, or as boggling the eyes in anger at the Other would be in the facial masks of Grotowski or in the aggressive technique of the Kathakali, derived from a martial art, where the Master calls – when the eyes seem already to be bulging out of the head – for more *force*. That boggling is a critical distinction. It has ideological force. It keeps the Other or the Double at bay. In our conventional theater, still *petit-bourgeois*, the Other tends to be mythicized into the Same; that is, in any face-to-face encounter with the Other, the Other is doubled over by the performer into a mirrored version of the Self, which itself mirrors the system of representation that reproduces itself.

It should be remarked, perhaps, that as the cycle is now mirrored in the repetitions of theory, the tautology seems to spread over the whole field of reproduction, and we run into the question as to whether there is any system of representation that doesn't reproduce itself. (Surely the Kathakali does, as if the double in the theater is never kept at bay.) Whether this is good or bad, thinking makes it so, and the requirements of history. There is surely more to be said on behalf of the self as the historical triumph of an otherness from which it wants to be relieved, but there is an immediate issue in the troublesome mirror.[9] As the performer in this system, eyes with gazing fed, is caught up in the gaze, what would seem to appear in the eye of the beholder is ideology itself, the immediate material or material cause of a society's consciousness of itself. As it happens, this is also the wobbling pivot of Althusser's thought, the point at which he equivocates about the spontaneously lived ideology, its use-value, the presupposing of "an essential identity (which makes the processes of psychological identification themselves possible, in so far as they are psychological)" (*For Marx* 144). The presupposing is, of course, the threshold beyond which in the theater it must undergo a critique, as in the dramaturgy of Brecht. With the reluctance to get too close to the alibis of psychology, the lies and sublimations of bourgeois consciousness, we are left somewhere between a "dialectic-in-the-wings" (142) and the familiar double bind: without such ideology there would be no mirror of self-recognition, and yet that is precisely the mirror which must be broken if there is to be real self-knowledge, historical knowledge, and not its illusory surrogate, "the image of a consciousness of self living the totality of its world in the transparency of its own myths" (144).

As in Castoriades' concept of the "social imaginary"[10] – without which there would be no symbolic networks, no sense of augmented being – the mirrored reflections may be seen as something other than a deathtrap of specularity. But if there is any major problem with the social imaginary it is, in the inversion by Baudrillard, the imaginary social, which seems to have disappeared (if it ever existed) through the superplenitude of

51

image into the commodification of otherness itself, or the silent power of indifference, inert material of the spongy mass: aegis of simulation, the hyperreal. If that presents us with images at all, they are images in which there is *nothing to see*. In the aesthetics of the hyperreal – whose sublime agency is the eye of the video tube and the reign of "informatization" – we are no longer dealing with a mirroring truth. Whereas ideology corresponds only to a betrayal of reality by signs, simulation is the short circuiting of reality and its reduplication by an overdose of signs.[11] Without necessarily going for the moment as far as the hyperreal – with its bleakly ecstatic fable of the end of representation – we are back to the question raised by other theorists, and ubiquitously over the centuries within the theater itself: what happens to the real theater when only theater seems to be real?

According to Roland Barthes, the *real* theater – Artaud's cruel spectacle, Brecht's tribunal – is the place where the Other always "threatens to appear in full view," but even this anointed or judicial place is threatened by the mirrors (*CE* 151). The ideological force of these mirrors has dominated the history and sensibility of our theater. The Brechtian techniques of alienation, by decentering the image of ideological consciousness, aimed to break their force, but the plays of Heiner Müller, a mordant fusion of Brecht and Artaud, suggest in all their poetic virulence just how unbreakable the mirrors are. With a similar virulence in the brothel, that had already been done by Jean Genet, who stopped writing plays after *The Screens*, which in its gleeful imagining of the end of representation, as if from beyond the grave, seems to multiply the mirrors in laughter where you'd think they would have an end.

CONVENTIONS OF APPEARANCE
AND THE APPEARANCE OF INDETERMINACY

So far as the theater is a model of life that takes its cues from the theater it has dominated the activity of perception as well: what we see and what we are prepared to see, even by the recurring pretense that pretends it is not pretending. But there is in the mirrored show an ideology of perception which in turn affects the ideology of performance. We stage our lives, in or out of the theater, in accordance with the description available of the perceptual process itself. When, for instance, principles of indeterminacy began to absorb the scientific imagination, conveying a view of the material universe that no longer corresponded to the expectancies of empirical cause and effect, the possibilities and strategies of performance were altered to correspond. That became in a sense a newer realism. (Within the play of indeterminacy and its paradigm of expectation, the passage from abstraction back to psychology might be represented in dance, say, by the mutations of movement from Merce Cunningham to Pina Bausch, though her work is hardly the older realism, and with psychology still abstract.) Since what appeared to be so was not so, or at least seriously questionable, appearance itself was submitted to another kind of reality testing, which involved a discourse *on* appearance as part of the substance of changed appearance in performance. At the same time surface appearance – what was hitherto accepted as real – was deconstituted into the more undecidable grain of the real, in such a way that indeterminacy became both reality and method. As a result, we can think of it now as a virtual *convention of appearance*, including the undecidability.

We can think of it so, but we're not sure we can see it. It will obviously take a little time for this newer realism to solidify itself in the marketplace, which operates according to its own principles of indeterminacy. (It is, to be sure, a market that moves fast, and while it took some years for Merce Cunningham to get there, among the current vicissitudes of the avant-garde is the fact that both he and Pina Bausch are now, for all the quick movement of commodities, solidly established.) Meanwhile, the determination of what we see and what we are prepared to see seems to me, at this historical moment, the most urgent activity of a self-conscious theater that is ideologically uncertain, bewildered – not sure, to be perfectly honest, whether it is really seeing anything at all. ("Do you see nothing there?" "Nothing at all, yet all that is I see" (*Ham.* 3.4.131–2).) At its best that apprehension may enter the structure of performance as its self-reflexive subject. The enterprise of perception reflecting upon itself can be more or less articulated or conscious, more or less imbedded in the structural rhythm of a performance, but there is still in most of what we do a floating apprehension. This is all the more true in the American theater where, without any theoretical continuity or critical exchange, we each take our own chances. We take them and leave them, going it alone, as if the dialectic were a fantasy still waiting in the wings.

The thing is that we are not so much acting today *in principle* as acting, more or less consciously, *through the competition of principles dispersed in unbelief*, all claims weighed, next to drained, exhausted – and you are out there where the acting is, in the domain of appearance, with nothing but informed nerves, wishing yourself luck, *then* choosing. To *think* ideologically *in* performance – to make performance itself not merely expressive *of* ideology, victimized by its own unthinkingness, not really knowing what it thinks – we must realize that no performance can occur today outside the dispensation of mirrors; which is to say, all performance occurs in an ideological blur. That is why when Brecht, distrusting the political unconscious of the bourgeois actor, says we must act *above* the stream not in it, I can only respond by observing (as before *in* the theater work) that it is like saying you cannot step into the same river twice, which you cannot do because you cannot step into it even once, you are always already in it, and that is where the thinking has to be done, treading water. Which does not mean you should stop thinking. I realize that in describing all aspects of the theater as socially produced and having in turn, at the most unconscious levels, ideological consequences, is to fall into still another, tautological, double bind. But, as I said, we were already in it. To recognize the tautology is not to alleviate it and, for some, made nervous by the ideological repetition in the stream of consciousness, an excuse to ignore it.

BETWEEN A MIRROR AND A BLANK WALL: REPETITION AND HISTORY

If we can believe the history of modernism, we are living in the double bind, the repetition that always repeats itself. To think thus is not necessarily a matter of mere opinion, nor of cultural pessimism, the point at which modernism "comes to grief against its own material underside . . . ." For Fredric Jameson this is one of the intolerable options in the critique of late capitalism, its "final and most absolute contradiction, the 'situation' that has become a blank wall, beyond which History cannot pass,"[12] leaving no political option. But even Jameson has to concede, while assessing the power of negative critiques of ideology (Adorno, Tafuri), that "the anxieties provoked in almost everyone by such an implacable and absolute position are probably healthy and therapeutic in one way or another" ("Architecture and the Critique of Ideology" 58). The same issue arises, with the same anxieties, in trying to rethink catharsis through the Brechtian critique of tragedy. In any event it is not modernism that ordained repetition in history, nor can any therapy or theory exclude the offending term, for the name of that repetition is History, which does not allow us to escape its recurring and mirrored appearances, in terms of which we struggle to discern and articulate any political option.

If, as Jameson says, the philosophical formulation of a postmodern aesthetic may be properly founded on the idea that "difference relates" (59), there is still a critical difference between a mirror and a blank wall, no less, say, the Berlin Wall, through which history in the form of appearance had also managed to pass (not least in the images of West German television). These confronted us, even before the Wall collapsed, with the appearance of political options, which turned out to be, far more swiftly than expected, something more than appearance. If I am playing somewhat with the idea of appearance, that is merely to stress – whatever the bias toward distinction in the social imaginary – that there is nothing infallible in the necessities of perception. Between the modern and the postmodern, as in the matter of political options, we have had to learn to *wait* (as we still have to wait for the straightening out of prospects in the ruined economies of the old Soviet bloc, or, in the new master planning for the future of the Middle East, the working out of animosities *within* the Arab bloc, and the developing of capacities to imagine a future). Was that not the political lesson of Beckett's apolitical play, which was in the apparent futurelessness of a postwar world, the lassitudinous discharge of its *nothing to be done*, a virtual handbook of activating strategies for postmodern performance? Appearance may alter imperceptibly through the precipitations of time, or the autism of repetition (minimalist dance, Warhol's films, the ragas of Steve Reich), of which we first became conscious, perhaps, in Beckettian practice. As for Jameson's concern with a postmodern aesthetic, it can also be said to have been founded with a signature of uncertainty on indecisive ground. Speaking of how "difference relates," there was also the enactment there of how – as if unavoidably in the activity of perception – we slip, slide, decay, and maybe (with old modernist anxiety in the new age of precision-weapons) perish with imprecision.

So far as the theater is concerned, it has always seemed to me as if Beckett's practice occurred, with a certain virtuosity, in the space left empty, the precipitous silences, of the drama of Chekov. And I have written elsewhere about how – no matter how mordantly, or on the edge of parody – we are enjoined by Chekov to think better than we do, and later by Beckett to think (if failingly) better than we can: think! think! think! use your head, can't you, you're on earth, there's no cure for that! Moving on in thought, or mortified by it, between a mirror and a blank wall, one comes eventually to the theater of Genet (whose plays are being restaged in Europe and South America, probably elsewhere, and even now and then in one of our regional theaters, around questions of power and oppression, including sexual politics, in the demoralizing transition to a postcolonial world). It was apparent, when I first directed their plays years ago, that there were considerable differences between Beckett and Genet. But on one thing they seemed to concur: in a world confounded by the failing repetition of reflection itself there is no way to contend with the supremacy of appearance except, as the Bishop says to the mirror in the brothel, by the most immaculate intelligence.

Most of us will, no doubt, emulate the Bishop in falling short of that, but that's no excuse for denying appearances or, as a more sinister voice in Genet would have us do, giving in to them. There is, of course, a certain intelligence that can be too immaculate. With the Envoy from the missing Queen, we're into a stylistics of performance thriving on appearance, the play of mirrors or mirroring play, which carried over into the artworld with the incursion of performance. As that shifted with further refractions into the styles of popular culture – with the technology of appearance for its commodified masquerade: the capacity to reproduce the entire repertoire of polymorphous play – we may have a sense of reality more or less playing around. Like that literal amplification of appearance, the wrap-around giant screen with Dolby sound (for films dubbed in several languages to be marketed around the world), this can take on the oceanic immensity of the fascination-effect itself, with the vast seductions of its coming attractions. Or, as Jameson describes the alternative response to the massive contradictions of late capitalism, there are various temptations to relax within it or to invent "modes of perception in order to 'be at home' in the same impossible extremity: the substitution of a plus sign for a minus, on the same equation" (60).

THE IMMINENCE OF A NOT-YET

Actually, there is in any mirror a similar substitution in the equation, since when we look in a mirror we come back to ourselves reversed. And it is within the circuit of denegation that Pinter makes his peace in *No Man's Land* with the timewarped mirror of the archetypal modernist, T. S. Eliot, whose rhythm was adopted above as a sort of memory trace. The slip, slide, decay is like an atomic half-life of lost possibility, though some of us would resist the maybe imaginary loss in the slippery signifiers of what maybe never was, the timeless time before the fracture, which was itself only mirrored in the "dissociation of sensibility" that came with the baroque. (Or, as Benjamin remarks of its "panoramatic" appearances, its "unparallelled virtuosity of reflection."[13]) Yet given the undeniable inheritance of fracture, Eliot knew the hazards of perception.

We live in a world which, having the look of something that is looked at, seems worn down by the looking. Our thinking itself seems but a dim echo or reflection in the mirror, heard or seen before. That is why, from Brecht through the phenomenology of postmodern performance, we have learned to bracket certain ideas or put them into quotes. We saw such quotes, literally, in Brecht's earliest plays, *Baal* and *In the Jungle of Cities*; and when he took the inverted commas off Rimbaud he put them around the social *gestus*, that moment of historicization, bracketed or framed, which reminds us to think twice. The social *gestus* carries along with it as a dialectical proposition not only what went before but – in a very different sense a moment out of time – the imminence of a *not-yet*. So far as there is a utopian element in that imminence, it may not be redeemed in eternity, but the question remains, as it does in Marxist thought, whether it will ever occur in history.

If this is something that needs to be bracketed too, Brecht asked from the beginning of his career an essential (if not essentialist) question to which he returned in the provisional summing up of the *Short Organum*: What should our representations look like in the culture of productivity of a scientific age? The counterquestion has to do not only with the legitimacy of that *should*, its ideological imperative, but with the question of representation itself, *its* legitimacy, since it compounds the appearances, making it harder for truth. Just as Einstein's science demands that the relativity of the frames of reference be included in the objects studied, so must performance

56

relativize, first of all, now, the relations of the perceiver and the perceived. When I say in this context that the audience is the major problematic of the theater, I am not thinking of drumming up a subscription for another regional theater, but reflecting the idea that the agencies and instruments of perception alter the nature of what is seen. That is actually what we have come to mean by technique in a cybernetic age.

We may now think of human beings as desiring machines and technology no longer as machines at all, but as another conceptual power. As I've said, the elusive nature of that power is undergoing, first outside the theater, now in it, a good deal of ideological analysis. So is the theater itself, in the critique of representation. But it's as if we've just begun to hear what the theater has been telling us all along, in all the repeated manifestations of its fitful seeming. In short, the theater is being seen in its *seeminess*, the duplicity of its appearances, as an agency and instrument of that elusive power, as well as its hapless victim. This is particularly true of the actor who is of course victimized by the profession. With the advent of robotics, the actor remains labor-intensive but, without necessarily knowing it or conceding it, *specifically* ideological. Most actors think of themselves as unpolitical, adaptable to all kinds of roles. But they are no more neutral than the robot, by no means value free; and even determined to have values, victims just the same.

One of the major ironies of our theater, as of the other media, is that the dissidence of the performer may simply be absorbed into the ideological apparatus. It makes no difference whether a lifelong socialist aspiring to play King Lear was selling soap with good intentions through Norman Lear, no more than it does when an offbeat filmmaker attempts in the repetitive slowdown of a nighttime serial to improve with artfully insidious images the quality of the soaps. The system of reproduction that reproduces itself can, like Jarry's debraining machine in *King Ubu*, reprogram a former member of SDS[14] to anchor the evening news, or those still aligned nostalgically with the counterculture to read out the future as a utopia of the status quo in the image of *E.T.* What we keep looking for, I suppose, is something in the grain of performance that will convulse the ideological field in which the enunciation of power invisibly prevails. That, too, is easier said than done, although it is being said with some frequency in the cadres of cultural studies, its new materialism (as if rhetoric itself were the fundamental asynchrony, the CP violation (charge × parity) that left a world of matter, rather than antimatter, after the Big Bang). Yet even when there is a disruption, so powerful is the grip of the apparatus upon the attribution of truth and credibility, the accreditation of the natural, that even F. Lee Bailey's lie detector affirmed it some years ago on TV, before it was thrown out of the studio for its own questionable truth. To signify otherwise, however, is to be like some feeble specter of the actor/victim in Artaud's transfiguring flames. The flames themselves can be

57

reproduced at will by the apparatus, as we might see in rerun videotapes of "Burn, baby, burn!" or the simulation of a rocket launching in the studio, which seems like the real thing, rising parabolically into the orbit of the ideological field, where it makes a safe landing in the code.

As the failure of the Challenger – with video reruns of the fireball in the sky – opened up the difference again between the programmed simulation and the intolerable fact, there has always been a dangerous impulse in performance, which proceeds within codes, to spill its ideological content by means of the *traumatic*. Moreover, when the codes are too oppressive there is something like an upsurge of rage. In the economy of rage, which is the disfigured function of the economy of death, we can see today the shadows of Artaud and Genet, even among those who never heard of them. In his book on subcultural style, Dick Hebdige used Genet as a study guide to teddy boys, skinheads, and Rastaferians, whose rage, already a performance, was doubly played over in reggae and punk.[15] If performance can shock or outrage, spill over, so to speak, from the code, it might seem for a traumatic moment that the categories of language by which we observe the Law have been suspended. But it is only for the illusory moment, and then the performance is reappropriated like the wildest conceits of punk into the omnivorousness of the code – as Genet knew it would be all along, and as Barthes once said of Genet himself after Peter Brook's production of *The Balcony* at the Théâtre du Gymnase, on the once-grand boulevards of Paris.[16] What Barthes saw realized in that production is an inflexible law of the avant-garde, its serial liquidation by eventual accommodation, a process whose efficiency has so improved in the postmodern experience that it seems to occur by instant satellization or the speed of light. Or more parodically down-to-earth, like the ubiquitous pratfalls of the performer in Bill Irwin's *Regard of Flight*.

There are, nevertheless, historical moments when certain kinds of performance do seem efficacious, as Marx shows in *The Eighteenth Brumaire*, when he reminds us that the French Revolution was enacted in Roman dress, or when we remember that the Boston Tea Party was performed by bourgeois merchants in feathers and bare chests. So with the costumes and performances of the sixties – the happenings, action events, guerrilla theater, Be-Ins, Love-Ins, "actuals" of all kinds and varieties of the Living. They were enlivening not because they were accurate in their definition of unexamined propositions or in their reflective assessment of objective conditions or because of their respect, in a world which seemed total theater, for the theatrical facts that would not disclose their secrets. If they had any potency at all, it was because what they projected politically was desire, which, even if wanting in reality, is an ideological motive, also utopian, so long as it embodies the *truth* of desire. If the desire is merely a desire for performance, it seems somehow to run out of truth.

GROUND ZERO OF DESIRE

The power of popular forms is ideologically contained in their relation to that truth. They resist deprecating analysis because they arouse consensus of feeling at some unspeakable level of desire. If they resist our better knowledge that's because they are so deeply ideological, lodged as desire is in the operations of the unconscious. When the historical moment is right the unconscious speaks its own mind. And it speaks in another language, in touch with the source of desire. It is the level at which political energies can be mobilized, as they were for a glorious moment in the unfortunately short-lived history of the student uprising in Peking. We might remember that this was not entirely foreseen, as if the censor were asleep, or deceived by secondary revision, since the gestures and slogans *were* in another language. Whatever the language, however, there is never a guarantee that political energies will be mobilized for radical ends, nor that the censor won't awake, like Deng Xiao Peng, who seemed to be sleeping for quite a while as the demonstrations proceeded in Tiananmen Square.

As we saw some years ago with the Moral Majority – whose constituency, God knows, but we forget, was also aroused by desire – considerable energy may be mobilized for the gross reinforcement of the code, which operated with the Gross National Product to shift our radicalism to the right. There was very little in our theater that, before the election of Ronald Reagan, gave us an early warning signal on that. But you could hear it in, say, country music, which found a way of articulating the pain of certain truths while affirming the ideological system out of which it grew, and which – in Reagan's vision of a little house on the hill – seemed like a utopian truth. If Black Monday seemed in its abrupt panic to put an end to that truth, there were (in the dirty campaign of George Bush) "a thousand points of light" to indicate that there was still some life left in the myths spontaneously lived. As a matter of social class, leveraged buyouts and arbitrage are not exactly themes for country music, though it would have hardly been surprising if for other painful reasons "Black Monday" had become the title of a song.

What is a major problem in the susceptibility to any truth is precisely what makes it susceptible: the inability of the desiring subject to elucidate his/her own truth. We see that with harrowing understatement, like the ground zero of desire, in the mutes and mutants of the earlier drama of Franz Kroetz. The nearly subhuman characters of his plays are, if not brutalized on the farm, robbed of speech by urbanization and do not, like other victims of political oppression, have even the relief of speaking in tongues. The plays are chilling and should have been chastening to certain political illusions. When, during the sound/movement fantasies of the sixties and seventies, we found bourgeois actors yielding up their speech in

59

order to bring in the millennium *by* speaking in tongues, we had a political aberration in the theater of the oddest ideological dimensions. It was unfortunately traceable to Artaud, who had often felt like ripping out his tongue because the words were stolen from the instant of speech, as if they were stolen from birth. That theft was powerfully theorized into the theater of cruelty, as it was not in, say, *Orghast* at Persepolis, one of the memorable experiments of the period, though with a rather naive view of some phonemic continuum of language across centuries of cultural difference pointing back to a primal source. There was the additional political irony that those animated material murmurs in the air, indebted to Artaud, were being financed by the Shah who, for the exiled followers of the Ayatollah, had done the stealing from birth.

Kroetz once objected to the capacity for speech in Brecht's working-class characters, only to concede later that without such speech there would be no possibility of a dialectic in the plays, and no class awareness, nor any way of articulating the utopian shape of desire. One would have thought that Heiner Müller, in the years behind the Berlin Wall, would have been committed to such a position. But on the evidence of *Quartett* or the *Hamletmachine*, he may never have had the temperament for the utopian shape of desire. We have at any rate seen in his work varying degrees of disenchantment, anarchy, and some experiment with "presenting" the text (or having it presented by Robert Wilson) through the spatial refraction or dispersion of speech. We shall turn to other aspects of Müller's work later, but there are times when he seems not only indifferent to class awareness, but without any faith whatever in the collective substance of language. Yet there was a time when Müller's working-class characters were, like Brecht's, more or less articulate, and often eloquently so, and this is mainly how we see them – with certain brutish inflections and deranged figures of speech – in his own recent staging of an early play, *Die Lohndrücker* (*The Scab*), with a dialectical standoff in all its perverse dependence between the power of the workers and the power of the State.

Without updating ancient drama and putting it in modern dress, Müller has frequently in his plays cut across history as if *it* were hallucinating to draw poetic sustenance from its bloodstained myth. There is a similar movement in this play from postwar East Germany to Empedocles on Etna, by elliptical images on film and invocations of Hölderlin. But what is really unexpected in the volcanic dialectic of baffled power is that the last words are given not to the workers but to the secretary of the Party, who tries to imagine a state in which power would not be needed at all. The utopian dream of the secretary Schorn is spoken, however, with perfect legibility over a loudspeaker, the actor seated down front listening, not as a member of the audience, to the withdrawn prospect in his gaze. What is manifest, however, in the lucidity of the impersonal voice is what, before the total opening of the Wall, kept Müller shuttling from East to West:

the ambivalence of the dream increasingly left behind, the nightmarish awakening to a world of perfect order: not an incident against the State, not a crime, people behaving just as they do in the unbanned books and Party journals. "I want to see that OR I do not want to see that." More and more one suspects that Müller doesn't, and never did. And he has been, with acerbic displacements of personal anguish, very articulate about that in the sometimes brain-damaged speech of the later plays, indebted as they are to Artaud, who of all the enraged witnesses to this century, Müller said, understood its savagery best.

SPEAKING THE REMAINDER: AN INFLECTION OF GENDER

The symptoms of the theater of cruelty were, indeed, a spectacular diagnosis. But without being seduced again by the insidious glamour of the Plague, let us stay with the issue of speech. Within the more sensational and mythic aspects of his theory, Artaud was making an ideological distinction of considerable importance: not when he seemed to abolish words but when he assigned them an appropriate place in the reimagining of the theater. As with the "rolling alphabet" (*T&D* 67) of the Balinese dancers – the whirling and murmuring signs in a "perpetual play of mirrors" (63) – the words are situated between eye and ear, dream and event; that is, between the linguistic structure of the unconscious, with its metonymic distortions and transformations, and the materiality of history as it repeats itself.

The shape of that depends on who controls speech. As we can see from the rudimentary cruelty and almost sensory devastation of the characters in Kroetz, and in the brutally silenced women of Pinter's *Mountain Language*, there is no alternative but an assumption of speech by those who could never speak for themselves or those who feel bespoken by a colonizing power, the words flying up, the body bereft, a power not really their own. As for those of us inhabited by speech, there seems no relief from that. Nor from the invisible force of the logos that only repeats itself. And if the theatrical facts *did* disclose their secrets, what we fear is that they would only reveal – as Pinter's plays reveal, subversive as they once seemed – another version of the Same, what we take to be inevitable and unchangeable, *that power* – what indeed makes bourgeois culture, even if secular and restive, look as if it were ordained.

The terror of that ordinance is endemic to the no man's land of Pinter's plays, which may seem abstract and ahistorical when compared to either Kroetz or Müller. Here we encounter again the ideological distance from those endowed with the privilege of repression. The dramaturgy of Pinter converts the eventuality of history into what seems – through the jigsaw puzzles of his elegantly schizzy language – a place of uniform inertia, "which never moves, which never changes, which never grows older, but which remains forever, icy and silent" (*No Man's Land* 153). My own temperament is only too susceptible to the metonymic aura of that icy opacity in which argument inevitably fails. But there's something rather facile in the allure of the highly regulated play of signifiers – "It's gone. Did it ever exist? It's gone. It never existed. It remains" (108) – that signify virtually nothing except the permutations and combinations of its own self-encircling and empty play. I say that with some hesitation. There are few enough dramatists with Pinter's skills writing similarly evocative drama, rather than plays (or other texts) in which the emptiness can hardly be said to approach the conceptual. (I should add that the verbal content and incipient dramaturgy of many performance pieces seem to me, with whatever avant-garde, postmodern, or political claims, retrograde in comparison to various segments of Pinter's drama that, like Beckett's, are virtual models of solo performance or other aspects of performance art.) Nor do I mean to insist that there is nothing remaining in Pinter but the repetitive figuration of a feeling of impotency, although it is certainly possible to feel that – what Jameson worries about as the material underside of modernist doubt.

Without the benefit of a doubt, whose benefits are part of the problem: there is a hint in Pinter of another prospect in the dying fall of the *remainder* that maybe changes the exhausted subject and maybe doesn't. True, it's nothing like the moment of arrested meaning – what Barthes calls the *pregnant moment*[17] – in the dispersion of questionable value that (ideally) constitutes the ideological in the *gestus* of a Brechtian play. But Pinter does give the barest suggestion of a sort of not-yet, the frail imminence of something other, in the surprising inflection of gender at the end of Spooner's speech about the poetry reading projected for Hirst, "an evening to be remembered by all who take part in *her*" (108; emphasis mine).

It's not much of a space for the feminine to move in. And it seems to come pathetically out of the Eliotic past. And in any event it still has to be theorized, ideologically thought through, as it *is* being theorized in the critical intersection of psychoanalysis with radical feminist and homosexual discourse, at the decentered crossing of which is the unfillable gap of which Hirst speaks early in the play. It is a play with a not at all illegible homosexual presence (focused in the actor for whom it was written) and a certain fear and trembling about the feminine, not-yet-there, as if it were the returning repressed. For those who know the discourse, that gap is another name for what Freud called the dream's navel, where in the act of interpretation the dream passes out of sight. Another name for the gap is the *lack* explored by Lacan in his revision of Freud. While women are keeping their distance from the gap that defines their being in terms of castration, it is the lack which produces desire and the ideological subject who/which also passes out of sight, as if the subject were created in the (dis)appearances of the dream. "Who was drowning in my dream?" asks Hirst, as he imagines the figure of a feminine absence. "No-one is drowning" (108). Which doesn't relieve the dread of absence. "No one has power," said the Bishop in the mirror imaging of Genet's *The Balcony*, with its baroque allegorization of desire, whose subject is also an absence, the missing Queen, embroidering and not embroidering.

The feminization of recent thought is obsessed with the embroidered absence and the power of the desiring subject (even its power to overcome the status of an empty signifier by *determining* its disappearance as an image). Out of the absence, a flood of desire which threatens, anonymously, to blot Hirst out and all he represents, including the structure of representation, the image-repertoire itself, those images that yet fresh images beget, in the image of repressive power. "Who is doing it?" asks Hirst. "I'm suffocating. It's a muff. A muff, perfumed" (108). And if you care to look into it further you will see without question that it is an ideological muff that is caught up, theoretically, in the subject of power.[18]

It is a subject about which there will be more to say as we proceed, but as we become more acquainted with the discourse of power – not in theory, but in politics – it is easier to believe what the theater instinctively believes, even when more realistic, that the real is as imagined as the imaginary. Actually, that is what theory has also come to believe, which is why it appears to behave like theater. If you have been following the literary battles over deconstruction (revived with somewhat gleeful antagonism by the revelations about Paul de Man) the charge is that there has been a subversion *by* performance of the autonomy of the text, which is seen as a text of power. This is no longer a covert operation in reverse, as with the amplification of the subtext by the Method actor who is playing a private moment, with a kind of palpable secrecy, as if it were illicit emotion.

The private moment, to be sure, was a preface to the pregnant moment, not in the Brechtian sense (except as critique of its subjectivity) but in the solipsistic sense of the autoerotic performance that spans a couple of decades now – as well as the more extreme gap between the artworld and the theaterworld – from Vito Acconci plucking out his pubic hairs or masturbating under a ramp to Karen Finley's *The Constant State of Desire*, where *she* gets the "ultimate erection" *and* "the ultimate orgasm" from the fantasy of her father masturbating, in black stockings and garters, mirrored, as he hangs himself from the shower stall.[19] If these private moments are pregnant (and not all as sensational as that) they are, as Derrida says of writing and play, a pregnancy *without* birth, for birth is a kind of closure, a meaning embodied in an (apparent) identity and thereby undeferred. As for the prerogatives of the text, what they are worrying about in literature is what they are worrying about in the theater (when they are not worrying about funding) as directors revise the classics; that is, the arbitrariness of interpretation, which for guardians of the canon seems like a scandal of history.

FETISHISM OF THE SIGNIFIER: THE MISSING TAPE

But let us reflect for a moment upon the politicians, among whom scandal now seems like a commonplace of history, the revision seeming to occur almost as quickly as history is made. (Indeed, it seems to be the way in which, quickly, the most revisionist history is made, like the shredding of documents by Oliver North.) But what is this history we are talking about – whether in the canonical texts or the course of human events – about which we can never seem to have the last word, as if the past were nothing but footnotes and postscripts and the present always escapes? It is as if those who make history are, when they write about it themselves, reshaped to a common discourse that attenuates the real and becomes a mirage of abstraction. It was the outcome of this demiurgy that Marx described as phantoms of the brain, which under the rubric of false consciousness is pretty much what ideology is when not more or less prescriptive dogma. Still, it is possible in the dramaturgy of Marx to have good phantoms and bad phantoms and, in revisionist Marx crossed by Lacanian Freud, phantoms just about as inscrutable as the ghosts we encounter in the cellarage of our theater or the scene of writing in the unconscious, which Freud thought of *as* a language that is also the *site* of speech.

That is why we may think of ideology today, with our semiotic addiction, as a fetishism of the signifier[20] which – through the words, words, words – traps the ideological subject, the subject of desire, in the articulations of a code. Saussure had described the arbitrariness of the signifier. As if the words had their own mind, the fetish is a *word-thing* that seems to be telling another story, a *fabrication* or *fabulation*, an alienated projection of appearances and signs which passes like a phantasmic performance into the mechanisms of exchange. It is a stock exchange, however, which is already glutted with appearances and signs. Voyeur at heart, the fetishist has to have a performance, but there are times when, in its superfetation of image, the eroticized spectacle is almost too much, as after being fastidiously stuffed *mit blutwurst* by a voluptuous paramour, the performance artist John Kelly-as-Egon Schiele multiply crucifies and, in numerous scandalous postures, replicates himself.

To pick up, however, on the other scandal, let us resort to some more or less recent history or, among the best sellers of recent years, the making of history (with large "advances") in the accounts of the making of it. Take the memoirs, for instance, of Richard Nixon and Henry Kissinger. We are only too prepared to believe that we're dealing with myth when it comes to the Nixon era, with its undercover scenarios and worldwide dramaturgy of illusion, culminating in that poignant scene in the personal tragedy of Nixon, where the two master politicians are, like the Duke and the Cardinal in Webster's play, on their knees praying together. But what is most disturbing about the memoirs, even now with some distance, is not their contradictions, apologias, or cover ups – which our cynicism expected – but rather that they are fabricated with a rather perverse desire to reproduce exactly the system which entrapped them, that is, within the same *economy of truth* as John Dean's *Blind Ambition* or H. R. Haldeman's *The Ends of Power* or, for that matter, the still unverifiable revelations of that other phantom, the original whispered source, Deep Throat – who might conceivably have been a fiction but is surely a fiction now – or the later scourging of Kissinger by Seymour Hersh in his book *The Price of Power*, about policy-making in the Nixon White House. From all accounts it was a structure of appearances that might be the consummate model of postmodern performance, including as it does among the myriad fabulations an interval of silence that might have been composed by John Cage, the eighteen minutes of missing tape.

The price appears to be throughout the discourse a certain delirium of truth in which we try to maintain our collective sanity. But like the dynastic representations of power on television, the story is not over when it's over, and there were later complications when that honest man in the White House, the Great Communicator, appointed the peripatetic statesman, the Master of Secrecy, to formulate our policy below the border.[21] The art of covert operations is such that it immediately appeared on the surface, along with cruisers and maneuvers, that we were dealing with a hidden agenda, merely confirmed some years later by Colonel North. For all the subsequent exposure, that agenda goes deeper than we know, and even if it didn't the grounds of suspicion are such that we are prepared to believe almost anything. Or in a curious warp of perception, it's as if the Doctrine of Credibility had produced the very opposite of a willing suspension of disbelief. In this regard, what George Bush called "the loop" would seem to encircle us all, and if he remained outside, as he said, nothing else appeared to be. For the loop seems to expand with an autonomy of its own, or as a function of information. The drama of the nineteenth century was, in its glaucous revelations, already in the loop, which spreads like a grid of misrepresentation in the structure of our theater. But haven't we become aware, in the critique of representation, that it's the other way around? For the charge against the theater has been that it is the long historical repository of deceit and distrust, contributing its expertise, if not to the specific actuality, then to the reflexive habit of an utterly dissembled truth.

But somebody must be telling the truth! we are still ingenuous enough to think, even the most jaundiced among us. My father, a plumber (not of the Watergate variety), used to read the newspaper from beginning to end, every word, advertisements, classifieds, obituaries, everything. He had a

65

working man's response to the problem of authenticity (which will be a major theme of the last two chapters). "They're all liars," he would say, as he folded the paper, though he would read all the way through the next day – editorials, gossip, letters, captions, checking out the weather in places he would never see – to confirm his unswerving conviction. "They're still liars," he would say, only the box scores, perhaps, passing the test of accuracy. This was, to keep matters simple, before the age of steroids, free agentry, and widespread scandal in sports. ("Say it ain't so, Pete.") So much for the certitudes of the proletariat, who can also tell it like it is, though none of us is quite sure whom to tell it to, and *they*'re not sure what to do about it. True, it becomes harder to determine the proletariat as ideology breaches class and money ideology in a country where dispossession is as much a psychic condition as an economic status. Which is not to say the status can't still be miserable, at the level of material culture. If the proletariat is less identifiable, the street people are not, and we also have the "new poor" not yet out on the streets, who never anticipated the dispossession that compounds the psychic condition *because* they are running out of money. Yet even many of them, hoping with whatever hope that the economic indices would be authentic, twice supported a presidency that, starting with the image of teflon and ending with the "sleaze factor," seemed to be the model in the semiotic flux of what we think of as the slippery signified.

Which sticks on the question of truth. It is the question that shadows our theater today like those mysterious illnesses of our time (legionnaire's disease, herpes, AIDS) which seem to replicate the question. Nor is that because we've had a quick series of plays on and off Broadway on the demoralizing subject of AIDS. Still, with our tenuous bourgeois convictions (bolstered in theater or theory by the fictions of another politics), we look for a little piece of truth here, a little piece there. The problem is compounded by the very sense of relativity, that dis-ease of liberal thought upon which the history of modernism has exponentially upped the ante, until the very act of looking seems, as I've suggested, to add its problematizing portion to the slippery problem of truth that is the sticky alibi of history. So far as I know, my father never read Nietzsche, who more than shared his opinion that you could hardly believe a word. According to Nietzsche, we are *all* liars, know it or not, like it or not, since we live in a dispensation of error that is engrained and enshrined in our language. "What then is truth?" he asks, in a keynote of current theory. "A mobile army of metaphors, metonyms, and anthropomorphisms – in short, a sum of human relations, which have been enhanced, transposed, and embellished poetically and rhetorically, and which after long use seem firm, canonical, and obligatory to a people . . . ."

Here is the entropic downside of the ideology spontaneously lived. Not only have we forgotten the substance of our truths as the illusions they are – a process intrinsic to our idea of theater even as the theater exposed it – but the metaphors are exhausted by long usage, like our plots and characters, which have been divested as well of their signifying power, like "coins which have lost their pictures and now matter only as metal, no longer as coins."[22] It is an irony of the exchange mechanism in which our meanings are made that it seems to function like the theater in which, for all its power of representation, the pictures disappear. What Marx and Freud added to this analysis is a view of the ideological system of representation, in the economy and in the psyche, through which we can see how the very means of telling the truth, including the words by which we swear it, are bought and sold or always already corrupted or repressed.

Swear! says the Ghost, to the one who can hardly believe a word, no less the suspect tale of a phantasm in a place that stinks to heaven.

THE NEW SHAPE OF POWER

When we grow weary of the disorder of the world whose disorder spreads through our language so that we grow exhausted, we retreat to or look for energy in the apparent order of art, its ingrown autonomy. Music is unmeaning, poetry is a play of words aspiring to the order of music, theater is theater, not politics, however it may remind us of the world, which grows weary of a politics that looks like theater. The less we can depend on the appearances of things or approach anything like a consensus on what they mean, then the more likely it is that in the intangibility of political process, as in the immateriality of performance, what happens in the world will be repeated, signified in established ways. This is all the more so when there appears to be an event in the world which seems questionable, undecidable, unpredictable, which appears to break for the moment our expectations about the world. Since there are always disingenuous forces and self-disposed interests – very powerful and unexhausted – they are likely to interpret according to their interests, reshaping the unexpected into the frame. This is itself the new shape of power, ideological power, which determines how events are signified, like the power behind the play-within-the-play who even authorizes what the ghostly father can speak.

The power to signify is not impartial either in the theater or the world. And what we are beginning to realize – far more outside our theater than in it – is that cultural objects acquire social force to the degree that they are aware that differential meanings are woven in social and political conflicts. This backwardness of theater, or delinquency, would appear to be strange given the fact that actors and directors have always been involved in the task of differentiating meanings. You'd think a developed competence would be transferable, except that we also have a developed example in the *production* of plays, their *interpretation*, of what

67

Marx compellingly argued in the second part of *Capital*, that no production is possible, nor a sustained social formation, that does not reproduce (*as it produces*) the material conditions of its production, including the means of production allowing it to produce. While production and interpretation remain cognates in the theater, there has been a shift of emphasis – in the displacement of a privileged text, by altered or rejected content or revisionist strategies of production – that corresponds to the necessities of social and political conflict. In the age of the media, the signification of events is a good part of what is being struggled over in the world, not only the right to life but the right to determine its meaning. It is in this perspective that ideology, the ghostly speech of the phantoms of the brain, is to be seen as a material force, as real as the acting body, real not only as carnal, but real as history is real, in its signifying *effects*. The ideology we have in mind as a predisposition to meaning depends, then, on the balance of interpretative forces, in performance as in politics, *at this point in time*, as they said in the Watergate inquiry, speaking more accurately of historicization than they knew. For it was in the theatricalized reality of such an event, as well as its current fabulation, that we could see how the theater itself is implicated in the politics of signification.

A theater may or may not take sides on the big issues of war, ecology, space, labor, international trade and protectionism, crime, poverty, abortion, drugs, the rise and fall of the dollar, the possible revival of fascism and the immanence of racism, fundamentalism and terrorism, unresolved colonialism, genocide and triage, and the right of all those born and living – incontestably past the demand for the fetal right to life – to some barebones security and minimal dignity in the passage of life to death. In an early interview in *Tel Quel*, Barthes took the position that an "ideological theater" such as Brecht's *should* take sides, but not necessarily with a "positive message." There are still theaters in parts of the world – precapitalist, nomadic, or village cultures, but also subcultures of the industrial world – that can no doubt justify such a message, as they can justify the deployment of aesthetic forms (realism, constructivism, expressionism, or any level of abstraction) that in a local context will be estranging, critical, serviceable, instrumental. While there is certainly a point to American feminists or urban blacks arguing among themselves the ideological propriety of certain forms, elsewhere the notion of justification is little more than a non sequitur or simply irrelevant – as the justification for terrorism may be, with all its theatricality, for those who live *inside* the terror. Justifications become a problem as adaptations begin to occur, and we have certainly seen over the history of "liberation movements," from the Irgun zvei Leumi to the PLO, the repeated historical turning where continued "gratuitous" violence will be argued ideologically within a movement before it is renounced, theatrically, before the world.

All of this is relevant for theory, but retrospectively, from a distance, as we think through again the questions of aesthetics. What troubled Barthes, of course, in the positive message was what prompted him later to put the idea of performance, the *actio*, the whole risible stereophony of the body at the ideological center of *jouissance*. We can surely see now that the libidinal body and the subsequent lover's discourse were ideological reflexes and consequences of the sixties, positing the incremental perversions and infinitesimal delights (or illicit *délits*) of the pleasured body against the monadic, rationalizing, culinary forms of egoistic bourgeois power. (More about the pleasured body, and other variants, in the next chapter.) It wasn't only a matter of saying it, but of showing it as well, which Barthes himself did in the guise of *écriture*, presumably displacing or dispersing the message into performance. (There is in the apparent dispersion a decisive formalism that again poses itself against the statedness of "content," a holdover from modernist technique that, making a virtue of reification, thought of the most abstract form as material content, by indirections finding directions out.) Yet on the earlier question of an ideological theater, focused in the praxis of Brecht, the message was clear enough: however the issues were brought to attention, meanings elided or even writ large (emblematized, say, in banners over the stage), there had to be the challenge of *interpretation*. As we might expect, the taboo for Barthes was a "theater of the signified." A theater could be considered appropriately ideological only when its issues were problematized by performance, the world seen as an object to be *deciphered*. Which is not to say that it will be, for there are no guarantees of meaning, no ultimate secrets, nor explanatory origins. With the Marxism suspended as a question, what Barthes saw in Brecht is a process that produces meaning without any meaning at all unless interpreted and (how *in* the theater? when and how *outside*? still needing interpretation in Brecht) acted upon; in short, a "theater of the signifier" (*CE* 263).

A DOUBLE STRUGGLE AND THE SPLINTERED HEAP

There is more to be said of the liabilities of the signifier, especially when it floats or freely plays; the liability of action, particularly revolutionary action, is that it puts an end to that. But pending that paradox, the determining energy in the relationship of ideology and performance marshals itself in/for a double struggle:

First of all – in the theater as in the older industrial world – a continuing struggle for the means of production, which is what the playwright/dramaturg Richard Nelson was despondent about some years ago in two issues of *Performing Arts Journal*.[23] Nelson's analysis of still-current practices can hardly be disputed, but it is in the longer view of the regional theaters that, as a cultural study, his essay is wanting. For the theaters he is writing about – which started emerging in the fifties – were *never* revolutionary, as he says, not when I was exhorting them to be in *The Impossible Theater*, not my own theater in San Francisco (more adventurous than most), not even the Group Theater earlier, which was for all its legendary social conscience always ancillary to Broadway. Whatever the adventitious ways in which this movement was potentially liberating, the most to be said of it now is that it remains with rather vague promise on the scene, which is more than can be said of the "alternative theater" of the sixties. Actually, the nature of its accomplishment has never been accurately assessed, so much of it overestimated at the time – the best of it without continuity because untheorized, or crudely theorized as experimental with the worst.

The struggle must occur, moreover, with awareness that in the praxis of performance we are doing a relatively medieval sort of work. This is all the more conspicuous in a mediated world with systems of information that, despite the hardware, seem weightless and vapid, made out of signs. We may talk about performance within that system, as video image, or in the theatricalized behavior of everyday life, but the problem remains that of sorting out the appearances, deciphering and interpreting with a finer sense of distinction. In this regard, one distinction to be made is that, develop as we will a semiotics of the body, the body is not, with information or image, part of the same delivery system. And even if it assumes in a given production the fiction of a mere function – with no more intrinsic value than light, color, fabric, or other objects in space – there will inevitably be the friction of resistance, with somebody calling it ego, this impediment of the body refusing to be a sign. Whatever the accretion that looks like ego, it seems to materialize in the *mise-en-scène* of the unconscious, as a lamination of theater or theatrical construct, which leaves us with the necessity of another distinction:

As we turn to the signifying task, we may do so with the ideological suspicion – or is it ontological awareness? – that in or behind all systems the theater is doing its work, disarming function, and transforming the real as only the theater can. This suggests that there is no way to *produce* meanings in performance, except adventitiously (with or without messages but in any positive sense), without knowing that there is, in the field of knowing, a scrim of theatricality over our lives. It is precisely that, moreover, in all its indeterminacy that may prevent us from ever making the finest distinction, as to whether the scrim is ideological or ontological, or some indecipherable weaving of both – which would seem to be the impasse that, whatever we think of it, sustains the theater as theater. The element in the equation that we tend to forget, what signifies the impasse itself, is that if theater gets in the way of theater it is, whatever the measures of power, thinking that makes it so.

Which is in the Hamletic nutshell the perplexed fate of consciousness brought to ideology as well. Even the most powerful ideological consciousness will – in the confusion of realms: language and nature, reference and

70

phenomenality – be undone by theater, as in the case of Althusser. As a systematic theorist, Althusser gave us the formulae, acronyms, and descriptive theory of the RSA (Repressive State Apparatus) and the ISA (Ideological State Apparatus), developing beyond Gramsci their inter-relations and respective indices of effectivity. At the same time, he worked through the elusive notion that ideology has no history, which he read in Marx as a negative thesis, committing him in *The German Ideology* to a view of ideology like Hamlet's contracted vision of infinite space, the empty vanity of a dream, and a bad dream at that. Althusser tried to understand ideology as something essential and vital, like the air we breathe. If not pure air, it was not, as Marx would have it, an etherizing vapor, but that which, because we share the same dawn, the same abyss, the same history, solved "the false problem of identification" from the beginning.

Despite this perception, Althusser nevertheless worried about the effects of ideology in so far as they threatened a scientific discourse on ideology and, in a fully developed and rectified Marxism, scientific knowledge itself. If he now and then seemed to despair of such knowledge (perhaps undeterr-ably so at the end), that would surely have been a liability as he displaced the conception into the terminology and structure of the unconscious. I don't want to labor here the question of psychoanalysis as a science, but if ideology presupposes, as he thought, a real (lived) relation to the world profoundly invested in an imaginary (lived) relation, the false problem solved from the beginning keeps recurring in all its falsehood as something very real. Which is why, in the remarkable essay on the theater that I have already referred to,[24] he can't avoid the onset of self-consciousness in self-recognition, with the renewed incursion of a mirrored reality. Thus he is finally constrained to ask, with a certain ideological poignancy, about the prospects of the important work done for dramaturgy by Brecht and Strehler:

> What will become of this ideological self-recognition? Will it exhaust itself in the dialectic of the consciousness of self, deepening its myths without ever escaping from them? Will it put this infinite mirror at the center of the action? Or will it rather displace it, put it to one side, find it and lose it, leave it, return to it, expose it from afar to forces which are external – and so drawn out – that like those wine-glasses broken at a distance by a physical resonance, it comes to a sudden end as a heap of splinters on the floor.
>
> (*For Marx* 150)

Is this another bad dream? It is perhaps only one of those slips that psychoanalysis would pick up, and no doubt exaggerate, but there is in the last sentence not even the consolation of a question mark after the splintered heap.

71

WORKING THROUGH:
DO YOU GO TO THE THEATER OFTEN?

The heap, the little heap, the impossible heap . . . the Beckettian cadence of *Endgame* came a few years before the shattering of the wine-glass in Althusser. But even before the subsequent profusion of aporias in postmodern performance, most of us in the theater had been willing, since the advent of modernist drama, to put aside the certitudes of scientific knowledge. Perhaps too reflexively so, since few of us know much about science (or have the tenacity for its methods), except perhaps that it distrusts itself. Or so we've come to think, all truths subject to the ethos of suspicion. If that came into our culture with Oedipus, the more immediate patrimony is from thinkers like Marx and Freud who pursued in elusive fields an impossible science. But to stay within the parameters of our own elusive field: if the certitudes weren't already disposed of in the scabrous disaffections of (prematurely modern) Jacobean drama, they surely had disappeared before the lost documentation of the last conceivable certainty, the evidence of an origin, in Pirandello's *Right You Are, If You Think You Are!* What is being looked for, I'd guess, in a world of confounding appearances, is the outside possibility of a stateable truth, a truth you can live with in candor. But we know we cannot live with it, however well stated, if it is not worked through, as they say in psychoanalysis, though I mean it *as theater*, which of course operates in the dramaturgy of analysis, as in the scenography of the unconscious, with its insubstantial pageant fading . . . leaving to Freud what Prospero didn't define.

Shakespeare might also have left to Freud, who never took it up, the still missing motive for his leaving the theater. Whether or not Prospero's farewell to illusion is his own valedictory, the drama he left us raises the ontological question as to whether, if we are such stuff as dreams are made on, one ever leaves it. "Canst thou remember/A time before we came unto this cell?" (*Temp.* 1.2.38–9). Whether the cell is in the beginning, as on the island of *The Tempest*, or at the end, as in the prison of *Richard II*, we are inevitably dealing in Shakespeare, as later in Nietzsche and Freud, with the circumference of illusion, the merest pinprick of which is as vast as the sky's seeming or, as in psychoanalysis, "the dark backward and abysm of time" (1.2.50). So it is that from the spectacle in the cell of the fantasy of the wreck (spelled: wrack) to the almost indelible evocation of the theater's reality as disappearance (leaving not a wrack behind) there seems to be an affinity with the "structure" of the unconscious: the space without boundaries, a nul, a nothingness, thus returning us to ideology, which is precisely nothing, the void that cannot be explained, yet as Althusser remarked, omnipresent and transhistorical.

Strangely too, as with the pedagogy of Prospero, there is an estranging instruction in the form of negation, which is like the theater itself a negation in question. Thus we learn from Shakespeare to Beckett, as from the pedagogy of Zeami in his protocols of the Noh – with its inscription of evanescence, so conscious of the void – that the nothing at issue is, maybe yes maybe no, on the margins of indeterminacy a nothing to be done. There is always the liability that it will be much ado about nothing, or that in its infinite repetitions we have seen it before, or that, as they say of the landscape while waiting for Godot, there's rather too much of the void. Yet there has developed on that bleak datum a self-reflexive momentum in the theater that, in turning attention to its own processes, eventually saw them as ideological, though increasingly so as constructions of history. If there is meanwhile some reluctance to identify ideology with the structure of the unconscious, that's the obverse side of the desire to rid the theater itself of too much obsession with its fascination-effect, or in a reality almost saturated with performance the vision of life as essentially theater. (The saturation does have the effect of diluting what was once intrinsic to this vision, "the direful spectacle of the wrack" (1.2.26) in its tragic sense of human suffering: the body in pain, human sacrifices all around, barbaric delights, what outraged Brecht in the *Short Organum*. Despite postmodern indifference to this painful view of the spectacle in which it is otherwise at home, the barbaric form so disturbing to Brecht still weighs upon the theater. It has also returned as an issue in critical theory, nobody much liking the awful necessity in its metaphysics of power, but having to deal again with the question of tragedy.)

There was also, in a simpler vein, the association of a more objective kind of truth – if not exactly scientific, less hermetic – with the urgencies of a social and political theater. It was along these lines that we saw in the seventies and eighties, after revivals of Eugene O'Neill, an even more avid engagement with Arthur Miller by socialist directors in England, as well as a more theorized reworking of realism in the French and German theaters. This was not only a matter of new approaches to the tradition of bourgeois drama, but of interrogating in the theater its own problematic, the reality of representation and the immanence of illusion, restating itself in the process, not as the reification or sublimation of a mystery, but as a cultural invention, the theatrical fact as a fact of history. Which doesn't mean that it eliminates the problematic, since it is not yet an incontestably stateable truth that the suffusion of reality with theater is merely an invention, whatever the construction one puts upon history. Along with the effort, then, to revive a social drama, there are now realistic or naturalistic plays being done that in the process of inquisition are as equivocal as Strindberg's preface to *Miss Julie*, where he wants all the mechanisms exposed, magic box open, showing the strings attached, as if he were Brecht, yet speaks disparagingly of the audience's dwindling capacity for illusion, refusing an intermission – that is, an alienating break in the action – because he wants to sustain the illusion and thereby preserve the mystery.[25] There are other productions, however, that have nothing equivocal about them. The magic box may still be open, but with a strong ideological disposition, and no patience whatever for either the illusion of reality, the fake method of realism, or the reality of illusion, which is real enough, widespread, and just what needs to be exposed.

I spoke earlier of Matthias Langhoff's approach to *The Duchess of Malfi*; what he did with *Miss Julie* was a sort of preface to that. Before commenting on this production, let me turn for a moment to an aspect of Strindberg's text. When the (unseen) Count returns at the end of the play, the debased heroine, whose hysteria seems to have diminished to catatonia, tries to summon up the energy for the denouement by a fatal act of acting, an enforced theatricality – by the character, by the text – the culmination of a series of reflexive references to the lethal play within the play, as when Julie says to her lackey seducer during an early teasing exchange: "Where on earth did you learn to talk like that? Do you go to the theater often?" (*Five Plays* 68). Jean soon gains the advantage in the psychosexual economy of the drama, but never the complete mastery he desires, and there is toward the end a virtual stalemate when they are psychically exhausted, both depleted. Julie wants him then to order her to use the razor, but his impotency is a paralysis, an instinctive powerlessness, brought on actually by the Count's voice over the speaking tube. "Then pretend you're he," she says, "and I'm you! – You gave such a good performance before when you knelt at my feet. – You were a real nobleman. – Or – have you ever seen a hypnotist in the theater?" (101). Whereupon she causes him to enact with her what she wants him to cause her to do. Before we reach, if so disposed, any level of abstraction or iconicity in the imagination of its staging, the text already suggests that there are various ways you can go, for it appears to have, at minimum, the quite radically divided consciousness that can also be seen in the preface, a manifesto of naturalism, where Strindberg can't quite separate the physiological from the psychological, character from characterlessness, a candid theatrical awareness from the "multiplicity of motives" in the "soul-complex" (52–3), or, in the usages of illusion, the mystery from the demystification.

As we might expect in Langhoff's production, the intention was, as with Webster, relentlessly to undo the mystery, in a kind of exacerbation of techniques ingested from Brecht, a theatrical analytic whose boldness is mixed with a disgust for theatricality, or at least the sentiments of a decadence that have no other form. Langhoff works almost instinctively, too, within the German tradition of the grotesque, and there were callously comic details in the materiality of the staging, from the cutting up of a large fish on the woodblock tilted over the apron, and the cleaning out of its guts, to the ribald squirt of blood on Julie's dress from the decapitated bird, which shouldn't have disturbed her too much since we'd seen her earlier gnawing sanguinely on a slab of raw meat. Crude as that may seem to be, it was performed with the broad exactitude of an image in the later painting of Philip Guston, all of it underlining the severely reductive view of a ruined social order, whose every reflex is soiled, crass, too absurd to be corrupt, with the style writ large, almost mockingly, on the curtain: A NATURALISTIC TRAGEDY.

For Langhoff it wasn't a question of an old-fashioned dramaturgical balance of forces, with even a token deference to the nobility in decay. Or if he materialized anything of that, it was only the decay, so far gone that it was, when the bell rang for Jean, already down for the Count. There was virtually no issue here of logocentric power. As it came down the speaking tube even the Name of the Father was a laugh. The Count's boots, once as ominous in Strindberg's text as the General's pistols in *Hedda Gabler*, were never anything but haplessly encrusted with mud, as if Jean had never cleaned them and didn't give a shit. As for Miss Julie, she was played (by the same actress who did the Duchess: Laurence Calame) with a kind of dicey wit, post-punk, but with an occasional holdover of spaciness from the acid trips of the sixties, which made the seduction a redundancy because there was, any way you look at it, really nothing to lose. Yet you wanted to look, or at least I did, with very little left for conventional voyeurism, since there was in the working through of the text a kind of working it over, laying it waste, with a sense of universal abandon or nihilistic power in the sometimes savage but stubbornly articulated indifference of it all. It's not the way I'd approach the material, nor work through the possibilities of a stateable truth, but one knew in this production, as in the collage of *The Duchess of Malfi*, that the text, however "violated" (no collage) had been intensely studied by someone with a harshly "realistic" view of its world, asserted through the text as theatrical fact.

Quarrel with them as one might, Langhoff's productions are carefully thought and informed by each other, and easy traffic between England and the continent has allowed a certain amount of cross-reflection, with Artaud and Brecht still in the background of much of the inquiry. Between England and Germany, Shakespeare is also in the background, or often at the center, of the inquiry, because of the long German connection to his plays, increasingly shared by the French because of the more feasible translations by Jean-Michel Desprats. As for the still-current rethinking of the drama of realism and naturalism, none of it would mean much if it hadn't been preceded, surrounded, and followed by the search for alternative theater forms and reinterpretations of the older classics, more or less radical, but on the whole, today, more dutiful to the texts than Langhoff, or than directors were during the seventies and early eighties. (We simply do not have the same theoretical apparatus in the American theater, nor enough reflective variations on the same texts, in successive stagings, to expect anything like a similar development, although we can well use, given its literary incapacities, a rethinking of American drama as *social text*.) To the extent that reinterpretations are still a function of experiment with theater forms, the interrogations are a replay, in the aftermath of poststructuralism and revival of the Frankfurt School, of the Brecht–Lukács debates on realism, brought to a Beckettian standstill by Adorno. The issues at stake were again cognitive and epistemological as well as aesthetic, and applied to more than the drama of realism. If we think of the debate as being picked up where Adorno left it (as we shall do somewhat in chapter 4), we can now see, perhaps, that notoriously modernist impasse as not exactly a dead end.

One would like to say the same about the theater itself, whose status has been continually threatened by what Adorno named the culture industry and, like the billion dollar deal between Sony and Michael Jackson, the escalating dominance of the media. "Do you go to the theater often?" That many have never gone, and that those who have, even in countries with established theater traditions, are going elsewhere or, with cable and VCRs, staying home, is also theatrical fact, a datum of practice – and a not inconsiderable reason for the reassessment of the drama of realism, which in the days of its dominance appeared to have what can now hardly be said to exist: a public.

RADICALLY NEW IN EVERY RESPECT: TRAGEDY'S UNSTEADY STATE

It was not the realistic drama in itself, but a combination of political disappointment and philosophical realism that inevitably brought about – as the conjugation of impossibility in Beckett does – a rethinking of tragedy. Not, however, in Langhoff's naturalistic mode, nor as usually performed at, say, the Comédie-Française, but in a sort of conflation of the art invented by Diderot with that invented by the Greeks. As in the sixties, but for other reasons, there was particular attention to Euripides, with *The Bacchae* as the most favored drama over the course of a generation, though feminism has turned attention again to *Medea* and, with a rethinking of pathos as well, to the rarely performed *Iphigeneia at Aulis*.

What attracted both directors and theorists to Euripides is that he was not only critical of established power, but by taking Dionysus as his subject he forced the theater to think – not only ecstatically but *realistically* – about itself, as an almost untenable reflection of institutional process, including the tragic festival in which he was conducting his critique. (This attention to the realistic substance of the tragic, with a more naturalistic behavior and depth psychology, and an implicit criticism of the institution, was actually represented at the Comédie in a controversial production of the neo-classical *Bérénice* by the German director Klaus Michael Grüber. With the restoration of conservative vigilance and renewed "respect pour le texte," it seems to have been dropped from the repertoire. The realistic substance of the tragic persisted, however, into Antoine Vitez's last production before he died, Brecht's *Galileo*, which was powerfully performed by Roland Bertin as a drama of psychological realism, with historical specificity, but few – almost gratuitous – alienation effects.) This movement of thought in the theater was anticipated by the scholar Jean-Pierre Vernant, who had written of Greek tragedy that it was not merely a confirmation of the *paideia* of the city-state, its truth, but "something radically new in every respect."[26] As the city-state itself was apparently very different from what Marx thought it was, tragedy confirmed not so much our accepted version of an archaic unification but rather its threatened and unsteady state.

This unsteady state, irredeemably threatened by the replication of an originary division, is what Artaud seemed to understand in his intuition of an essential drama, with its "infinite perspective of conflicts." For him, in the organized anarchy he thought of as "true theater," philosophical battles were still raging over the volcanic appearance of unremembered unifications (*T&D* 50–1). As Vernant saw it, the emergence of tragedy reflected a tumultuous change in consciousness *about* community that "could be neither thought, lived, nor even expressed otherwise than through the form of tragedy" ("Greek Tragedy" 284–5). The problems thus perceived as we rethink the tragedies – notions of hierarchy, origin, bloodlust and vengeance, war (the money changer of dead bodies), human responsibility and agencies of power, the quest for self-knowledge, the nature of the law, the meaning of appearances, and the question of truth itself – could not even be posed without the tragic form, which was a provisional solution to a horde of contradictions upon which the social order was constructed, like the oedipal complex with its incest taboo that still possesses our theory.

The meaning I am talking about is not, then, that of the play, the dramatic text, nor of the characters within the text, nor even that of the actors who – tired of playing what the character wants – prefer to play what *they* want and make up their own text, the subjects of desire who want to be spoken themselves; or those who, within the system of representation, have not been represented as they see themselves. That is likely to take the form, as with minority groups and women, of the forms we have seen before. Even with other content, or the content of otherness, it is likely to be insufficiently embroidered to escape the conventional fabric. It is, to be sure, a necessary stage in the restagings of thought. But what I am referring to is a deeper contestation with the ideological power behind the text, whether in the institutional theater or the apparently autonomous solo performance in a marginal space; that is, the structure of expectation, social and political, from which it emerges and which is likely to be reproduced even in the corporeality of performance, even in body art, below the level of words, for the body too is only too willing to lie.

There is after all nothing more coded than the body, and all the more now that there is around the body – a fantasy of itself, an ideological formation – an unabating discourse with a repertoire of devotions (through the essentialism of "difference") to its (singular) truth. It's as if the body were the new locus of received opinion, ghosted by the discursive accretions of common sense, habitual reflex, the conservatism of the instincts, and – as we have always seen when speaking of truth in acting, even improvisation, *especially* that – the established view of reality, the taken-for-grantedness and unexamined propositions, about life, about language, about the politics of behavior, about the acting and truth which define that truth. The body is, thus, the surpassing subject of the next chapter.

SYMBOLIC CAPITAL AND REVISIONIST PERFORMANCE

To repeat: what we recognize as credible in performance is more often than not what we have come to accept as credible in that closed circle of the ideological which, even in much experimental theater, produces not perception and knowledge, or even a change of heart, but the confirmation of what we already know and believe. The ideological matter amounts to this: we are as much spoken as speaking, inhabited by our language as we speak, even when – as in the theater of the sixties – we sometimes refused to speak, letting the bodies do it, or spoke too much, letting the words fall as they may, indifferent to meaning and the distinctions in language upon which the production of meaning depends.

That we are inhabited by language as we speak, words *and* body, would not be particularly disturbing, even cause for pride – has it not given evidence of being a beautiful language, one of the great "cultural pro-ductions"? – were it not that culture itself has been put in question. Or compounding that, what outraged Artaud: the sense that in being spoken there is an invisible presence in our speech whose voice is not, so to speak, speaking on our behalf. Or, if not with the paranoia of Artaud, the sense that we are nevertheless being stripped of the "symbolic capital" that determines authority in a culture. (This is a concept developed by Pierre Bourdieu, suggesting an economy of linguistic distinction within the "sys-tems of durable *dispositions*" (or *habitus*) that operate as a virtual principle of generation for practices and representations that are not only regulated but desirable. The products neither of mere obedience nor of thoughtless servitude to an overmastering structure, these practices and representations are, in the conscious orientation of the *habitus*, "collectively orchestrated," with a disposition to structure themselves.[27]) To have symbolic capital is to be available for those performative transactions or *transposable* dispo-sitions that, however adapted to the arbitrariness of a culture, keep us (the actors) from being mere dupes of the social structure. Whether or not the capital was to begin with an illusion of the structure, the exchange mechanism for "symbolic violence" (itself a cover up for the culturally arbitrary), the Foucauldian discourse on power sounded an alert, and we have since seen in critical theory – most markedly perhaps in feminism – the development of precautionary measures, which may be more or less paranoid, more or less aggressive. (Which may suggest that in any conceivable performative transaction there is no symbolic capital without some measure of paranoia and aggression.)

Thus it is that we are made aware that how the speaker is positioned in language determines how ideology declares or articulates itself. That positioning came to be thought of as the major operation or mechanism of ideology. What we are talking about is a history in the making, with a critical disposition to the history that has been made. So it is in performance with regard to a classical text, whose ostensible meanings may no longer be acceptable and from which, for diverse purposes, meanings may be produced (about which some will complain, of course, these have nothing to do with the text). Released from canonical fixture as from the artifice of eternity, these are now representations in the service of history. The question persists, however, as to whether it is a history one can live with or the history of which we are still unconscious agents while, as Marx said, the conditions in which we make history pass behind our backs.

Meanwhile, the arguments continue about revisionist productions, the simplest reason for which is that in the movement of history all production is revisionist, although most of the productions that we see, even those which purport to be experimental, revise us back to the simply unaltered. Thus we may have skateboards, wheelbarrows, and a bicycle built for two in a staging of *The Marriage of Figaro*, all of which have as much semiological legitimacy as powdered wigs, face patches, and fluttering fans – so long as there is some critical semblance of the class consciousness, its rage, that in Beaumarchais' time caused Louis XVI to declare the play contemptible and insist it must never be performed, and that in our own time – when most of us couldn't care less what bothered Louis – suggests why it must be played; or if played, what in the critical distance is being significantly seen. Even then one wonders what, in any revised classic, might be sufficiently destabilizing. Or make it necessary to go to the theater. When, by the way, Beaumarchais' marvelous play was staged by Jean-Pierre Vincent a few years ago for the Théâtre National Populaire at the Palais de Chaillot, it won the first Molière award – Parisian equivalent of the Broadway Tony – in a skillful performance without either the benefit or the challenge of revisionist devices. There is a certain undeniable pleasure in watching good acting, but all told there is not in such productions, however amusing and gracefully staged, much more illumination of the text, or special insight, than one could get from a well-imagined close reading, which might conceivably be more incendiary. Vincent had been among the cadre of innovators in the seventies who are now, in more conservative times, pulling back from previous audacities with the text. When staged a year or two later by another one of the innovators, Antoine Vitez, for the bicentennial of the French Revolution (his first production as head of the Comédie-Française), the revolutionary play was at best a commemorative drama.

However the classics are approached, under whatever historical circumstances there is, nevertheless, no respite from the retextualization that is always going on in performance. Playing it straight, as they say, hardly avoids it. And like the most ordinary conventions in theater practice, the curtain, a monologue, the use of a bench for a throne, an intimate scene that can be heard in an eighteen hundred seat auditorium, the whole taken-for-granted panoply of commonplace signs, such a performance (if you think about it) requires trickier things of the mind than a more radical performance, or treatment of a text, that in one way or another refuses the convention or tests it or deploys it for other purposes, or to suggest the possibility that in a society of the spectacle all the tricks are known and the conventions undone by an excess of performance. Under these circumstances, the argument over revisionism would seem to have reached a point of diminishing returns, although that's not at all true of performance itself, which seems to be wherever you look, not only revising the text but becoming the text, the social text, almost more of it than we might wish. I say this with mixed feelings about the current ubiquity of performance in the social formation of our lives, real performance and meta-performance, performance on the stage and on the page, in therapy, fashion, marketing, politics, the whole panoply of posture and play, confu-sing the boundaries of performance, "all kinds of performance in motion," as Barthes has written in the self-reflexive performance of *Roland Barthes by Roland Barthes*. With all this performative energy, the problem is that "free production remains clogged, hysterical, and somehow bewildered; most of the time the texts and performances proceed," the ones we care about, "where there is no demand for them,"[28] like a vanity of hopeless desire.

Still, we take our chances. I do not care in what form, really, the meanings occur, and it should be clear that so far as performance is at issue I've never expected them to occur *as* meaning, but as action, image, impulse, sensations, affects, the ideography of a neural bias, or inflexions of seeming conviction that are no more (as Nietzsche said, defining *values*) than judgments of the muscles. Yet discursivity itself – an irruption of cognition in an articulate quest of thought – may also be a powerful image, and it may be driven as well by thought's own function as a recuperation of language. (Need I say that this is not merely a matter for playwrights?) As implied, I do not care whether the prospect of meaning is mantic or semantic, although I cannot imagine a theater form of any magnitude or ideological consequence that does not hold discourse among the modes of meaning and, if there is not in the very act of performance something of an analytic as well, the self-reflexivity that not only spins wheels but also suspects its own motives.

That, if an objection is to be raised, is the one I would make to Matthias Langhoff's productions, the absence in the ideological conviction that leads, in the summary behavior of *Miss Julie*, to the gratuities of the grotesque and the cool, punk, or savage indifference. In his case, the conviction is palpably there, but unexamined. Shifting to another sphere of performance: sometimes, as in the sly demeanor of Laurie Anderson, the motives are suspected with an air of indifference that keeps the wheels spinning around the mere appearance of an ideological valence. But coming back to an institutional setting: no such temporizing was apparent in Liviu Ciulei's last production before giving up the directorship of the Guthrie Theater, a self-excoriating study of *Midsummer Night's Dream*, as if it had been written by Heiner Müller at the time of the *Hamletmachine*. Neither a Peter Brook circus nor a Reinhardt romance, it might have been a reflection on the roadblock to what Artaud called "true theater" in the heartland of America. Whatever moved it in conception, it went to the prophetic entrails of the play's enchantments: Oberon a sadist, Puck's magic a ministration of horror. What the production demonstrated in the process is that it's still possible for a ruthless critique of a canonical text to seem far more threatening, if not avant-garde, than self-consciously ruptured postmodern forms tearing apart bourgeois hegemony or phallocratic power or commodity culture, in a catechism of criticism, while having a good time ripping it off. Ciulei's staging was uncompromising: it spared no one, neither the theater nor the performers, neither the audience nor himself, nor did he merely reverse the dramaturgy with a corrective politics and give the critical edge to the artisans when they present their makeshift play. Which is not likely to be anymore a major contribution to class struggle.

Let me be clear: I'm not suggesting that all productions must be self-incriminating, but rather aware of their own premises, overstatements, gaps of knowledge, and the outside limits, if not makeshift longevity, of any ideological position. So far as Ciulei's autocritique is concerned, if our regional theaters could sustain a theatrical inquiry of this order they might take on meaning in our culture that, so far, they've never had. But then, the production seemed at least partly motivated by disappointment and frustration, in short, the necessity of Ciulei's departure, and the unlikely early prospect of the millennium coming to pass.

THE RESISTING SUBSTANCE OF PRODUCTION

What are the grounds for assessing the meanings we might produce? There are those within the ethos of process who seem to know, with theoretical strictures against closure, what nevertheless *should* be there. For want of a correct politics, however, or some reflexive anachronism of utopian thought, that still depends, I think, on the resisting substance of production, in the very genesis of thought its *refractoriness*, as when Brecht remarked in early conjecture on the epic theater that the viscosity of petroleum resists the five-act form. Even with a (more or less suspended) correct politics, he spent a lifetime thinking about that, especially as he realized (which he did as early as *Baal*) that it was something more volatile than petroleum he was dealing with, not a product but a "pure phenomenon," more like the cracking of the atom itself (which, as suggested before, accounted for the revision of *Galileo*, and a harsh revision too, maybe unduly harsh, in which Brecht seemed to take out on his character something more than the scientist's guilt; but we're only guessing at that). What this points to, in assessing meanings, is that if there is anything like nuclear energy on a stage it is inseparable from the complexity of issues that, testing perception in rehearsal – exhaustively there – also test it in performance, in the imminence of meaning which, giving no assurance, always seems to escape. Here we seem to be, again, at the perceptual limit of theater when, assaying its own substance, it inevitably fails itself. Yet, in the (un)seemly repetitions of that cautionary tale there would seem to be a measure of meaning that – whatever you see on stage, or on ideological grounds would like to see – is itself worth thinking about:

The acutest perception is at best a partial truth, or a partial object with a disposition to truth, "[t]he clear eye's moiety and the dear heart's part," as Shakespeare wrote in one of the sonnets (46.12), making as always, since we must, the acutest allowance for desire. But even if it were the whole truth and nothing but the truth, it would still have to be, given the irreversible factionalism of the world, the truth *for me* and not the truth *for*, the bias in history-without-a-subject that points the way for history regardless of the subject. It is not, then, some delinquent relativity that makes me say in assessing meanings that I speak only for myself. There is, moreover, in this insistent (or resistant) subjectivity a fairly clear awareness that there is something in the infrastructure of thought which puts, for all my vigilance, a certain threshold on what I can think and accept. The realization, however, that thought is overdetermined may in itself be a motive compelling thought to self-assessment while making demands on what we see, as if ideological correctness were the form of such demands.

When I encounter, therefore, the theatrical fact that does not disclose its secret, I want to push back the threshold. When I sense a limitation in something I see I want to be sure it is not the reflection of a boundary in the back of my own mind ready to head off the next stage of somebody else's work. If I am not a Marxist, I believe as Marx does in the *Grundrisse* that there are no sacred boundaries and that preconceived conditions of production are likely to keep the productive forces from developing. I want to encourage those forces that, surprising not only my weaknesses but what I had thought and imagined, help me to understand history as a process and to conceive of nature as the real body of my desire. I also know when that desire is disappointed, as it is by much of what still passes in performance as body language and, in the drama that is not *rethought*, most of the words I hear. I know the same old gestures when I see them and the same old story when I hear it. Yet, if the truth were known, there *are* times when I find it comforting and attractive, which also says something about desire, though not quite adequate to what I am addressing now, which is the truth of my desire.

I can't honestly say that I always trust that truth. And in the next chapter, reflecting further on the body, I shall have more to say about the competing claims of desire, which has been after all, in the infinity of its perspectives, the obsessive subject of the theater and, wherever it occurs with any complexity, the impelling power of performance. On that issue, the traditional drama in the conventional theater – with all the ideological liabilities of false perspective – still seems to me a good deal more profound, and realistic, than its critique, in so far as the analysis of repression and domination has also produced a liturgical agenda or doxology of desire. The drama has shown rather extensively that an obvious liability of the truth of desire is that it can be uncharitable to the truth of somebody else's desire. That's why I hesitate to say, still pursuing the theatrical fact, that I know the evasion when I see it, the hedged bets, the alibis, the cheats, the things you can get away with, the unexamined propositions, and the sort of stumbling erratic thought which is for me the major scandal of our theater, sloppiness of mind, which leads quite obviously – without splitting any infinitives in our superobjectives – to falsified emotion.

I am referring again to the American theater, but you see it elsewhere as well. No matter where it is, if the proposition is unexamined, anything gotten away with, reputation helps. Earlier I spoke approvingly of a certain inquiry in the French theater, in which Patrice Chéreau was one of the major figures, particularly in the devout, impeccably realized, forbearingly intimate productions that he did of the plays of Bernard Koltès. Just about the time of Koltès' death, Chéreau's production of *Hamlet* received the second Molière Award, like the Tony in New York similarly staged for television. The two events were a sad coincidence, and while there is always for the serious theater practitioner an ideological problem with such awards, it is too obvious to labor. Problems of ideology have, like power, their own microphysics, and we shall be dealing with subtler judgments of the muscles later on. I want to focus here, however, on a very obvious effect in the production of *Hamlet*, an effect which received enough critical attention to have been one of the reasons for the award.

I saw the production at Avignon in the summer of 1988, and surely its most impressive moment, for the moment, was the appearance of the Ghost on a huge flexed modular platform like a hyperextended Japanese Noh stage, multiply trapped and resounding, in the courtyard of the Pope's palace. This was no mere furtive ghost, like the dilatory figure in the drama of the Noh, making his voluminously eerie entrance down the length of the *hashigakara*. It was rather abrupt, spectacular, clamorous, for the actor was riding a horse: a real horse. Now, what can we say about the "ideological content"? I have thought much of that image, and I'm still not sure what it was all about. All told, the sensation over, I don't think it was about very much. When I said it was obvious I meant just that, something you couldn't miss, either its presence or its meaning, for what we had was a sign of power. So far, however, as it was meant to represent the oedipal father in all the remembered splendor of his martial glory, it was still vulnerable to the traditional problem that we used to define, in reduced scale, by the real dog on stage (the phenomenology of which was recently rethought in a fine analysis by Bert O. States).[29] Given the dispersion of value – and the *dispersed perception of value* – in the dubious unity of any audience, I am usually reluctant to say what other people are seeing, what not; but simply put: it was hard not to watch the horse, which was understandably skittish, as the play went by. If it remained nevertheless a sign of power, that had more to do with Chéreau's status at the Ministry of Culture, for this was a very expensive production. Except for the horse and the platform, and an unexpected blast of rock music, it was also, in the working out of relationships, characterization, style, etc., a rather nondescript production on the oedipal theme, leveled out psychologically, with the durable disposition of French actors toward a monotonic intensity that signals passion.

There was very little in the production, however, that resisted its partial truths, or for that matter the hyperbolism of those truths. Chéreau, it should be said in all fairness, is quite capable of doing things with impressive scale, as in his Bayreuth production of Wagner, in collaboration with Pierre Boulez. And if I'm making an issue of a single excess in the staging of *Hamlet*, that has also to do, I suppose, with the ramifications of the production as a cultural event. Whatever the implications of the Molière award, there is also a problem today in the atmosphere of an international festival, which seems in retrospect a voluminous preface: the prices, the hype, the crowds, the worldwide circuitry of received opinion, the resonance of the event, so that the amplification of expectation seemed to be embodied in that horse. I couldn't help contrasting it in the mind's eye with the stagings I saw in that same courtyard thirty years before, in the year that Camus was killed and Sartre wrote about it – past their broken friendship, over the Algerian War – as an "imbecilic death": a shape, egregious, faint, against a wall, farflung light marking out the unencumbered space of existential being, embodied in previous years by Gérard Philipe, but the splendor largely conceptual, and then suddenly, adventitiously (nature dead imagine!), the storied wind of Provence coming over the ramparts, to supplement the austerity in the theater of Jean Vilar.

As I'm well aware that Vilar, Sartre, and Gérard Philipe are dead, and that existential being has been for some time theoretically subject to doubt, I trust I don't have to explain that, despite the perceptual jeopardy, I have nothing ideologically against a theatrical image with a real horse or dog or any living thing (all of which are likely to be more reliable than that wind). Nor any monotonic passion for a parsimonious stage. I was talking, however, of unexamined propositions, of which the horse seemed to me a galvanically large example. What is far more distressing, however, in the development of a production is the experimental notion, or idea of considerable substance, that turns out on stage – for reasons sometimes that nobody understands – to be a massively hollow mistake. And it's just as well, though it hurts, that you don't get away with it. If ideology may be defined as false consciousness there are, unfortunately, conspicuous examples of it in theater practice without the excuse of its being merely in the imaginary: the pretense of experiment and the pretense of inquiry, as well as the kind of performance which is a self-deception from beginning to end.

Sometimes it is innocent and sometimes it is not. I am no longer making theater, but there was something to be learned there, from the great compulsive substance of the drama and the always delicate matter of working with actors, more or less gifted at being what they're not, about my own capacity for self-deception. I know it could come upon me like the appearance of ideology, incognito, while history made its way behind my back. Yet there were times, too, sitting there in the dark, when I saw it in front of my eyes, and then there was, with whatever residual blindness, the obligation to address it, as a propriety of method, in the working out of performance: the always insufficiently fine and often embarrassing labor of doing it and doing it again, until it is exhaustively thought through, the only time in theater work when you're properly exhausted. It was when I was not sure, however, that I was deceiving myself and wanted to think otherwise, or forget it, that I was likely to be close to some ideological repression that had to be tracked down and seen for what it was. Anything else is, in the activity of performance, ideological neglect. That may sound like it came from the great compulsive scenario of rectitude, but I should think it would be true from any ideological perspective.

Here it's a matter of looking for the resistances, as much as anything the resistances in yourself. There's no guarantee, of course, that what you're looking for is going to be seen, and while those who work in theater still put a high premium on the wisdom of the body or thinking with the body, and those who work in theory have developed an ideology of committed bodies (by race, class, gender, etc.), you might not even see it if you put your body on the line. Which is why we find ourselves doing it and

3

THE SURPASSING BODY

THE REVOLUTIONARY BREAK:
BIOMECHANICS AND PHANTASMAPHYSICS

"When one breaks a hand or a leg," writes Trotsky in his chapter on futurism in *Literature and Revolution*, "the bones, the tendons, the muscles, the arteries, the nerves and the skin do not break and tear in one line, nor afterwards do they grow together and heal at the same time. So, in a revolutionary break in the life of society, there is no simultaneousness and no symmetry of processes either in the ideology of society, or in its economic structure. The ideological premises which are needed for the revolution are formed before the revolution, and most important ideologic deductions from the revolution appear only much later."[1] If the critique of futurism is a symptom of the asymmetry, the final chapter of the book is an ideological deduction from the revolution that turns from a qualified defense of traditional forms (tragedy, e.g., without God, or submission to a mysterious authority) into a futuristic fantasy of psychophysical development – to which we've had, with more or less system to the fantasy, correlatives in the theater.

While the breaking and tearing continued, through the anatomy of modernism, as the structural principle of artistic forms, there were as a preface to postmodern performance various notions of body consciousness or disciplines of the thinking body or the signifying body or, amidst the baffling semiurgy of exchangeable signs, regimens of the body as its own authority in the rhetorical struggle to assure a future. One might have thought that Meyerhold's biomechanics was, in its articulation of signs, an important part of that struggle, but about that particular system in the theater of his time Trotsky is not at all sanguine. And as he questions the historical necessity of this apparent innovation – which impressed both Brecht and Eisenstein – it's as if he were writing off in advance the body language of the American theater of the sixties, when it was under the spell of Artaud and Grotowski and, in a more populist mode, the messianism of the Living Theater. While "the passionate experimenter, Meyerhold" was

at the outset (unlike Stanislavski) a committed Bolshevik, he is referred to
as "the furious Vissarion Belinski of the stage," who teaches the actors,
inept as they are in dialogue, a combinatory (or compensatory) set of semi-
rhythmic movements: "the result is – abortive" (*L&R* 134–5).

Despite the dismissal of biomechanics as a form of "provincial dilettant-
ism" (135), the body and the machine are embraced, and embrace each
other, in the higher synthesis imagined by Trotsky in his exhilarating coda
on education. While the machine becomes in the socialist order a virtual
fact of nature, so unopposed to the earth "that the tiger won't even notice"
(252), the somatic and psychic molding of new generations is to be the
apotheosis of social thinking. Undoing the stagnant traces of a "worm-
eaten domestic life," it is education that will be the source of "an endless
collective consciousness," including the liberation of woman from "her
semi-servile condition" (253). If the nature of man is still secreted in the
darkest subsoil of the elemental, there will have to be further investigation
of the processes of the unconscious so that human beings shall not be
subject to the blind heredity of unknown sexual laws. As the mystifying
elements of this blind inheritance are driven out of economic relations,
where they have most heavily settled, the drive toward emancipation will
turn toward the body itself, to create (as if Mayakovsky were the model,
purged of the faults of futurism) "a higher biologic type, or, if you please,
a superman." This will involve a planned economy of the body: distributed
labor in the organs and a sort of amortization of body parts, not only
accounting for wear and tear, but also preparing the organism for danger
and the inevitability of death. "There can be no doubt," writes Trotsky,
"that man's extreme anatomical and physiological disharmony, that is, the
extreme disproportion in the growth and wearing out of organs and tissues,
give the life instinct the form of a pinched, morbid and hysterical fear of
death, which darkens reason and which feeds the stupid and humiliating
fantasies about life after death" (255).

Biomechanics, indebted to Taylorism, yields in this economy to a new
technology of the body. As the revolution tries to stabilize itself, Trotsky
is understandably cautious about the darkening of reason. But so far as
he is attentive to the processes of the unconscious (subsoil of the elemental
out of which the revolution arose?) his conception of the psychophysical
management of the organism begins to resemble in certain aspects the
"phantasmaphysics" of poststructuralist thought.[2] By releasing and then
controlling the energy flows, anonymous drives, condensations, pulsations,
explosive semantics of the imaginary – the entire repertoire of primary
process – the revolution will have brought into the life of society what
otherwise is lost, trapped, dispersed in the unconscious: along with the
fungus growth of repressed emotion, the fractious theatricality of the factitious body.

What happens in the microcosm is reflected in the macrocosm, as it was

88

by Eisenstein in the polyvalent structure and surging movements of the crowd. As the Rabelaisian spectacle of the crowd is described by Bakhtin or, in all its protuberant and menacing excess, *compressed* by Canetti into the psyche, it becomes in turn a monstrous paradigm of the libidinal economy of performance art, from the insurrectionary events of the Viennese Aktion group, with its public orgies and mutilations, to the solipsistic solo performance that was, in the sublimations of the seventies, the polymorphous retrenchment of the volatilized social body. During the period of retrenchment this volatilized body was displaced, with the redoubled dream of revolution, into a rhetoric of transgression. We have seen it again in both theory and performance, with more or less wishfully imagined perversity in the almost ceaseless discourse on the body. (This is the dominant aspect of the displacement into theory of an erotics of theater that, at the same time, is a critique of the reproductive structure of the oedipal drama.) Meanwhile, in the fantasy text of the postmodern – at the dead end of representation or the possible death of the social – there is still the living image of the participatory spectacle itself, the carnival or the festival, where the dismembered body politic would be transformed from an amorphous silent mass into the vociferous equity of the crowd.

DESIRE EVERYWHERE:
ANTI-BODIES AND THE CRITICAL MASS

The festival remains, with various antecedents on the great stage of history, a memory trace in theory of the theatricality of the sixties. But "the theoretical problem of ideology has always been determined," as Étienne Balibar observes, "by the same practical problem; that of the constitution of a revolutionary force (or form)."[3] The theoretical problem of revolution has always been that once the force is there it becomes, with any radical assumption of power, very much a matter of form. We see it in the aesthetic limits placed on the participatory multitudes, whether in *The Festival of the Supreme Being*, ordained by Robespierre and designed by David, or in Trotsky's rejection of a socialist art overcharged with collective passion in which, as he thought of Mayakovsky's *The 150 Million*, "the parts refuse to obey the whole" (152). (Or worse. "Carnival! Carnival!" says the revolutionary plumber in Genet's *The Balcony*. "You know well enough we ought to beware of it like the plague, since its logical conclusion is death. You know well enough that a carnival that goes to the limit is a suicide!"[4]) Every revolution has to assess in the stagings of its power the degree of permissible license in the instrumentality of the crowd, not only the temporal moment but its critical mass of desiring bodies. For those still trying to think revolution within the precincts of advanced capitalism, the problem is compounded by the diffusion of the crowd into a statistical mass with "a sort of phantom content," the excess of information that is, according to

Baudrillard, information's absence (into which, before the emergence of the silent majorities, the bourgeois concept of a Public disappeared). In the now familiar process of egregious simulation, we have the electronic avatar of the crowded festival, an anti-theater of communication in which "the desire of the audience is put on stage" only to have its immense energies deployed, through "the integrated circuit of the negative,"[5] in avoiding the brutal recognition that instead of being reversed in the mirror of production the real has been abolished. Or is not sufficiently real. Or too much so.

What is real enough, to be sure, is that some desiring bodies are so disaffected, so (visibly) marginal or extruded, yet so raveled in the loop of the integrated circuit, that they are hardly even statistics, more like anti-bodies. Such bodies were already part of the scene in Gorki's lower depths, but they are now in all the metropolises a burgeoning aspect of the spectacle, within the circuit to the extent that they are among the empty signifiers, both replicated and dematerialized on the TV screens. While they convey, no doubt, quite basic forms of desire, there is still the leveraged appearance of a postscarcity world, where poverty and victimization are overshadowed in the general excess of reality by the material energies of mass culture and consumer goods in abundance. There are, of course, levels of dispossession, and while there are those whose deprivation is such that they seem, in some last classless reflex of degraded pride, to have opted out of the system, there are also the victims who want the bounty and gratifications that go with our cultural politics: the sensory fallout of surplus value, its high decibel count, boombox or bust, what the crowd goes for in our cities, plate glass shattering, like some imploded fractal moment of the production of desire, whenever the looting begins.

"Desire everywhere," writes Baudrillard, "is only the referential of political despair. And the strategy of desire, after having been tried out in the marketing industry, is today polished up further in its revolutionary promotion in the masses" (*SM* 88). There have been more or less subtle attempts to theorize difference in desire (largely in terms of *gender*, somewhat less with *race*, here and there with *class*, now if belatedly with the coming of *age*), but whatever the differences the discourse of the body proceeds through an ideology of desire and, with a premium on performance, claims for the subversive potential of postmodern dissemination. As with the psychophysical exercises of a generation ago, the model and motive power is the liberated economy of the unconscious, the seeds of the psyche's history spilling over the stage, confounding representation and, in the play of body parts, disrupting the hegemony of the specular with oral drives, anal drives, labial, olfactory, epidermal, duodenal.

"Spit out yer teeth," said Crow to Hoss in *The Tooth of Crime*, while putting him through the corporeal catechism absorbed by Sam Shepard at the Open Theater or (with unpurged sense memories of the self-indulgent

Method) from the various praxes of the body that also produced, in the communitarian ethos of a few years before, *Dionysus in 69.* "Ear pulls. Nose pulls. Pull out a booger. Slow scratches from shoulder to belly. Hitch up yer shirt. Sex, man. Tighten yer ass. Tighten one cheek and loosen the other. Pull off yer thighs to yer calves. Get it all talkin' a language."[6] For Crow, the gypsy marker bred on image, this language is a surface, a sort of punk-rock glitter of manipulable codes. But if you pull out the booger long enough it may more than scratch the surface, the outside becomes the inside, which seems to release energies from the repressed contents of the unconscious. Meanwhile, this is the language still quite visible in the musicated spectacles of popular culture or, in all the plenitude of lubricious desire, the libidinal economy of MTV, all the tightened asses open, competing for the gold. What happens in the macrocosm happens in the microcosm, but the subsystems of the macrocosm differ around the world, with the politics of the unconscious itself, its dependence on representation.

None of this is to minimize the thwarted claims of dispossession, nor to forget that in the emergence of any revolutionary mass there will be disparate and dubious forms of desire. (As we might remember from Dostoyevsky, some of them may be, even before the inevitable derangements of the revolution, utterly despicable and palpably corrupt.) As for the rhetoric of transgression, so far as it occurs within the repressively tolerant structures of late bourgeois capitalism, it's hard to say just how far it wants to go with the body in the gratification of desire, nor in what conceivable political space. But as we theorize once more – in a pluralistic society with multiply agonistic and maybe repugnant desires (e.g., the pornographic) – the prospect of a liveable public sphere, the unavoidable question remains as to the allowable level of energy flows or, with remedial breaks and tears in the body politic, the threshold of legitimacy of the formerly repressed. (The issue remains in the spontaneously lived life of any society, including the utopian extremities of popular culture, even if you think that the desire for a public sphere is merely recidivism or bourgeois asceticism, a nostalgic holdover from the dialectics of the Enlightenment.[7])

This is also a question of scale, its feasible magnitudes, as we saw with the crowds flowing in the gentle revolution of Eastern Europe through expectant breaches in the Berlin Wall. That was for an ecstatic moment the site of celebrations, happenings, performance events, none more vertiginous than the sequential spectacle of collapsing power. ("History has begun to develop very quickly in this country, now we have this fantastic speed," said Havel,[8] after accepting the virtual surrender of the repressive regime that had put him in prison recurrently and banned his plays for twenty years.) Yet even as the barrier of repression was being lifted, inviting not only dissidence but primary process, the nervous question arose: how much space will there be for the imaginary before the barrier

91

is lowered again? The more violently total the revolution the quicker it's likely to be, as in the killing fields of Cambodia or the zealotry of Iran, where in the semiotic *chora* the immediate price of transgression was not merely the floating fantasy of a dismembered body but the actual loss of body parts: a finger, a hand, a head. There was the period after the expulsion of the Shah when Iran seemed to be the bewildering model of what appeals to postmodern thought, a dispersed and centerless, undecidable power, after which we confronted under the rule of the Ayatollah the even more unsettling postmodern paradox of a televised spectacle in which the liminal body of desire seemed to embrace not free markets but fundamentalist repression, while the promise of salvation awaited another, less satanic world.

DAMN IT ALL! CORPSES!

There was nothing here, of course, like that euphoric period after the Bolshevik Revolution when the avant-garde identified itself with the will of the proletariat. At the time *Literature and Revolution* was published, Meyerhold was still passionately experimenting, and Trotsky might even concede through his most caustic critique that futurism was a necessary link in the formation of a greater and more emancipated art (159). Where there was common ground he was also concerned, as I've said, with a technology of the body. The futurists had more of an instinct, in their romance with technology, for unmediated desire and immediate gratifications, but Trotsky was hardly contemplating the prospect of radical human change with anything like the attenuated vision of Chekov's Vershinin, a hundred years, a thousand years down the road. Yet, while he is rejecting the humiliating fantasies of a belated payoff – no less the absurd expectancy of an afterlife – the vision of "a higher biologic type" is by no means liberated from an economy of death. Nor is he imagining, even when he later speaks of a permanent revolution, anything like a "body without organs," as it will come to be – by way of Artaud, Judge Schreber, Büchner, and Beckett – in the schizoanalytic mutations of Marxist thought.[9] His own unembarrassed aspiration is to make the instincts transparent and, by extending "the wires of [the] will into hidden recesses," to attain a new superhuman plane, where "the average human type will rise to the heights of an Aristotle, a Goethe, or a Marx" (256).

That is not exactly the millennium of the desiring-machine in the rhizomatic space of a thousand plateaus.[10] With dematerialization of the machine in a culture of information that spreads its dominion over the earth, Trotsky may have been right, however, about the tiger not taking notice. Keeping an eye on the ecology of the jungle is a necessity now in defining the postmodern condition. (Speaking of fantastic speed, perspective changes radically in the agricultural economies of a preindustrial world – as soon, indeed, as the boomboxes are there, and the aerials rise like splintered totems of commodified information.) Yet, while the wires of the will seem to have been connected in the short circuits of history to the "electrobody" of corporate capitalism, the current plane of body consciousness in the average human type would seem to be fairly conveyed on a recent billboard in the Parisian Métro. It shows a gorilla with arms full of sporting goods, tennis racket, running shoes, boxing gloves, etc., and this message from the great department store Samaritaine: "Vous avez un corps. Essayez-le."

This is in its down-to-earth reminder of "our body's *nature-for-us*," something other than what Sartre intended by the phrase when he concluded "that the body is perpetually the *surpassed*." We may think of the body as the thing most real to us, what gives immediacy to any truth, but it is only in the surpassing, according to Sartre, that it becomes the sensible datum or center of reference "for its own fixed immobility." Which is to say, "since it is surpassed," that the body "is the Past."[11] With bodies sprawled on the platforms of the Métro, spaced out, drugged out, indigent beyond repair, secreting more past than we may care to remember, it would appear that life after death, the consummation devoutly wished that was once a serious question, is no longer even a humiliating fantasy. (It's as if "your body, the thing that seems the most real to you," is not even "doubtless the most phantasmic," as Barthes observed about the reflexive mythos of a nature-for-us that is the originary site of a "natural" body.[12]) If there is any resemblance here to the abjected body of "grotesque realism," which reveals its essence to the outside world with all its apertures open, gaping mouth, running eyes, unbuttoned belly, breasts, genitals, it is not quite "the ancestral body of the people" celebrated by Bakhtin "as a principle of growth which exceeds its own limits only in copulation, pregnancy, childbirth, the throes of death, eating, drinking, defecation."[13]

This is the underworld, rather, where eating, drinking, defecation, and the imminent throes of death may remind us that the word 'somatic', from the Greek root *soma*, originally designated a 'corpse'. It has been translated as body, but it designates rather what remains of the body when its life-force and vital functions are gone, and there is only the inertial figure, waste matter, or at best – for the dubious imagination of impoverished myth – an effigy.[14] This might have been once redeemed by the lamentations of dithyramb or in the paradox of tragic display where, after its mortification, the ritual figure disappears into its invisibility. But here it is merely *refuse*, more or less insisting on its presence *as such*, visible, cadaverous, proliferating, not about to disappear. "FLESH LIKES TO KEEP THE COMPANY OF FLESH among the bums around me," says the figure who "was" Hamlet, amidst the ruins and babble of history, in the "Family Scrapbook" of Heiner Müller's *Hamletmachine*. " . . . I laid down and listened to the world doing its turns in step with the putrefaction."[15] We might look upon that, as Julia Kristeva does in her essay on the abject, as "true theater, without makeup or masks," where body fluids, refuse, and corpses, "this defilement, this shit," *show* us what we "permanently thrust aside in order to live."[16]

This is what Brecht showed us at the end of *Baal*, in what seems a corrective *gestus*, or ideological move against the almost irreducible nihilism of the play. "Damn it all! Corpses!" says one of the woodsmen[17] as he wipes the spit off the forehead of the dying Baal, whose polymorphously bloated and stinking body has become, through the ful(some)ness of its perversions, more like the offal than an effigy of itself. It may be that "there's something about that pale lump of fat that makes a man think," and therefore susceptible to the A-effect, but they don't think about it very long, spitting on the body and kicking it aside, since the wind has died down and there's work to be done in the forest. Back in the windless depths of the urban landscape, as we sidestep the bodies that accumulate around us, there may be an unadmitted responsiveness to that other sentiment in the Brechtian scene: "Try to schedule your stinking tomorrow" (56). On the border of the abject, of such dimensions, it often seems better not to think at all. And as we try to forget it or pass it by, this body or that extricating itself, "as being alive, from that border" (Kristeva, *Powers* 3), it is parody (privileged genre of the society of the spectacle) that comes to rescue us from paranoia.

After all, we also speak of the subways as jungles. With the gorilla, however, that might be a performer on *Saturday Night Live* – the origin of the species merely another element in postmodern pastiche – the body is proposed not as past or future but, at the most rudimentary level, in the commodified immediacy of its own pleasures. As the promoter said of the world of boxing, where in the most ferocious discipline of the commodity the body *is* surpassed: "Sanctioning bodies don't make champions, the public does" – that aggregate of the average type with its susceptible purchasing power, whose pleasures are produced, like boxing on Home Box Office of cable television, through the image-repertoire of the fantasy machine.

THE BODY COUNT

There are times when the machine that seems a virtual fact of nature, more voracious than the tiger, is the spectacle itself, image consuming image like the expenditure of bodies in the human waves of a holy war. It was the Vietnam war, however, that intensified awareness of the vast consumption of image as if in deranged proportion to the body count. We have come to think of the spectacle as desensitizing perception and dematerializing the real, but to the degree that the mutilated body, a finger, a hand, a head, is felt through the mediascape as something more than fantasy, not mere simulation, it may sustain a view of history as hysteria, as in the cannibalistic text of *Hamletmachine*: "Somewhere bodies are torn apart so I can dwell in my shit. Somewhere bodies are opened so I can be alone with my blood. My thoughts are lesions in my brain" (57).

There is a savage moment when the text, with the corpses piling up behind it, the ruins and babble of history reeking with putrefaction, seems to direct the century's rage against the ideologies of revolution and the scriptural figures of the communist world: Marx, Lenin, and Mao. The play was written in 1977; a dozen years after, we have seen the renunciation, sometimes peaceable, sometimes vengeful, of Marxist-Leninism (Mao went sooner) all over the Eastern bloc, from the turn to free markets in Poland to the merchandising of the Berlin Wall to the abolition of Communist parties to the efforts by Mikhail Gorbachev, amidst the spread of *perestroika*, to salvage Marxism for theory (like American scholars who have recently discovered history). But whatever the impact of these events on Müller, the self-incriminating ferocity of *Hamletmachine* suggests that the lesions are unlikely to be healed as the site of revolution shifts to tribal, ethnically divided, preindustrialized parts of the world and to other categories, such as race and gender, in the imbecilic spectacle and bloodbath of history. Which requires its quota of bodies like Jarry's debraining machine. Or like the frenzied crowd in Dracula's Transylvania – after the apparent liberation of Rumania by the execution of Ceaucescu – with that astonishing bit of performance art, televised, where the crowd dispersed in pursuit of more bodies while a man with a bludgeon gave one last casual blow, and tossed a bouquet of flowers onto the plaintively rising figure that subsided as a corpse.

Back in the *Hamletmachine*, there are three naked women on stage when, after the tearing up of the author's photograph, the TV screens go black and the busts of the patriarchal heroes of socialism are axed. This brings us back to the floating fantasy that would, in its assault on phallogocentrism, undo the structure of reproduction and bring an end to history. "All the cocks have been butchered. Tomorrow has been cancelled," says the figure who was Hamlet (who seemed to have lost the capacity for action even in the present tense), as if announcing the end of the phallic when the Wall was still rigidly there. "I want to be a woman," he says (54), but the necessity of abjection is such that he dresses in Ophelia's clothes while she puts the makeup of a whore on his face. *Hamletmachine* ends with the bound figure of Ophelia speaking as Electra, and ejecting for all women the sperm she has received. The speech is a perverse conflation of terrorism and feminism, with reference to Ulrika Meinhof and the last line from Squeaky Fromme (the Manson follower who tried to assassinate Gerald

Ford): "When she walks through your bedrooms carrying butcher knives you'll know the truth" (58). As Müller no doubt realized, not even then.

A couple of years later he published *The Task*, in which Liberty is "the serpent with the bloodthirsty vulva," which engenders no truth except the desire for more blood. The play opens with a figure who dissociates himself from the revolution and the desire for power. Of butcheries, he says, "I have seen enough. I know the human anatomy inside out" (86). After such knowledge, what forgiveness? Eliot's question about the depravity of history lingers in the bloodstained mimicry of Müller's drama, where in a virtual orgy of theatricality heads fall, bodies are gutted, and under the blade of justice the executioner rips the bandage from the dream – as if the imaginary were lusting for more.

It was anatomy, we may remember, that provided the model for the incisions and dissections that, like the slit eyeball of *Un Chien andalou*, precipitated the modern – the rupture, cutting and tearing that have since been assumed as the virtual structuration of structure (the redoubling of division into the radical thinking of play) in the transgressive strategies of the postmodern. So far as anatomy tears open the organism and spatializes it, undoing appearance by dispersing interiority and displaying, instrumentally, its operable parts, there is this anatomical element in the technique of alienation. "Why cut yourself in pieces like that?" says Shlink in Brecht's *In the Jungle of Cities*, before the technique was rationalized beyond the desperate ground of the other alienation. "Look: my body is numb, it even affects my skin. Man's skin in its natural state is too thin for this world, that's why people do their best to make it thicker. The method would be satisfactory if the growth could be stopped."[18] To the degree that technique carried over to the politics of desecration, Brecht was certainly familiar with the butcheries too. They come with knives at the end to get Shlink, whose skin has not grown thick enough to protect him.

Whatever the body count in the ideological distance between Brecht and Müller, there was a generational difference in their attitude toward the orthodoxies of the DDR, and the prospects there of a feasible audience in a defensible theater. As Müller moved around the West, he also absorbed a generation of drama and performance – from the hieratic bodies in the erotics of Genet to the more corrosive figures of body art – that worked its way into his flayed, suppurating, disfigured, and schizoid texts, along with the "language of pain" derived from Artaud. The flagellant body of Artaud's texts is for Müller "the terminal case" of the astonishing thought that began with the death of God, as if consciousness itself were struck by lightning and somehow, split asunder, miraculously survived. In the delirious imagining of a body without organs (more on that to come) he not only went beyond anatomy but liquidated the arrogant authority of a ludicrously swollen sex, what Genet later (de)allegorized in the limp penis of the Bishop as he descends from his cothurni, and the huge phallic

96

fantasy of the Chief of Police: "[Artaud] wrested literature from the hands of the police," said Müller, "the theater from the hands of medicine. His texts blossom under the sun of torture that is shining with equal force on all continents of this planet."[19] Or if not with equal force, in a system of displacement which guarantees that, however the practice is mitigated in one part of the world, the sun will be shining elsewhere.

A FULLY ACCEPTED LESIONISM

Meanwhile, we continue to see in new performance, as in the operations of the unconscious, an obsessive articulation of the *dismembered* body, which came into the postmodern (before it went into the Métro) from the cruelty of Artaud and the aphasic mutants, mutilations, amputees of Beckett, and later the bodiless figures in the funerary urns, the otherwise organless corpses that, along with emotional memories, appear to have a brain. There was a certain ideological distancing and change of tone – extruding both memory and emotion – in the period of minimalism and Judson dance, but that the mind is a muscle was demonstrated in the flesh by Yvonne Rainer before she turned to a form without organs and started making films. More or less conceptual, attenuated, Beckettian, with variable images of the residual body, there has been – from Robert Wilson, Squat, and the Mabou Mines to Pina Bausch, Criquot 2, and the lunar and solar effigies of Poppo Shiraishi (eyeballs distended, painted in gold) – an arresting extension of the processes, dilatory as *différance*, circuitous, repetitive to the point of hallucination, that may in the momentum of conventional dramaturgy pass us by in the theater. This may be in the extremity of its body consciousness, or imaging of consumption, more or less morbid or hysterical, as with Kantor's mortuary theater or the mummified fetuses of Sankai Juku or the obsessional cross-dressed violence in Bausch, or in the compulsive singularity of certain figures of performance art: from the vomitous swallowings of Gina Pane or the hunger strikes of Stuart Brisley to the bulimic fantasies of Karen Finley or the prophetic entrails that seem to be ripped, with its plague-ridden ostinato and horrendous keenings, from the voice of Diamanda Galas. Not to mention the actual animal entrails and live rats, with exploding firecrackers, on the vociferating body of Joe Coleman, in his nearly berserk outbursts as Professor Momboozoo. Spitting blood at the pregnant belly of a woman, squashing and beheading the rats as though he were tearing himself apart, Coleman screams through the audience like some raving Titus Andronicus in the age of acid rain, as if in one bilious denunciation of the despicable in us all the world might come, epileptically, to a decent end.

To rephrase, however, the Aristotelian formula, it is the morbidity and hysteria, instead of pity and fear, that would produce another catharsis, purging those emotions, rejecting the bourgeois vanity of evasive pity and overcoming fear in an economy of death. This kind of performance would seem, indeed, to have been worked through "by the death drive," as Josette Féral has remarked in an essay on the demystified subject that, as it meets the video screen (which commonly documents or appropriates such events), is "frozen and dies" and returned to the system of representation it has tried so desperately to escape. What is performed is the outcome of a conscious practice deliberately consented to, "the body belonging to a fully accepted lesionism" – a critique of ideology or beyond ideology; instead of Marx's phantoms, Müller's lesions in the brain. The rupture, cutting, and tearing are not performed, however, "in order to negate [the body], but in order to bring it back to life in each of its parts which have, each one, become an independent whole."[20] The body parts or obscure details may be recorded, caressed, extruded, replicated, magnified, cloned, or otherwise resurrected by video or film. There are still those who, while preserving the lesionism, resist the mediatization, as a more or less desperate measure to stay outside of ideology. So it was, some time ago, with Jochen Gerz when he wrote on a wall with his finger the quite literal description of what happened when he wrote: "These words are my flesh and blood." More often than not, however, more likely now than then, the bloodstains of such an event will be part of its documentation.

Body art emerged through the seventies as a function of conceptualism,[21] but there is in the existing plurality of these events a range of configured experience that seems to be a grotesque inversion of the birthing rituals of the sixties, with their synesthetic imagery and collective swapping of body parts, women with penises, pregnant men, in an ideology of liberation. Or as if shattering representation with an increment of the inexplicable, turning AID (artificial insemination by donor) to AIDS (the horrific acronym of a defenseless system), which is the explicit subject of the wild Cassandra-like ravings of Galas in her trilogy of the Red Death. (Given the emotional pitch of her performances, the vocal chords of Galas are always in peril, but this work was suggested to her by a stricken friend who had, as if in some ironic and innocent penance for the attack on logocentrism, gradually lost his voice.) Such events are not quite representative, however, of the pleasured body that has also been a dominantly indulged figure in alternative modes of performance, as it has been in the discourse on sexuality and power. "The rallying point for the counterattack against the deployment of sexuality ought not to be sex-desire, but bodies and pleasures," wrote Foucault,[22] shifting the emphasis of his own discourse from the microphysics of repression to the partial objects of "biopower," in the ambitious work he started before he died of AIDS.

Where body fluids are concerned, things may be proceeding now with more discretion, but up to the brim of danger (as after Christ in urine, grants at the NEA[23]) the indulgence is still there. Where new possibilities in performance are being explored around bodies and pleasures the rallying-point remains situated not with any conventional bodies, but more or less *in extremis* those of feminists and gays, who are deconstructing and recoding the ideology of gender. As for the imaging of dismemberment, that remains in the erogenous play of floating body parts the vertiginous but equivocal source of euphoric pleasure. We may still find the mimicry of birthing rituals as political statements by radicalized women, either as parody in, say, the lesbian subculture of the Lower East Side or quite seriously still in the emerging new theater of underdeveloped countries, where we may also see its inversion. While Third World women are still lightyears from the camp and masquerade of a "butch-femme" aesthetic (neither class nor sex specific, undoing gender roles),[24] there is a common dissidence at the level of bodies and pleasures, in the *refusal* to "break waters" and, while its intensity varies, the animus against men. That was the volatile substance of the lyric performance of a Haitian play where the women abuse, fondle, excoriate, rage with the desire to tear apart the life-size effigies of the men who, through centuries of oppressive pregnancy polluting the land, have poured scum into their bodies.[25]

There is in some lesbian performance another level of consciousness where the body is in a sense *deactualized*, killed off ideologically, so that it might be rediscovered, more or less exultantly, but again and again, as in the disengendering artifice and iconography of one of the more remarkable plays of the genre, Holly Hughes' *Dress Suits to Hire*. Here the floating phallic presence is the hand of one of the women, named Little Peter, who/which chokes her at the outset and does the body in (as Eliot's Sweeney said every man has to, needs to, once in a lifetime). About this conversion of an old vaudeville routine to the purposes of gender critique, the stage direction reads: "*In fact she is dead for the rest of the play.*"[26] But she is not by any means abjectly, or apologetically, a corpse.

While *Dress Suits to Hire* was conceived for performance away from its usual premises, the WOW theater café in the East Village, most such plays are likely to have a restricted audience, within the provenance of lesbian culture with its generic strategies and underlying codes. With other performances that reflect an ethos of pansexuality or polysexuality, including the bondage and domination or sadomasochism that were, with more or less actualization by the actors, allegorized in Genet, the audience or participation may also be relatively exclusive. Or there may be, for those somehow attending with other tastes, an ideological challenge to examine, with the censorship apparently lifted, the range of pleasures self-denied, including the pornographic. Since the censorship, however, is never really lifted, but only displaced to the point where desire can measure up to desire before it's thwarted again, the challenge may be aggressive. Or, as with the "open cunt" Cynthia of Kathy Acker's *The Birth of the Poet*, sticking razor blades (verbally) up her arms, it may be mockingly obscene, an inverted form of self-contempt turned into aggression. Or with different personalities and a panoply of erogenous zones, it may be more of an invitation. It may also be, as with the performance artist Marina Abramović, who presented her body without any resistance, an unerotic invitation with *real* razor blades.

While S&M and B&D have through the history of theater and into slasher films an undeniable specular appeal, for most of us, I suppose, they don't yet quite work in the participatory mode. But there are other body shows in which what appears to be threatening turns out to be benign, or in which the apparently repellent is, when examined, the better part of a life. So it is in the shamanistic exhibitionism (or "eroplay") of the paraplegic Frank Moore, reminiscent of the James Joyce Liquid Memorial Theater of the sixties, but as if the grotesque body were Love's Body itself; or the fantasy sex of Annie Sprinkle, who "went at hooking with a heart of gold"[27] and will perform it as you wish, or let you, publicly, perform it on her (as in Richard Schechner's *Prometheus Project*); or the ecological inventory by Rachel Rosenthal of her aging body, and particularly the disarmingly triumphant moment when, bending over toward the audience, she lipsticks a gleeful 60 (that was her age when I saw it) on her momentarily forbidding and utterly shaven head.

The floating and the extension may be more or less literalized and, curiously, even more invitational, with the incursion of technology upon performance: filmic image, video feedback, lasers, and electronic prostheses. But in the age of simulacra, with its floating viruses too, the invitation and its feedback can make you a little nervous. That's why there is a certain comfort today when the body *is* screened, kept at a distance, the dismembered play of Eros – in the full surrealist scope of ideologized desire – displaced to MTV. It is there, in the fractured plenitude of a vacuous figuration, the liquidated layering of image and ravenous devouring of object-parts, that we are as close to a body without organs as Artaud ever dreamed. There we may find in all its fatal attraction the utmost thrill of abjection and, through whatever promiscuous imaginings, the ultimately safe sex. As the statistics accumulate, however, with selective inattention, Artaud's notion of the essential theater emerging through the plague no longer seems the mere febrile prophecy of a disintegrating mind.

COUNTERGRAVITY: THE OLD MAID HISTORY
AND THE QUEEN OF SHOWERS

Apocalypse itself may be attractive at a distance. Some of us were smitten a generation ago by the corporeal license of an imaginary pestilence, "as much moral as social," that provided us with a paradigm for the theater whose purpose would be "to drain abscesses collectively." But we are likely to have very mixed feelings today about the confirming evidence of "a superior disease," dark and insidious, but "infallibly identified with sexual freedom which is also dark, although we do not know precisely why." From "the human point of view," as Artaud wrote in his notorious essay on the plague, the essence of theater may still be, like the plague, to impel us to see things as they are, causing "the mask to fall," revealing "the lie, the slackness, baseness, and hypocrisy of our world" (*T&D* 30–1). So it is with the current epidemic, though the ideological benefits may not be, from the human point of view, sufficient to offset the ravaged bodies.

There were other visionaries of the theater, like Heinrich von Kleist and Gordon Craig, who felt the body as an encumbrance and, what's more, not the sacred vessel of a superior disease but an irredeemable source of pollution. Kleist attributes this to "the disorder that consciousness could produce in the natural grace of humankind," and his preference for the puppet has to do with the advantage of "*countergravity*," the inanimate doll being exempt from the "inertia of matter"[28] or, not only in the exertions of the dance, its *waste*. There was, too, in the preference for the puppet a distrust of mere human emotions that elides, curiously, in Craig's theory (as in his relation with his mother, Ellen Terry[29]) into a distrust of female emotion. This carries over to our own time, somewhat equivocally, in Tadeusz Kantor's manifesto on "The Theater of Death (1975)," which acknowledges Kleist and Craig, and the aesthetics of symbolism, as it resists the disruption of art by unpredictable emotions and passions. The manifesto opens with Craig's fable of the two women who, somewhere along the banks of the Ganges, forced their way into the shrine of the Divine Marionette. After spying on its movements and gestures, the jealously guarded secrets of the True Theater, they managed "by cheap parody . . . to satisfy the vulgar taste of the mob." Kantor eventually declares Craig's idea about replacing the live actor with a marionette as invalid for us today, but as he goes on to discuss the appearance of mannequins in his own work, he leaves us with a creation myth of the modern theater (nowhere revised) as a debasement by the women of the appropriated powers of the non-human body: "At the moment when they finally ordered a similar monument built for themselves – the modern theater, as we know it only too well and as it has lasted to this day, was born."[30]

There is a sense, of course, in which one can say of the emergence of realism that it was inseparable from the dramatization of hysteria, the unruly emotion that was the characteristic symptom of, say, the heroines of Ibsen's drama.[31] One can also say that it was the characteristic symptom of the heroes of Strindberg's drama, particularly the Father. Whatever the gender of the emotion, it infected the drama and, with ergotropic symptoms in the body, corrupted acting as well, which is why Duse said – agreeing with Craig, anticipating Kantor, in terms that resembled Artaud – that if the theater was to be saved all the actors would have to die of the plague.

101

This was an apocalyptic sentiment sometimes shared by William Butler Yeats, who also detested realism and the banality of its emotions, wanting ecstasy instead of hysteria, and a certain kind of woman.

With a symbolist's interest in countergravity, Yeats also wanted severed heads for the ritual dance of his final drama, *The Death of Cuchulain*. But how could that be achieved, short of the grossest naturalism (or the bodiless surgery of film), with anything of flesh and blood? As for the dancer herself, there might have been, for such a dance, a proper dancer once, who might have looked timeless, almost inhuman, requiring as the adored object of her tragic gaze no more than "a parallelogram of painted wood." But the intemperate Old Man who seems to represent Yeats in the prologue – "I am old, I belong to mythology" – despairs of that. Nothing now, he says, but the dancers painted by Degas, with their "chambermaid" faces, spinning on their toes like pegtops, but as if emptying the slop of that "old maid history," on which in a rage he trebly spits.[32] With the bodies of these dancers, there are none of the thrilling questions arising from the Ledaean kind – O body swayed to music, O brightening glance! – there's too much flesh between the dancer and the dance. Yeats, of course, had the wildest ambivalence about the biological/historical body, sometimes wanting it purged, abstracted, geometrized, at a byzantine distance in God's holy fire, and sometimes – as with the revels of Crazy Jane – in all the immediate visceral fervor of the reversed entropy of waste, born again like poetry in the rag and bone shop of the heart. Or, as Jane says to the Bishop of the mansion of Love, pitched in the place of excrement.

Thrilling as that may be, as Sartre shows in his massive study of the saintliness of Genet, biology and its functions are always on the verge of discrediting the body as either the sanctuary of a self or a purified vision of theater. No wonder the fastidiousness of the ceremonious whore in Genet's *The Screens*, who worked stylishly for years at cleaning her teeth with the extruded eloquence of a gilded hatpin. "Completely decayed," she says, spitting something out. "The whole back of my mouth is in ruins." To deal with the body in the desolation of its decay demands a great performance, whose magnanimous ectoplasm is thoroughly prepared, as through the artifice of the centuries, a kind of viscous *excess of materiality*, baroque, funereal, achieving its countergravity by painting an inch thick, thicker, the white on the ankles, and then the gown, as if poured from gold, hair coiled up in a blood-red chignon, and the armory of bracelets, without which she feels like a coffin with a hammerstroke missing: "I have to be heavy."[33]

As Benjamin says of mourning in his study of the baroque cult of the ruin, we are dealing with "a state of mind in which feeling revives the empty world in the form of a mask" (*Origin* 139). And from this strange operation of affect there is a certain enigmatic satisfaction in daring to contemplate what is there, as the Envoy suggests enigmatically beside

102

the brute flesh of the corpse in the Funeral Studio of *The Balcony*. Benjamin, too, might have been describing Genet, the allegorist, when he wrote: "the allegorization of the physis can only be carried through in all its vigour in respect of the corpse" (217). Through the delirious laughter at the end of *The Screens*, we see enacted what should have been apparent from the beginning, that Genet was writing, so far as can be seen, from the point of view of death, and it is precisely that which, for Benjamin, defines the enlivening mortifications of the baroque: "Seen from the point of death, the product of the corpse is life. It is not only in the loss of the limbs, not only in the changes of the aging body, but in all the processes of elimination and purification that everything corpse-like falls away from the body piece by piece" (218). With the cutting away of dead matter from the living body, there is the apparent end of biological function, though Benjamin observes with a sort of mortuary empiricism, shared by Genet, that nails and hair continue to grow on the corpse.

What we have left, however, in the physis is the baroque iconography, as it were the incised or graven memory itself, the emblematic formation of a memorial. Or the fetish that is a fantasy of a preoedipal order, part objects, erotogenic zones, not the bourgeois fetish of male genitality, but the fetishistic mimicry of the phallic mother, as in the grand ablutions of Warda in *The Screens*; or the chalice of Duchamp's *Fountain*, the recycled urinal; or the waxwork spread of the voluptuous body seen through the peephole of *Étant donnés*, vagina exposed, but the illuminating gas like an erect candle in its hand; or the anal objects of postmodern forms, fetishizing the feces, as if in, say, the sculpture of Jeff Koons the excrement were silvered or, as if prepared for the eternal freezer – designed, performed, photographed by Cindy Sherman (in surburban wig) – saran-wrapped. As Warda says, in her own solemn preparation of this fetishizing ideal, it is not a matter for loose emotion or improvisation. Nor solipsism, since it's a question of making sacred the detritus of the secular. Nor the unadorned innocence of the body, the naked transparency of the thing itself.

Concealment is at issue, but not as mere seduction. Without her grease paint and finery Warda can hardly spread her legs to piss, but "rigged up in gold" she is, as she says, "the Queen of Showers" (18), insisting that the men keep their distance before – as they must, gravely – emptying themselves into her. (As into the urinal/fountain of pregenital desire.) When the revolution breaks out, however, she gets "a bellyache to the very bowels of the earth" (128), since the long-prepared spectacle is undone and all decorum is gone, the men actually coming to fuck her, instead of admiring the stoic ostentation of her pink petticoats and watching her maneuver with finesse the long pointed utensil between her teeth. "It's a regular factory," she says of the ravenous appetites of the body (130), as the economy shifts from the service of fascination in a communion of the specular to mere service, worse yet, culinary, fast food, nothing but exchange, "the space and time circulating about us ... like any other." With this invasive disregard of the body, the fascinating body, "The brothel's no longer the brothel and, so to speak, we're fucking in the open" (131).

THE SOVEREIGNTY OF ABJECTION

Haunted by a sense of catastrophic violence, a cataract that will destroy the world, the baroque has only a theory of the imperiled body in a state of emergency. As Benjamin remarks, "the baroque knows no eschatology" (*Origin* 66), and as a result the impulse of exaltation is, as with the belly laughter of death in *The Screens*, turned into something like derision in the end. Or, through all the varieties of abjection, into something obscene. So it is with Genet, in his passion play of absence, in which the hereafter smells of the rot of the world and the sordidness, the shittiness of its hero is embalmed.

The scatalogical vision of the play, where the soldiers fart in chorus over the body of their dead lieutenant, is focused, however, in the fugitive character of Leila, who makes waste matter into something of an art form, and of whom the Mother says, "What interests her is the holes. The more there are, the better she likes it" (67). Ugly beyond belief, with one eye out, her body itching and covered with scabs, she virtually eats shit, though in a moment of perfect stillness amidst the "muck" and "crap" of the revolution she says, "Go away, stink! ... Who told you to stand beside me?" But then, considering the matter soberly, without pretension, she addresses the stink as if it were some humbled figure of death or, with some remembered dignity in the body's decay, a once exalted stranger in exile from itself: "Oh well, sit down there if you like, and don't move, sovereign" (156). If there is, along with the deference to sovereignty, the residue or inflection of a naturalistic gesture, almost parodic, "a variation of the same idea is touched on," as Benjamin observes (quoting Wilhelm Hausenstein) in the passage on sovereignty and eschatology, "by the insight that the naturalism of the baroque is 'the art of least distances . . . . In every case naturalistic means are used to reduce distances,' " as if some unavoidable intimacy of the actual – and what more intimate or actual than shittiness itself? – might " 'revert all the more surely into formal elevation and the forecourts of the metaphysical' " (*Origin* 66).

Where we also find Artaud. Of all modern dramatists Genet conceived a theater that in the ideographic splendor of its sense of decay, the infection of the human and its impossible stink, the ordure, bad faith and smell of western culture, most profoundly approaches the sovereignty of abjection in Artaud's theater of cruelty. Such a theater requires an immaculate conception, "the most rigorous intelligence," as the Bishop says in *The Balcony* (1), as if he were quoting Artaud. There is a bodily piety in Genet's perversions, but if it were possible for Artaud there would be a metaphysics of the flesh without the functions of the body – a pure body, then, of such utterly materialized intelligence that it is, like the exalted Ideas in the painting of "The Daughters of Lot" (*T&D* 33), without the stench of excreted thought. For Artaud, the pure body cannot shit, for what shits is the glue of minds, the "implacable stickiness" of the doxa that, for Roland Barthes, is "a kind of unconscious: in short, the essence of ideology."[34]

Yet if excrement is the abhorrent sign of originary separation, the filthiness that occurs within separation itself, the awful truth is that existence cannot be without the body and its detestable organs. As awesomely displayed in tragic drama, like the guts of Ajax doubly speared, by the gift-sword of Hector and the noonday sun, this schizoid bind may be a self-evident archaic truth, but what has always been haunting about Artaud is the fierce scruple of his scourge upon the body that gives us – with the seminal trace of the essential theater, site of a body that is only body – exemplary access to the "marrow's *delicacy*,"[35] the quick of thought in schizophrenia itself. Artaud was fascinated by ritual but in so far as its erotic function is not accessory: he wants the body there in its delirium, sonorous flesh streaming, not as representing but in the absence of (its) representation. Because the alchemical theater would dematerialize the body and its parts so that, at the incandescent edges of the future, nothing might resemble a fetish-object, it seems to go in conception even beyond what Artaud saw in the Balinese theater. He would have disdained, at any rate, the ritual contrivance, the decorous severed heads of Yeats' theater, its aestheticized violence, or Craig's symbolist recourse to the *Übermarionette*. What we may feel, even in Artaud's writings, is his own ravaged figure, rather, compelling us back to the body while flaying its muscles, whipping its innateness, refusing to accept *this* body as *his* body, which disappeared somewhere in the black hole of birth.

Paranoiac as this may be, it has had an almost brain-dazzling influence on the radicalized sexuality of recent thought, including feminism, by way of Derrida, Kristeva, and, in their *Anti-Oedipus*, Deleuze and Guattari. It is the disarticulated body of schizoanalysis, the phantasmaphysics, that has been carried over as the (most unrealizable) model of postmodern performance: no mouth, no tongue, no teeth, no larynx, no belly, no anus, only the epidermic play of perversity itself, the body only body without need of organs; or in the metonymic autonomy of the feminine the lips of the vulva speaking, flesh keeping the company of flesh. We are reminded, perhaps, of the Mouth of Beckett's *Not I*, its erotic babble. There is in the monstrous pregnancy of his figures, those ceaseless figures of speech, an asepsis in Beckett, and about the degrading incapacities of the body, that absurd dysfunction of the fiasco of birth, a revulsion of its own, "nearest lavatory . . . start pouring it out," excretion turning into logorrhea, "the brain . . . flickering away like mad. . . . "[36] Even when constipated, like

105

Clov, something is taking its course: brain fever, relieved only by the convulsive body's compulsive laughter, the laugh laughing up its sleeve or, as he says, the *risus purus*, afflatus of the rictus, laughing at itself. And when that dies out, a murmur a rustle, there is the tempering agency of the *nostalgia* that from the ideolect of silence, up the snout, roaring, reflective gape and grimace, starts it all over again, it all, it all, begging the mouth to stop.

There is, in cruel proportion to the thief who was saved (but not, as Didi hermeneutically reminds us, in *all* the gospels), a reasonable percentage of irreducible sadomasochism in Beckett. This is a matter of the *pensum*, the interminable sentence (of language) in which the body is engrailed, as far back as the "fontanelles." For Artaud, however, all the perverse possibilities of the mind released by the plague and localized in the body are accompanied by a corrosive puritanism that, as the inexhaustible source of self-lacerating pain, seems to go unrelieved. If he makes provision in his metaphysics of the flesh, as in the *mise-en-scène* of the unconscious, for the suspect powers of speech, that is because everything depends on the *interdiction*. Paranoia is prescience. Artaud promises the ductility of a speech that is a body, a body that is a theater, but the theater of cruelty, like Kafka's vast and labyrinthine psychoerotic burrow, is as much a defense mechanism as a desiring machine. Cerebral, cruel (gray room, gray matter), the setting of Beckett's *Endgame* is something of a burrow too. And with all the compulsive geometry of paranoia, it is marked by *the fear of touch*, which is, if primordial, the precise measure of an inviolable distance. According to Canetti in *Crowds and Power*, what is also measured in the fear of touch is the psychic basis of the audience, as if there were another interdiction, favoring specularity, keeping us at a distance.

THE ETHOS OF PLAY: A DISSEVERED STORY

Endgame is a play so localized in the body that it can hardly move. Beckett spoke of it as his most "clawing" play. If the apparently disjunct, regressive, and improvisational elements of *Waiting for Godot* gave us, through its elegiac clowning, the structural paradigm for an ethos of play, we can see palpably in *Endgame* another side of *jouissance*: play is deadly. If it abrades upon the body, it is impacted with specularity, like the accretions of memory in the "blindness" of Hamm or the "envenomed stare" of Clov, as if *he* were the infant described by Augustine, in the phrase appropriated by Lacan for his account of the scopic drive. We may speak of a cutting look, but as Beckett seems to understand, in his Augustinian way, there is no look which is not cutting, even the look which loves, loving itself loving, but wondering painfully at every moment: "Am I as much as . . . being seen?" That would seem to be the issue in the incriminative light of Beckett's *Play*, where the heads in the funeral urns, "mere eye," tell the dissevered story, "the whole thing there, all there, staring you in the face" (157).

What is staring you in the face is the cutting necessity, the fate of the body as a site of knowing, from the tragic *sparagmos* to the incision of anatomy, which affirms the propriety of violence (or violation) in the heuristic order of things. So far as it is thought as a body of knowledge, the body is subject to the severing light, dramatized by Beckett and theorized by Foucault, who has pointed out in his archeology that knowledge is not made for understanding, it is made for cutting. As for the phantasms created by fear and desire, those which pass through the heads of *Play*, it's as if Foucault were commenting precisely on them in his "Theatrum Philosophicum." They would only be phantasms, he says, in their "incorporeal materiality," unless they were allowed "to function at the limit of bodies; against bodies, because they stick to bodies and protrude from them, but also because they touch them, cut them, break them into sections" (*LCP* 169).

As for the punishing regime by means of which knowledge gets into the body, on that delicate subject Kafka has anticipated both Foucault's *Discipline and Punish* and Beckett's *pensum*, the interminable sentence that is an inscription upon the body. He conceives the process, moreover, as a piece of body art that requires not only careful preparation of the performance but some sophistication from the audience: "When the man lies down on the Bed and it begins to vibrate, the Harrow is lowered onto his body. It regulates itself automatically so that the needles barely touch his skin; once contact is made the steel ribbon stiffens immediately into a rigid band. *And then the performance begins*. An ignorant onlooker would see no difference between one punishment and another."[37] Meanwhile, however you look at it, the more you look, the facticity of the body cuts, *is* cut, both ways, literally and figuratively, is made for cutting, actor and audience, in the relentless light of its absence and ("You'll see it" (*Play* 157)) the apparent taboo in the telling: "Bite off my tongue and swallow it? Spit it out?" (154). What is *it*? we may ask again. Or with footfalls falling, "it all, it all,"[38] the whole thing there, all there (it: on the tip of the tongue?). Whatever it is it is a far cry, it seems, from bodies and pleasures, although there are, to be sure, peculiar or marginal pleasures in the most abused, maimed, stared at, or anatomized bodies of Beckett's drama.

If there is, in those partial bodies, only the most minimal consolation ("The mind won't have it" (155)), there is in the extremity of postmodern performance, along with valorization of the body, a utopian desire to do without it entirely. Or to claim it doesn't exist. The performance artist Stelarc, suspending himself by fishhooks through his flesh, has tried to prove by exquisite levitation that the prosthetic body has made the body obsolete. As with the schizoid body of the desiring-machine producing desire with no organs at all, it's hard to say what desire might be fulfilled by the auxiliary organs or ascetic discipline of the prosthesis. Since it's not exactly the resurrection of the flesh, it may be relief – by something other than the decrepitude of age – from the ageold burden of desire.

We'll come back to the imaginary of the prosthetic shortly, but meanwhile, on the alluring landscape of commodified desire, the trying out of the body in the plenitude of its own pleasures has turned out to be a trial. More than a trial, an international scandal, as in the labyrinthine operations of the Médellin cartel, with its global network of dependent bodies, sniffing, needled, up the nose, into the arm, through the womb, overdosed, ravaged, degraded, ruined at birth by drugs – the image of which on the nightly news, innumerable documentaries, and everywhere on the soaps is an appalling part of the spectacle which remains our major commodity. In the irreality of the body, the very "abundance of dispossession" (*Spectacle*, note 31), which we'd like to believe is *only* an image.

But with all due indulgence of its unexhausted pleasures, suspended perhaps but far from obsolete, the body has become again, as in the syphilitic nightmare of Ibsen's *Ghosts*, the ideological space of death-in-life, the killing field whose immunological systems are mysteriously breaking down. As the will is now wired with new prohibitions, and all the anxiety of a hollow rhetoric, to these hidden recesses, ideology has become in the proliferous exposures or venereal imagery of the society of the spectacle increasingly enamored with and immured in a politics of the body.

IDEOLOGY AND ZOOLOGY: THE TRANSPARENT VEIL

That it was the destiny of ideology to be thus attached to the body, and its politics, was perhaps to be expected from the early history of the term. When it was introduced at the time of the French Revolution, by Antoine Destutt de Tracy, he developed the elements of the concept on the premise that the study of ideology (like Samaritaine's view of the commodity) is part of *zoology*. As it happens, the historical repertoire of the body's images pays a good deal of attention to the birds and the beasts[39] which are presumably content with their bodies or don't think twice about them, no less as machines, desiring or otherwise, while the drama of humankind seems constructed on a grid of malaise, indulgence, self-hatred, detestation of the body or short-lived ecstasies, followed by remorse, as well as the monstrous knowledge of whatever *jouissance* that the prison house of language is constructed on the makeshift and mortal scaffold of insubstantial flesh and bone.

That may be why, with all the body-building and rhetorical building up, there are still very few people about whom we're inclined to say they are perfectly at ease with their bodies. And the same might be said of the new regime of preferential bodies chosen today on psychosexual grounds, no less those imagined in the ideological fantasy, with its surrealist imagery,

108

of the libidinal flow of a postoedipal theater. Such imaginings are actually quite useful in the theater, and have found their way into the psychophysical exercises to which actors have grown accustomed. In the experimental work of the last generation some actors developed remarkable abilities to think the body's organs as transposable elements in a combinatory set, or to initiate sound or movement as if enacting the credo of schizoanalysis or, with an imagined dissolution of organs, the uttermost wish of polysexual desire. But in the multiplicity of body rhetorics now sounded on the stage, within the universal spectacle whose apotheosis is noise, the one inarguable rhetoric is the inexorable force of gravity in the semiurgy of floating objects, the allegoresis of body parts.

It may be that in the reification of image diffused all over the world the exuberant body is happily rent, dismembered, disseminated, and that no human language or historical event can resist this diffusion, as it occurs through electronic memory with the speed of light. True, in the age of simulacra we have image-producing technologies capable of realizing what no actor can and the theater has only dreamed, a full fluidity of the body or total reconstruction, from the liquid(ating) fantasy of a body without organs to the sci fi promise of no bodies at all. All of this can be achieved, maybe even in cyberspace, with a semblance of performance, but not so far without its haunted referent: the resistless remembrance of the surpassing body, the body which is past, bringing its laden knowledge to performance. (The same was true, we might remember, with the referent in art, the overdetermined object or figure with a history, which was extruded for a time, then returned through the body by means of performance.) In the dematerialized imagery of the spectacle (or in conceptual art) the body may appear to give itself over to its utter dissemination or, like Ibsen's Peer Gynt, to the scenarios of liberation fashioned by desire, where performance forsakes the structures of drama for the hegemony of a purer play. But the knowledge it returns with is what we always knew, attending upon the absence of an empty stage, which in the ironies of aesthetics is the emblem of that knowledge: we are born astride of a grave and return to it in the end. This is not a mere *effect* of language, power, desire, or appearance, as Beckett tried to make clear through a burst of rage from the blinded Pozzo, shattering in the instant the ideology of play. It could be said, rather, that language, power, desire, and appearance are themselves the effects, the incorporeal materiality of the grave truth of material being, around which the idea of theater has consolidated itself. (Of course the play will resume, either to undo or reform the theater, or with the forlorn expectation that it will have deepened itself.) There have been in the theater, as we've seen, extraordinary imaginings of a counter-gravity, but even the mannequins are haunted by the grave, as in the manic obsessions of Kantor's theater. Or to return again to zoology, we are fastened to a dying animal (as Yeats well knew on the way to Byzantium), which inevitably makes an absurdity of any ideology of desire.

With Destutt de Tracy, who might have rejected countergravity as a manifestation of religious thought, ideology was from the outset kept separate from desire. In superimposing the materialism of Cabanis upon the sensationalism of Locke, he was extruding religion as a determinant of value or authorizing power and, in displacing morality into metaphysics, characterized the latter as a realm of illusion. Unlike the theater of the eighteenth century, however, no less Nietzsche's visionary conception of the ancient theater, it was a realm of illusion not destined for both gratification *and* instruction, which for Destutt de Tracy had to keep its epistemological distance from pleasure. In short, gratification is not knowledge and had nothing to do with his objective, which was to establish a science of ideas, an account of the natural history of the mind that was at the same time a critique of false value or absolute norms. However our thoughts are formed, Destutt de Tracy's view was that there is no supersensible reality behind. If not exactly destiny, biology is the basis of human psychology, and the materialism of the science of ideas was intended, through definition of the laws of human nature and sociability, to theorize the grounds of republican citizenship.[40]

As it happened, though, the grounds of republican citizenship had already been enunciated in the carceral theater at the cutting edge of the Terror, as Büchner understood, before Foucault, in *Danton's Death*: "The guillotine makes good Republicans!"[41] Despite his quite precocious historical understanding, Büchner may not have been aware that Destutt de Tracy was one of the group of *savants* appointed by the Convention in 1794 to administer the newly founded Institute of France, whose articles of faith had been articulated a year before by Condorcet in his systematic account of the progress of the human spirit. In this regard, the "ideologues" of the Institute were to bring the revolution into consciousness by infusing a new system of higher learning with the philosophy of the Enlightenment. "The Revolution must end and the Republic begin," says Hérault-Sechelles at the beginning of *Danton's Death*. And with a libidinal impulse to the libertarian vision derived from the Enlightenment, Camille Desmoulins declares with a kind of rapture against the threat of a renewed puritanism: "The Constitution must be a transparent veil that clings close to the body of the people. Through it we must see the pulsing of every vein, the flexing of every muscle, the quiver of every sinew" (1.1, p. 5).

Instead of Trotsky's image of uneven healing as a cautionary figure of uneven development, what we have in Desmoulins' conception of the Constitution is an erotic apprehension of the future in the instant, a premonitory image of Love's Body – what was to become in the polymorphous perversity of the theatricalized sixties the transcendent figure of totalizing desire. This was the constitution of the body politics of the Living

Theater, literally demanding the future in the instant in the production of *Frankenstein* or reaching for its apotheosis in *Paradise Now*, spelled out by the actual bodies of the performers. But as Nietzsche perceived, when he spoke of all value as judgments of the muscles, these judgments are caught up, with the vicissitudes of desire, in the will to power – as well as the insidious depredations of the body itself, subject as it is to the cancerous sedimentations of the indeterminacy of time. So it is in Büchner's character-ization of Danton himself, with his fastidious awareness of the body's stink and, with each minute crushing the vanities of desire, his equivocal resis-tance to the assumption of power.

GOD-KISSING CARRION: THE SOCIAL TEXT

I have written elsewhere on this aspect of *Danton's Death*,[42] which is also, along with Büchner's *Woyzeck*, a virtual index to the issues of postmodern performance as it consolidates itself around the phenomenology and instru-mentality of the body, that clinical object with a fantasy life: house of pleasure or prison house; interpellated subject or subject of entropic decay; elusive other of the living word or indeterminate antecedent of the sign; inescapable image of itself or, in the negative theology of poststructuralist thought, the memory bank of afterimage, its allegorical ground – in the spectacle of a culture whose symbolic is in ruins. Mere currency, passing strange, the body may be too unstable in the economy of exchange to be the last instance or material base – or, as it was with the valorized body of the antiverbal sixties, the tactile court of last resort. "I had things to say," said Jane Comfort, explaining why, not for the first time in dance, language was reintroduced, "I absolutely didn't know how to do with my body."[43]

While discourse on the body is as avid as ever, this is a significant departure from the assumption of body language as a repository of truth, or the notion of an unaccommodated body, the poor bare forked unme-diated thing itself. It should be said, however, that in the performative space between these two possibilities there is a good deal of conceptual sweat and methodological wrangling about the precise relation of the body to language. It is an ideological problem of no minor importance. The problem arises from the seeming inseparability of signifier and signified in the performing body itself, which appears to conflate sign and meaning in its very breath and gesture. Once more, Yeats has defined the issue in a talismanic question: "How can we know the dancer from the dance?" The line is usually read as a testament to the inseparability, but there is something in performance that also abrades against it, resists the rhetorical assertion. It is this resistance that Paul de Man reflects or shadows in his *Allegories of Reading*, suggesting that a more literal reading may be in order, which would lead to greater complication of what might be construed as the manifest content of the line. This complicating impetus has to do with the desire in reading to make the distinction that the rhetoric of appearances appears to resist. Dancer and dance are separable and inseparable in thought, "entirely coherent but entirely incompatible," like the dancer and the dance *in* performance. As the two readings of the line have to engage each other – the impossibility of telling them apart, the desire to tell them apart – so neither of them can be determined as having "priority over the other; none can exist in the other's absence. There can be no dance without a dancer, no sign without a referent. On the other hand, the authority of the meaning engendered by the grammatical structure is fully obscured by the duplicity of a figure that cries out for the differentiation it conceals."[44] One can say, of course, like Dr Johnson refuting Bishop Berkeley, that the callous or the shin splint knows the dancer from the dance, though the perceptual issue may be more complicated for us by the dancer's covering that up or forgetting it in performance. As the performer approaches a state of being that would, for Nietzsche, be outside of ideology, the condition of that forgetfulness is another complication.

There is still some carryover of Nietzsche in the move to a cultural politics, but this is not the sort of complication that current readings of the body are really prepared for, or concerned with. The condition of forgetfulness seems to throw the dancer again, inseparably, into the vertigo of the dance, which may be thought of as the dance of high modernism, or a form of indeterminacy through which, paradoxically, the body may assert itself as presence. That is, as we know, discomfiting to critical theory. What we are asked to be particularly conscious of now is based on this assumption: prior representations of the body merely disguise the fact that there is no pure phenomenological body or – without the inscriptions of social production – a natural human body as such. To our watchful semiotics such an idea would seem to be as bathetic as the Ghost's anguished outcry in *Hamlet* for the unscarred smoothness of his royal body. In this play so mordantly conscious of the body as machine or, with a residue of desire, god-kissing carrion, the body is with the king but the king is not with the body. Which is to say that it is not really *the* body we are talking about any longer, but a corporeal abstraction, the more or less emblooded projection of bodiless thought coursing through the (represented) body, derealized as it is by the wild and whirling words. Whatever the mysterious substance that flowed through "The natural gates and alleys of the body," leaving it "barked about/Most lazarlike, with vile and loathsome crust" (1.5.71–2), we tend to look at the crust now as mere dubious evidence of a bodily absence, to be read as a social text.

Marx made a distinction in the *Economic and Philosophic Manuscripts of 1844* between the senses of social man and those of non-social man, who lacked "the objectively unfolded richness of man's essential being. . . . " The unfolding is teleological, and there is a disturbing humanism here for those who are wary of any kind of *essentialism*, even that (ambiguously or retrospectively) produced by history. But there would be little misgiving, I'd suppose, about the idea that the five senses are formed by "a labour of the entire history of the world down to the present" (*Marx–Engels* 89). So, too, the body is now seen as a social formation or system of relations, discursive, material, and psychosexual, the distinct outgrowth of historical modes of production or, the body entangled with language, as the inscription of a personal history.

"Which body?" asks Roland Barthes, whose body exists for him, he says, only in two general forms, migraine and sensuality, "theatrical to itself only to a mild degree," and certainly not as the old heroic body of myth, which has passed through the overexposures of history and the dramaturgy of the unconscious into ideology. Nevertheless, he is "captivated to the point of fascination by the socialized body, the mythological body, the artificial body (the body of Japanese costumes), and the prostituted body (of the actor)."[45] With more or less fascination and (despite a view of language *as* body) rare displays of sensuality, all of this has come to be taken for granted by critical theorists. But like anything taken for granted the question remains whether, as counterideology, it is too much so. With a grievous sense of the body as socially produced, the theater has always been – even in the classical world, certainly with Euripides – obsessed with the question, as it struggles with the notion that the body is marked, written, overdetermined, nothing more than a text. For the moment, however, leaving that in abeyance:

THE POWER GRID AND THE PROSTHETIC

"If the new ensemble of terms and relations is established conjuncturally around a particular corporeal status," writes Francis Barker of the tremulous private body emerging (in Pepys' diary) from the political settlements of the seventeenth century, "this is not because the body is the essential foundation of the structure."[46] Nor is the body, in this conjecture, the irreducible thing left over when the codes have been deciphered and the ideology of presence dispelled. "The body is a power grid," write Kroker and Cook in *The Postmodern Scene*, "tattooed with all the signs of cultural excess on its surface, encoded from within by the language of desire, broken into at will by the ideological interpellation of the subject, and, all the while, held together as a fictive and concrete unity by the illusion of *misrecognition*" (26).

As a power grid, then, the body has its political history, its "nature" circumscribed by a set of historical practices and discourses. It is neither hypostatized object nor transcendental signified, nor is it the invariant datum of the Lacanian Real, what in its carnal knowledge takes the position of the one presumed to know by merely remaining mute. The

113

body is rather site, instrument, machine, process, or – as Menenius suggests in *Coriolanus* with the parable of the Belly – a kind of ecosystem, invested by the regimen of power and indentifiable as the body of specific historical thought. Thus, we speak now of the atomistic body, the Cartesian body, or the body of organicism that has come to be bureaucratized, the body of use-value, the surreptitiously tortured or polluted body, the body under surveillance, appropriated and pliable, bent to the purposes of an industrial order; or the disaffected bodies of that order: black body, woman's body, gay body, the body in its becoming, with the imagined body of androgyny poised against the unimaginable hybrids of genetic engineering and recombinant DNA.

Among all these – but especially for the disaffected with a jaundiced view of genesis – there is the problematic of the prosthetic body. I am referring to a particular corollary of the feminist critique of reproduction, as developed by the performance artist/filmmaker Valie Export, in a recent essay on the technologies of reproduction. There are various ethical issues raised by these technologies that are also being debated, but what is of greater moment to Export are the questions of power posed for the body itself, and especially the female body. As every made object may be thought of as a projection of the human body, there is a sense of the logic of the body producing its own technology: as with language, technology *as* body, which is in all its electronic avatars a triumph of technology *over* the body. Here, in the prosthetic movement from the mechanical to the robotic to the immaterial, we enter a shadowy realm in which the body is threatened by its new dimensions. The augmented physical organs of the deficient body launch its image into a sort of cyberspace, where it reproduces mastery over nature with other mystifications in a theater of astronomical scale. That might at some overreaching disjuncture of the speed of light, or unaccountable swerve in the Doppler effect, break into some unimaginable galaxy of non-representation. What troubles Export, meanwhile, is that the body may be outdistanced or absent, but it is not, as Stelarc thinks, obsolete either. Not *that* body, wherever it is, for the concept of the prosthetic, and its expansionist policy, remains inseparable from the widening dominion of culture and its discourse, arising from the imaginary, blurring into and determined by the symbolic, whose phantasmic content is still articulated in "the social grammar of masculine desire."[47]

So far as this is true it is a domain uncrossable by women. Export did her earlier work in the transgressive, orgiastic, and ideologically explosive orbit of Viennese Aktionism, and was on several occasions arrested for it. I suspect the collapse of the Berlin Wall, and the freer passage of bodies over all the borders of Europe, will not drastically revise her view of the prosthetic. Her essay was written before it could register all the uprisings, promise, and subsequent frustrations, and it puts the issue in familiar semiotic terms: "The traversing of the phantasm is thwarted by the phallic signifier" ("The Real" 12). As the Wall itself was in the lethal reality of its once unbudgeable presence a virtual phantasm, which is to say *ideology itself, made manifest*, the implication would appear to be that it was there even as it was torn down and sold by the DDR. Yet as there are mixed signals in that, there must be mixed feelings as well.

In her performance pieces, quite formalistic, but putting her life at risk – literally, in one event, subject to electrocution – Export has tried to thwart the phallic signifier. If that's an impossible project, she has conceived such events to demonstrate that if culture is the language of absence, the body belongs to the rhetoric of the real. She has in the process explored questions of social control of the body, and if there is any such thing as a natural body at all whether or not it can be reached. When she turns, however, to the prosthetic body, she is referring not only to representation in language and the reproduction of images, the restricted code of the body, but – drawing on Freud's *Civilization and Its Discontents* – the relation of body functions and tools, natural organs and their artificial extensions, the outside possibilities of the spatializing prosthetic. Reproduction technology, in this sense, is looked at ambivalently, as progression of the work of culture but also, since the prosthetic extension occurs under the masculine signifier, as a further nullification of the feminine – if not the canceling out of woman's being, the positing of being for woman only in negation, in the accustomed continuum of the lost signifier.

But if culture produces thus the non-existent woman, it produces her in a kind of reversed optic whereby the masculine projection of the human body into space is countered by "the feminine assimilation of the environment through the body," in parts, fragments, floating vesicles of being (16), as if she were the disjunct libidinal circuit of the schizoanalytic desiring machine. Such a figure (hysterical or anorexic) can only be represented in the differential experience of the body as opaque or ambivalent. "The opaque representation (of the difference) produces the enigma of woman and the enigma of the image" in which – whether or not as consummately as Molière's Célimène, whose eminence is otherness – "the enigma woman conceals itself' (20). In that respect, the circuitous doubling of the enigma in the binary domain of the masculine signifier (not to mention the amplified recycling of the signifier from stage to screen), the woman does appear to assume the exchangeable features of the commodity, and in the process is fetishized as such. As I've suggested before, feminist performance has tried to rectify this image, or do away with it entirely. Or to do away with it by moving away from the body. There are still, of course, types of performance that claim for woman a special, even hyperbolic intimacy with the body, either as the (un)canny site of self-replenishing masquerade or virtually erupting within as a kind of over-presence.[48] But as Jane Comfort indicated – parsing out once more the dancer from the dance – other women have found that there are certain

115

things they want to do that can't be done with the body. Or that nobody, man or woman, seems to know how to do, with or without prosthesis.

THE *HYSTERA*, THE TOOTH, THE PALM: IS IT POSSIBLE, HOW?

Here we might reflect again upon something distressing in the ontology of theater – or is it merely ideological? – that turns the lost signifier, irrespective of gender, into something of a lost cause or, worse, no cause. It is not entirely clear whether the woman described by Export, no more than an element in the grammar of masculine desire, might be said to have been utterly represented in her non-existence by the alluring emptiness of the image of Duse, who in her refusal of a rhetoric could hardly escape the destiny of a fetish. Once again we may ask: is that what great acting is? And if so, we can surely understand why, variously, in neo-Marxism, feminism, and a sort of postmodern Platonism, there has been so intense a critique of theater.

This is particularly exacerbated in the French connection between the oppressive logos of its hereditary rationalism and the classical glamour of its institutional theaters. This attraction/disdain for the institution and a psychoanalytical recovery of the *hystera* (the faceless, unseen origin) come together in "The Stage Setup," a revisionary parable of Plato's Cave, by Luce Irigaray. The stage setup is not merely the arrangement of the scene, but the scene of a certain arrangement – a sort of metaphysical sting or swindle – that occurs in "the invisible process of translating the *hystera*" into the myth of phallocentrism. The setup is acted out "between rehearsal and performance, repetition and representation, or reproduction," and if the woman is dispossessed in the process, divested of the signifier and made subjectless, no one of either gender is actually spared. But while the man in reproduction is "always already a captive of repetition,"[49] upon the woman falls, as it did upon Iphigeneia, the implacable burden of the sacrificial demand. Shifting to another theorist in the continuum of this critique: "It is always necessary," writes Hélène Cixous, "for a woman to die in order for the play to begin. Only when she has disappeared can the curtain go up; she is relegated to repression, to the grave, the asylum, oblivion and silence. . . . She is loved only when absent or abused, a phantom or a fascinating abyss."[50]

This is not exactly the abyss that Jean-François Lyotard addresses, but for him the theater places us right in the heart of absence or negativity, or within the nihilism of representation that raises the question of power. And he posits against it an alternative system where, as in the trajectory of the libido itself, the "erotic-morbid body can function in all directions."[51] In such a system the semiology that merely sustains theology would be dismantled and along with it, perhaps, theatricality – in which case, it could be said, the disappearance of Duse would not be required. Picking up cues from Zeami, Artaud, Brecht, and eventually John Cage, Lyotard tries to imagine a theater in which the libidinal investment of body parts, "the tooth, the palm," would no longer be bound to representation but would circulate in a non-hierarchical relation as nothing but "forces, intensities, present affects" ("Tooth" 109), all produced "without intention." But what he declares as "the business of an energetic theater," appropriate for our social and ideological experience of modern capitalism, with its economy of reversible value, is not after all a guaranteed business: "That is my question: is it possible, how?" (110).

If not entirely a fascinating abyss, seductive as only that can be, Duse appears to be a limit case. There is the view, of course, that the appearance of being without a rhetoric was, no matter what it seemed, only mere appearance: seeming, seeming. An intense consciousness of that, as in Shakespeare's plays and sonnets, is not exactly to believe – whatever the designated body – that there is no such phenomenon as an empty, authentic, or unfictitious body. And there are still the spiritual disciplines absorbed into methods of acting or technologies of performance that speak, as in the disappearing figures of the tai chi, of emptying the body or, wanting that, burning it away, as with the *asanas* of yoga. Or, in Artaud, the alchemical flame.

There are few theaters still around constructing an ethos of performance around such ideas, not at least with the conspicuous piety of Grotowski's Laboratory Theater, which borrowed techniques not only from Meyerhold, Dullin, and Delsarte, but from the major forms of the East as well, the Peking Opera, the Kathakali, and the Japanese Noh. These culminated in a discipline that aimed to minimize the organism's resistance to the psychic process of trance or "transillumination." What Grotowski sought, and Cieslak almost realized in the tortuous performance of *The Constant Prince*, "a tension towards the extreme," was a kind of moral and spiritual nakedness. Grotowski described it in the sacerdotal language of his early work as a *via negativa*, in which "impulse and action are concurrent: the body vanishes, burns, and the spectator sees only a series of visible impulses."[52] Whether or not the particle physics of those impulses corresponds to those of Duse is a matter for speculation, remaining as it does, across disciplines, one of the enigmas of acting method. If those impulses are, however, no longer so visible in the performing body itself with anything like the intensities and affects, ablutions or metaphysics, of Grotowski's theater, there has been a carryover of what his method shared with Meyerhold, and with Brecht: a sense of the "dialectics of human behavior," expressed in a "rhythmically articulated" system of signs, more or less artificial, ideogrammatic, and erotic (*Poor Theater* 16–17).

So, too, it was the psychophysical practices in the experimental theater of the sixties that were a preface to the sort of post-Marxist romanticism that, as in certain radical feminisms or schizoanalytic thought, dreamed of a sumptuously signifying body, with no zones or boundaries and unceasing eroticism, an illimitable body of incessant becoming that, in its imageless fantasy of non-representational desire, might produce still-unnamable pleasures without end. If there is still something alluring in this body so full of itself it empties into thought, it is more commonplace now to see upon the material body the inscriptions of ideology and investments of power, without imagining behind it all some prior or elemental body, like an untouched Rosetta Stone, smooth but porous, awaiting the first metonymic marks of the stylus of power. There is more attention now, in cultural critique, to the abject bodies of persecution and repression, but as we think of the body in its dispossession, it is always a matter of reclaiming it from the institutional practices and technical procedures by means of which it acquires a local habitation and a name. Whatever the weight of critique, it by no means eliminates the persistent question as to whether there is something about the body that is ontologically dispossessed.

(DO YOU SMELL A FAULT?)

At a time when invocation of the Holocaust, that mass site of the dismembered body, seems like a rhetorical device in the discourse of transgression – either its most loaded image or an irony of oppression – there isn't much talk of the Jewish body, once the honorific figure of modernist alienation. Not within that discourse. Or within the developing annals of alienated bodies. That's mainly because of the political power of Jews in the United States, associated now with bourgeois imperialism, and unswerving support of Israel, despite its paradoxical status as an oppressor in the Middle East. There is still, however, a Jew in the canonical literature that has been among the chosen figures of the new historicism, though largely for the way in which he exposes the structural contradictions of Shakespeare's time, and of Shakespeare's drama itself, contradictions that persist through the tradition of bourgeois humanism: "If you prick us, do we not bleed?" (*MV* 3.1.66–7). At the ontological level, perhaps. There is in Shylock's notorious question not only a reversed pun of phallic aggression, but amidst the current insistence on historically constructed, encoded, or textualized bodies, a reassertion of a universalism of the body, the essential body, which has become in theory something of a historical taboo. A little bit of essentialism doesn't hurt, some say, but when it does it would seem, perhaps, a little closer to history, which has also been defined as the thing that hurts. While there is a quite understandable historical expediency in modalities of performance that deny it, forget it, or deflect attention from it, the deepest conceivable performance still occurs in the order of that body, the essential body, over the unnerving prospect of an ontological fault.

This was, is, and remains the irreducible space of theater. We are reminded of that in the sexual banter that prefaces both the body's mutilations and the political divisions of *King Lear* ("Do you smell a fault?" (1.1.15)). It is also what Beckett seemed to know, in his aporetic way, even before he turned to the stage, a prescience that turns up again, along with the mutilations, in one of his later pieces of prose, what even in the imagining has to be performed: "No mind. Where none. That at least. A place. Where none. For the body to be in."[53] That at least, a place, intimating the fault. (*Pause.*) That pause may be more subjective, more specifically a figure of an ontological break, than the pregnant moment of a Brechtian *gestus*, but it is also a moment of arrested being in which we can hardly ignore the political economy of the body that also enters into performance. Nor the power relations that have "an immediate hold upon it," as Foucault observed, as if he were watching Pozzo and Lucky, and which "invest it, mark it, train it, torture it, force it to carry out tasks, to perform ceremonies, to emit signs" – and, one might add, to double over those signs in cultural production, of which the theater demonstrates more than any other form that the body, its own major instrument or technology, "becomes a useful force only if it is both a productive body and a subjected body."[54] If institutions and state apparati have recourse to the body through diverse procedures, methods, demands, so does the apparatus of theater, each acting method or performance technique constituting, ideologically, another set of demands and verifying by reproduction both a particular image of the body, its capacities and possibilities of freedom, and its systemic constraints.

The systemic constraints of the naturalistic actor are revealed, for instance, by Roland Barthes in a comparison of the "loveable body" of the Bunraku puppet to the disarticulating mimesis, "the abjectness of its inertia," in the western marionette. There is, for Barthes, no countergravity in this marionette. Reflecting instead the "inertia of matter" which Kleist attributed to the human body, it is "a caricature of 'life,' " affirming "precisely thereby life's *moral* limits" and serving "to confine beauty, truth and emotion in the living body of the actor – he who nevertheless makes of that body a lie."[55] Since it is still quite arguable as to whether the constraints of any system produce any more than the approximation of a partial truth, we may be talking, as Nietzsche believed, of degrees of (inevitable) fraudulence, or misrepresentation; and I shall return to the illusion of truth in the lie of naturalism in the next chapter. As I've suggested before, the measure of any method is the extent to which it remains convincing about the future of its illusions, or in the ideological extensions and curvature of time the way in which the constraints in a system open themselves again, unexpectedly, to history.

With the Bunraku, as Barthes perceives its "lesson in writing," we have another view of performance as a regimen of signs. It is not a matter of

119

the puppet aping the human actor, who hardly performs – that animal body impeded by (the forgery of) a "soul" – with anything like the subtlety of the manipulated doll. The dance of the chief operator (his face "visible, smooth, clear, impassive, cold like 'a white onion freshly washed' " (170)) and his two black-hooded assistants rids us of the physiology of the actor and "the alibi of an organic unity," which is, for all its claim of a visceral truth, the simulation of a body that is specifically bourgeois. The Bunraku puppet is neither this unctuous simulation nor, like the marionette, a mere facsimile of bodily gestures, the little phallic thing, a "genital swathe ... fallen from the body to become a fetish" (172). What it is, rather, is a concrete abstraction, not a body-fetish with its corporal illusion but rather the versatile instrument of a performative text "in which the codes of expression are detached from each other, pulled free from the sticky organism in which they are held by Western theater" (175).

The stickiness of the organism remains an issue in performance wherever live bodies are still alive (some are not), even through abstraction, like Warda below her blood-red chignon, or rather the actor below the signs of Warda, who is in the psychogenesis of acting an impertinence of signs. Within the mechanisms or paraphernalia of any performance, or beyond the nude uncharactered body itself, it is that impertinent presence which constitutes the expressiveness of codes or the apparent life-force or vitality of signs. This is so whether the apparency of the body is robed, masked, geometrized, armored with doubt or distanced, or removed from the stage entirely, and instead of its naked sonorous streaming realization, there is nothing but an electronic memory, as in the punctuation of Beckett's *Breath*, the mere taped vagitus of a cry. It is there that we may feel the cost, the tragic cost, of emptying the body to all appearances, pulling it free of its sticky organism, and thinking of it in its absence as a fetishized illusion which is better deployed in performance as *no more* than a sign. And this is not only true of the forms of western theater, since the organism sticks to all forms, however encoded, like the ritualistic appearances in the dance/drama of the East. As we have already observed, there are other, perhaps worse, things sticking to such appearances, like the social structures not only built upon a fault but that, through the depredations of history or scandals of power or perversions of faith amounting to a plague, also smell a little, or stink to high heaven. If this is often forgotten amidst the new sentiments about the performance of otherness in cultures remote or strange, the pull of the organism – its full gravity, the power of the fault – is a somewhat displaced issue on the postmodern scene, in the marketplace of culture and the political economy of signs.

THE IRREDUCIBLE MEASURE

With an inordinately playful consciousness of signs, and a mellower cooled-down version of the ecstatic becomings and prospective pleasures of the body without end, the performance artist Laurie Anderson has taken a cue, perhaps, from the opening of Dante's *Comedy*, where in the middle of the journey of life the dark wood is entered and the straight way lost. Since she also shares, however, deconstruction's resistance to closure, the errancy in Anderson is accelerated and the body is like a freeway: "I . . . I AM IN MY BODY . . . I AM IN MY BODY THE WAY . . . I AM IN MY BODY THE WAY MOST PEOPLE DRIVE . . . I AM IN MY BODY THE WAY MOST PEOPLE DRIVE THEIR CARS." The song is from *Americans on the Move*, in which she elaborates the parable of lost direction into a landscape of rain and ceaseless traffic and driving through the night to a place you've never been, with everything unfamiliar so that you pull "into the next station and you feel so awkward saying, 'Excuse me, can you tell me where I am?' "[56]

With more or less anxiety or existential angst, or as with Anderson a certain hip levity on the postmodern freeway, I suppose we've all been lost in the body just about that way. There is, however, a sort of counter-movement in which, as we think of the aging body, the body is lost in us. (I am not talking here of an ideological category. Excuse me, can you tell me where it went?) Which is to say that it remains in its unceasing disappearance (much too subtle to see) the irreducible measure of our biological existence, what remains in theater its inexhaustible sign, what *makes* it theater even when – in the always failing scrutiny of the gaze – it claims to be something else: either non-mimetic *performance* without hidden recesses or the *afterimage* that, for want of a better word, we think of as *life* – as in the myths of ideology the life spontaneously lived. This is the mortal measure of performance as it occurs in a tactile state, however phantasmatic or dispersed it may appear to be, as with the partial objects of dream which are instances or relations or states of the body, or the refracted appearances of floating body parts. I am in my body the way that is simply inescapable, not to be deferred or lost as on the freeway in the metonymic appearances of a referential chain, nor reconstituted in the eternity of ideology as a linguistic subject, though I am that, too, to all appearances, which keep us tautologically in the double bind.

"We are all frail," says Angelo in *Measure for Measure* (2.4.121), taking the plaintive measure of the former piety of his words into the libidinal fallout of his biological existence. What he is saying may be, depending on the acting, as hypocritical as anything he said before, the better the acting the more impermeable, as if all that went before were nothing but theater, with no guarantee at all that the rest of it won't be. Such an interpretation may arise, it's true, from the paranoia of theater believing

121

its own hype, and passing off on us, with a certain pathos, its own ambivalent vision of the omnipresence of appearance. We are all frail. If that's easily verifiable in the psychopathology of everyday life, theater remains the form most dependent upon, fascinated with, drawn, quartered by, and fixated upon the body, its vulnerabilities, pain, and disappearance. The body art of recent years tried, in objectifying the body or treating it impersonally, as an experimental object, to abstract the pain or play with disappearance to keep the pathos at a distance. But what was particularly striking in the focus on the body in the emergence of conceptual art – even the "theatricality" that instrumentalized the body – was that it couldn't quite escape the inheritance of theater, the grievous subtext of all performance: there in the flesh, the attrition of appearance upon appearance.

There might be meditative events in resolute stasis or "movement at any cost," as Charles Olson once wrote, "violence, knives/anything to get the body in,"[57] but once it's in, conceptually in, it's hard to escape certain archetypal images at the extremity of thought. Some of these were almost literalized with violence, knives, at the conceptual end of body art: Prometheus nailed to the rock, before either time (or the theater) began, or the rotting carcass of Ajax, impaled on Hector's sword, there like a grisly sundial at the meridian of ancient theater, as the unendurable measure of the brutality of human time. And what must have been or seemed forbidden: the access to knowledge, the specifically Promethean impulse that, even in the empiricism of certain forms of body art, must have felt in a hallucinatory moment like knowledge of the divine.

THE SUBJECT OF KNOWLEDGE: EXTREMITY OF THE ACTUAL

"Knowledge does not slowly detach itself from its empirical roots, the initial needs from which it arose," wrote Foucault, "to become pure speculation subject only to the demands of reason; its development is not tied to the constitution and affirmation of a free subject; rather, it creates a progressive enslavement to its instinctive violence. Where religions once demanded the sacrifice of bodies, knowledge calls for experimentation on ourselves, calls us to the sacrifice of the subject of knowledge" (*LCP* 163). Body art, as an ideological and existential manifestation of conceptualism, wanted to have it both ways: to be the subject of knowledge and yet a free subject. The artist who submits his or her body to the stringencies of form – and much body art was intensely formalistic – is on the political level resisting appropriation and refusing to be alienated as labor in the process of the work (and, at least before documentation, the products as well). With less symbolist expressivity than the dancer and the dance, the body artist in performance *is* the work, which doesn't exist outside

122

the performance. Which, of course, is what we say about all performance, though little of what we see causes us to feel that singularity with anything like the same degree of either psychic or physical risk, nor as a decisive intervention in cultural politics.

As a praxis, body art no longer has the ideological purchase or aesthetic currency it had in the seventies, but it remains at the existential level the nuclear model of all performance, where the art act is a war of nerves, with the body as a buffer between the artist and a corrupting economy. There are varieties of body art, alluded to before, that are relatively warm-hearted, inviting, and not overtly political, but even when seductive its independence depends on a certain anxiety and, at its most powerful, a form of terror: one resists alienation by demanding complicity. And both the terror and the complicity are not merely the strategies of a self-renunciating modernism, but have their antecedents in the practices of the ancient theater, figured most controversially in the notion of catharsis, which has long been at the center of arguments about the politics of form. To the degree that it was political body art was not, however, seeking a cathartic response, as an alleviation of feeling, nor could it count upon it, in a period of anesthetized feeling. There are kinds of body art that recognize, no holds barred, that they must work at extremities to have any impact at all. At the psychic level, what is taken as an objective is the illusion of mental health. The psychological and social order, which has been unceasingly questioned through the whole history of the modern, has been either so nauseated by the questioning or so desensitized that it has to be confronted with actual rather than surrogate risk. In the days of existential anguish, after the war, we could exhort ourselves to accept the moral tightrope, which very soon became merely metaphorical. Body art produced metaphors too, but with the literalization of danger at the extremity of the actual. As with Philipe Petit on the tightrope between the twin towers of the World Trade Center, there was a perilous distance in the extremity that could turn it into a figure with real symbolic force.

As an offshoot of conceptual art, much of this was theorized, here and abroad. There was, for instance, a high theoretical impetus in the sadomasochistic performances of the Viennese Aktion group: Nitsch, Mühl, Brus, and Schwarzkogler. The events they conceived were more orgiastic in their concerted extremity, as political manifestations, than almost anything we encountered in the United States, including the performances of the Living Theater, which for all its outrageousness had nothing like Brus' swallowing of urine or Nitsch's disembowelings of animals or the saturation of the performance space with excrement and blood or the self-desecrating violence of Schwarzkogler, who has been mythicized for, quite literally, killing himself in his art. In France, there were somewhat similar manifestations, if not quite so repellent, in Situationist occurrences or the revival of surrealism in the form of happenings, by Jean-Jacques Lebel (who in the May Revolution of 1968 also made a performance of the takeover of the Odéon from an older avant-garde figure, Jean-Louis Barrault). As with Joseph Beuys in Germany, there were pedagogical, mythicizing, and solipsistic tendencies too, sometimes picking up impulses from the aestheticized domesticity of Fluxus and turning it all into a political statement: thus Michel Journiac's *Mass for a Body* (1969), a reflection on (dis)affiliation and solitude, in which he drew his own blood to make a pudding to be offered in communion.

These provocations – for that's what they embody – are counterimages of an ideological order, in which the body insists (or is made to insist) on its *substance* as the most sacred of taboos, what was not meant to be violated, yet is nevertheless manipulated, mutilated, castrated, consumed by all ideology. There is in these self-inflicted lacerations a remorseless refusal of all restriction by repressive authority, including the traces of authority inscribed in the body itself, as an inheritance of senselessly self-depriving privative being. As with Journiac's Mass, the performer literally inserts himself as a communicant between the desire for thoroughly unobstructed being and the degraded system which would with impunity deny it. That there were Catholic themes and rhetoric in the body language of this sacrificial art was surely to be expected, but the religious figuration could be eclectic, as in Linda Montano's *Mitchell's Death* (1978), where the sound from an Indian sruti box (Hindu) and a Japanese bowl gong (Buddhist) were amplified three times over while a video monitor showed Montano applying acupuncture needles to her face in mourning for her dead husband. This event was not meant as a provocation but as a ritual of mourning, crossing the boundaries between art and life.

But to return from this communion to the empirical roots of the subject of knowledge, the heuristic passion of body art: Chris Burden's risks were no less that for the precautions he took to research how the body might withstand crawling over broken glass, or the precise point on the palm where a nail might be driven so he might be crucified on a Volkswagen without irreparable harm. What he was seeking, however, in this sacrificial image was not so much participation in a ritual, but a certain kind of knowledge and decisive awareness, in himself, in the viewer, of something more in the body politic than the limited contingency of pain, but rather its suffusion in social fact and history. As with Gina Pane, the submission of the body is a forensic act refusing the reality of pain in human affairs as a tragic and irreversible condition. They inflicted pain on themselves so that whoever took notice by being at the event was *on* notice that the only intolerable pain was that gratuitously or compulsively exercised by the social order upon the body. Here the body is conceived of as a final conscience. One can see how the body art of Stelarc might have been derived from this, with the notion of the obsolete body as a form of higher morality.

Pane, like Burden, prepared herself over a period of months for the extreme discomforts to which she submitted. There was an empirical regimen through which she learned, like fire-walkers or contortionists, to withstand the ordeal: swallowing rotten meat, walking up a ladder whose rungs have sharp cutting edges, barefooted, or crushing glass in her mouth. When performed, the activity was relentless, unmitigated, with no relief for the viewer from its implications, either the mask of indifference or, by censuring the risk taken, moral outrage at the event. If you watched it you were complicit, and complicit, moreover, with more than the suffering there. (With Burden, it should be said, there were morally dubious events, in one case at least, when his own body wasn't at stake, justifying perhaps more than outrage. That was the event in which he fired at a plane taking off at the Los Angeles airport.[58]) There was always the risk, as with any aestheticized violence, that it might be desensitizing too, or possibly lurid, as with some spectators who, if given a chance, will try to outdo the performer in inflicting pain, less likely upon themselves than upon the performer, as some did once with Marina Abramović – who did, however, present the temptation: a totally passive body with razor blades beside it. What impressed me, however, in such events – for all the behavior that could be almost unbearable to watch – was the almost Platonic insistence on the purity of thought, the integrity of conception and analysis, and a mastery of the body not unlike that in the spiritual disciplines, sometimes drawing specifically on those disciplines, or based on research of an almost scholarly kind.

When Chris Burden, then, had himself shot in the arm, the brutality may have been more or less extruded as an issue, since what he did was thoroughly prepared as a matter of choice. So, too, with the material interchanges of Denis Oppenheim (e.g., ripping off a fingernail and replacing it with a splinter) or the self-abuse of Vito Acconci or the ordeals of Ulay and Abramović. In such performance, the apparent pain is displaced into a sort of corporeal discourse on other issues: sexuality, power, authority, the family, freedom, terrorism and torture, and in the material duration of real time, the ordeal or transcendence of time itself. It is this discourse, aroused by the bodily sacrifice of the subject of knowledge, that connects these avant-garde experiments to certain figures of the ancient theater, dominantly the impaled Prometheus, who initiated discourse as the subject of violence, itself subjected, which is why those imaged atrocities, more or less mutated or sublimated in subsequent forms of drama, or – as the charge was eventually made – exhausted *as images*, are still unpurged in the mind.

At the same time they raise the kind of question that was prompted by Brecht in his critique of tragedy: is it ideologically regressive, even barbaric, to think of (or with) the body thus? Or if – through the mirror stage of Lacan or the endgame of Beckett or the dead ends of deconstruction or the reflections of Benjamin on the corpse-like body in the ruins of time – we are constrained to reassess the idea of tragedy: is it ideologically stupid to think we should ever forget? Or do we ever forget? Or is it that we've had along with talk of the death of tragedy a twisted version of an active forgetting: the invention of aesthetic strategies that would, indeed, either anesthetize us against emotions we found intolerable, or, as eventually in body art, confront us in such a way that they could be absorbed or experienced again? I am not saying that was the intention of those artists who made performances of their bodies, but it seems to me of historical consequence that their work had something of that effect, corresponding with the (impasse of) theory that would lead to rethinking tragedy, its fatal representation and suspect cause and effect.

It was the intimidating prospect of that causation, the apparency of an appalling closure, which yielded to another cruelty in the history of modernism: the techniques of anatomy – cutting, tearing, rending, fracture – until we came to take dismemberment for granted, with discontinuity and indeterminacy, as the critical feature of postmodern forms. If it seemed at first like a revolutionary break, it is by no means conclusive that we have superseded the painful syntax of the tragic condition, its visceral realism. Of the disposition to believe that we have – as the psychoaesthetic ground of an alternative to the bourgeois order, with a disjunct politics of the expressive body, autistic, schizoid, postoedipal, whatever – we may say what Brecht himself did about the libertarian sentiments and vertigo of an older expressionism by which some felt themselves carried away: "It was very soon evident that such people had merely freed themselves from grammar, not capitalism."[59] That the realism of the remark seems like a prophecy confirmed by current events is perhaps not so surprising as the fact that, with the severest strains upon it, by artists, mass culture, the grammar is still intact, and with it the issues we thought to deal with in the languages of performance. That includes, of course, the language invented by Brecht for the unresolved issue of the next chapter.

4

DISTRESSED EMOTION

INTROVERSION AND INDICATION

It may be, if Trotsky was right, that with more or less furious passion in the mechanics the bodily disciplines of Meyerhold were far from the model of objectifying technique that we associate with estrangement in Brecht. It may be, too, that Meyerhold aligned himself with the Bolsheviks – when Stanislavski, Tairov, and other artists resisted – in order to propagate his own reforms, which included the proscription of "authentic emotions" either on stage or in the rehearsal process of building a character.[1] Taking him, though, at his most dispassionate word, what Meyerhold had against the authentic or "experienced emotions" was quite the opposite of what in our acting classes today we usually look for there: intimacy, naturalness, credibility. What he saw instead was anxiety and muscular tension. The directors of the Group Theater, who brought Stanislavski's method to America as an instrument of social commitment, had not yet made their pilgrimage to Moscow. It's interesting to speculate on what might have been the course of American acting if they had, while absorbing the lessons of the master, been more attentive to the student's critique (aspects of which we'll return to at various stages of this chapter). For Meyerhold might have been describing what we eventually came to experience through its subsequent adaptations in the worst excesses of psychological process, making of Stanislavski's technique of "public solitude" a virtual ideology of introversion.

This actually came about, with the vanishing of commitment into legend and nostalgia, through the exacerbated paradox of an aversion to excess. The mediations of technique are, in Kenneth Burke's useful phrase, "attitudes toward history," and I could be referring here to the dissipation of the politics of the thirties in the devastations of World War II, leading in the temperance of the Eisenhower period to one of the recurrently wishful versions of the end of ideology. What I have particularly in mind, however, is the more or less phobic resistance to "indication" in acting (though representation is inevitably, as Foucault has pointed out, crossed by indication.[2] The resistance can certainly be seen in its intensity as an inverted symptom of the postwar period, but it is still endemic to realistic acting, where – as a correlative (if not exactly an "objective correlative") of the modernist spirit of indirection – emotions may be revealed but not exactly *shown*, raising the Hamletic question as to whether, if shown, they were "true" emotions; or, if true, could be shown at all.

The objection, of course, was to an involuntary showing, overacting, or the actor's underlining of behavior, which was scorned among Method actors as "playwriting." It remains a serious issue, in art and politics, as to whether indirections find directions out, but there was also in the aversion a preference for the involuntary: accident, intuition, "letting it happen," out of emotions deeply experienced, as opposed to the conception of acting as a "signifying practice" or the conscious formation of behavior as a sign.[3] As for the uses of indication among the abuses of history, we may see it in the epic theater of Brecht: like the colophon of a text, the finger pointing in the margin to what may be, provocatively, the substance of a doubt, the Brechtian *gestus* is a form of indication. It came belatedly, true, to the American scene, but it has been around at least since the fifties; yet for some years afterward one could go to acting studios or attend rehearsals where, in a room full of authorities on the "truth of emotion," it was hard to think of indication as a heuristic device. Given its pedagogical function, one may question the inquisitive status of the A-effect as well, but it is precisely in its signifying intention – or rather the precision with which it points to what's in question – that the indicative *gestus* may be something more than didactic, complicating emotion by discerning contradictions. What was in any case methodological principle in the alienation of Brecht or the constructivism of Meyerhold was – with a codification of behavior almost neurotic about indication – original sin in the Method. At its most extreme, however, what we saw in the emotions not-shown was a certain kind of emotion, whose ground was a fear of the factitious so intense that it amounted, with various degrees of muscular tension, to the tortuous disguise of acting itself. One might see extraordinary exercises that merged process with improvisation in what appeared to be, in the totally experienced fulness of representation, the selvedge of the unmimetic. But even at its best, as a reflex of absence disclaiming its appearance, it became, conspicuously, a reproduceable style.

As this is not quite acting without a rhetoric (nor, in the insistent recessiveness of "motivated" behavior, the strategic depersonalization of modernist art) perhaps we should speak of the *secretions* of process that masked the fear of a disappearing self – or the disappearance of the self *into process*: in the anxiety about the authentic (or the absence of acting jobs) holding on for dear life. Freud remarked that through the operations of the unconscious we betray ourselves at every pore. Some of us will remember a period when the proprietary solipsism of experienced emotions, focused in the fetishism of the "private moment" (not Stanislavski's, but Lee Strasberg's term), had its manifest content of public paranoia. While it can hardly be denied that some memorable performances seemed to arise precisely from that condition (there is evidence still on film) there were also among the mythic (and marketable) figures of the Method broken lives and impaired careers. When we look back upon them now they seem to reflect, in the technocratic economy of the Cold War, a crisis of identity that, far from the prospect of a socialized theater (rehearsed by Harold Clurman in *The Fervent Years*), seemed like a preface to the culture of narcissism, amplified by commodification into the clamor of the spectacle, the mediascape of the postmodern, with the memory of an echo dispersed in the noise. It's as if there had been a scene change in the process of achieving authenticity, from the Actors Studio to the recording studio, with its image of the performer achieving high fidelity, with headphones over the ears.

BECKETT'S PAUSE/MEYERHOLD'S PASSION

"None looks within himself where none can be," Beckett wrote in *The Lost Ones*,[4] as if summ(on)ing up the period, and in the seizure of the specular, its synesthesia, the sonorous impasse of psychological process. (*Pause.*) Nothing but echo? or no echo at all? It would be the ground rhythm of the postmodern if it weren't for the pathos that – exceeding all parody, even his own – rises from the crippled and mutilated figures of Beckett's work, with an undiminished longing for the life where none can be. If his drama is constructed, in all its broken corporeality, out of the unfinished contingencies of a life that can't be had, the vitiation of mental and physical faculties was, according to Marx, due to a single alienation, that of *having*. That's why the desire for private property had to be, even with regard to the body itself, surpassed. The same might be said for the body's emotional memories, which are in the circuitous rites of subjectivity of the Stanislavski system cherished and seductive elements of the actor's technique. There are certain seductions in technique itself, but if there was a strain of madness in the Method it was more or less concentrated around memory as the originary site of emotion, or the domain of inwardness for an autonomous self.

There was very little metapsychology in the Method that gave it pause on this account, as Beckett did, say, in the lapsing memory of *Godot* (its "deadbeat escapement") or the (un)veiled blindness of the figure of Hamm, like the blindness of insight itself. What we had in Beckett's theater – aside from the dismembered structures or paratactical model of the postmodern – was an anticipatory paradigm of critical theory, where the self is the merest (laughable) prospect of an entity, its (hopelessly) failing hypothesis, or a fiction of specularity, as in the *mise-en-scène* of the unconscious, with its repetitive and exhaustive imaging of amnesia. Such is the stage, it appears, of the deepest form of memory, history without a subject, everything remembered and no borders to memory itself: the site where none can be.

Sense memory is also basic to realistic acting, but unlike emotional memory, whose parameters are endless, it seems in its more or less pragmatic evocation of remembered sensations, however crude or subtle (sour milk on the tongue, the sound of a falling leaf), a relatively simple concept. Yet, like every other aspect of technique that is further examined – timing, voice, breathing, not to mention the grounds of credibility or truth – it will have not only ideological, but almost metaphysical implications. In this regard, it is like the affective permutations of the minutest sensory detail in a Shakespearean text, a yellow leaf, or none, or few, a mote in the mind's eye or the unnumbered idle pebble in the murmuring surge, the amniotic infinity of still-breeding thought itself. At some limit of apprehension it may take your breath away, crossing or confounding the senses, passing from eye to ear or, as if the lilies (of the sonnets) were festering in the enchantment of the gaze itself, going up the nostrils smelling far worse than weeds.[5] When we come to our senses, however, their constitution and particularity, we are reminded by Marx that the five of them were formed and differentiated by all of human history, each sense, then, an accretion of social memory, without which it would be the merest threadbare filter of wayward experience, which is neither a preaesthetic register of indeterminacy nor the path of travelling theory. "The eye has become a human eye," Marx wrote, "when its object has become a social, human object produced by man and destined for him. Thus in practice the senses have become direct theoreticians."[6]

Despite the mechanics derived from Taylorism, this is the spirit in which Meyerhold thought, as he formulated a curriculum for actors, that he was developing a corrective to the false consciousness of Stanislavski's method. In the externalization of performance he would achieve this directness: the emphasis would be on skill, dexterity, rhythm, form, instead of the self-serving mesmerism of the "inner life," or those phantoms of internal experience that make a travesty of selfhood while confirming the body not as the surpassed but as a troubled and ductile impasse or viaduct of confusions, or as Merleau-Ponty remarked in *The Phenomenology of Perception*, "the ever-present principle of bewilderment and absent-mindedness."[7] The displacement of experienced emotions was in Meyerhold's own appraisal of his method, a matter of relieving the absent-mindedness with a precise sense of the body's functions, which has recurred as a central ambition in alternative forms of theater, with more or less conscious indebtedness to Meyerhold (e.g., Grotowski) and variant attitudes about the functions of the mind.

"Don't your 'experienced emotions' disrupt the measure of your breathing?" Meyerhold asked the actors as he urged them to take on, with theatrical imagination, the corporeal exactitude of the juggler or the acrobat. The measure of breathing (or *breaking* its measure, as Merce Cunningham used to say) remains an almost talismanic datum for any method, but in working out a new political status for performance it was, for Meyerhold, time to reach "some conclusion about the question of experienced emotions on the stage." Whereupon, with a kind of *salto mortale* into another sphere of experience, he complicates the problem: "Admirers of Oscar Wilde will have found the answer already in the words of Sibyl Vane in *The Picture of Dorian Gray*: 'I might mimic a passion that I do not feel, but I cannot mimic one that burns me like a fire' " (*Meyerhold* 152).

THE CULINARY REVISITED

As our breathing returns, so to speak, through this burning out of mimesis, how do we measure the orders of emotion? Or the distinction between authentic emotion and such a passion (putting aside the orders of passion, like the 1,620 enumerated by Fourier or the merely 600 listed by Sade, or in Nietzsche the virtual infinity of passions, variable as illusion, in the differential calculus of the will to power[8])? If the intensity of the passion is not quite that of Artaud's visionary actor signaling through the flame, what are we to make of it? as well as the desire for an objectifying technique in a theater for the masses, who were not exactly in the picture with Dorian Gray? What we may see, even in the directest theorizing of the senses (no less the indifference of the masses toward the theater, or the emergence of the audience as a statistical mass), is that the question of emotion in the theater is never simple. Moreover, it intersects almost all the theoretical questions that have arisen in the theater (and in the self-reflexiveness of theory itself) since we became aware that the emotions we had taken for granted – the ones we were *moved by*, including the profoundest emotions of tragic form – had been looked at critically and found ideologically wanting, dismissed as culinary, in the conception of modern theater as epic theater by Brecht.

At the risk of contributing to a notorious case of already excessive abuse let's review – for variation on the site but not the theme, here in the concert hall rather than the theater – the now-familiar picture of the audience at its worst:

> We see entire rows of human beings transported into a peculiar doped state, wholly passive, sunk without a trace, seemingly in the grip of a severe poisoning attack. Their tense, congealed gaze shows that these people are the helpless and involuntary victims of the unchecked lurchings of their emotions. Trickles of sweat prove how such excesses exhaust them. The worst gangster film treats its audience more like thinking beings. Music is cast in the role of Fate.
>
> (*Brecht* 89)

131

As with the inevitability of tragic drama, this Fate is unanalysable and its victim woefully unalterable, but so far as its passive reception is concerned the worst possible case is not only a bourgeois German audience. "The place is swamped with idiocy," wrote Antonio Gramsci, even before Brecht, in a review of an Italian play, or rather its audience, where "the worst returns to laughter," like the atrocities in *King Lear* (4.1.6). Though the following passage was written just after World War I, Gramsci's drama criticism is pervaded with dismay and revulsion, as if in a premonition of the fascist period to come. There are, however, mixed emotions as well, to which I'll want to return:

> There is a palpable atmosphere of bestiality in the auditorium of the Alfieri. It emanates from the laughing faces, from the gleaming eyes, from the short and nervous bursts of laughter from the audience. . . . And yet, these spectators are not crude lumps of flesh and blood wrapped in skin. They are moved, they are able to be moved. . . . They can feel humanity, they can understand pain, they can take on an expression of seriousness, they can feel their eyes veiled by a deep sadness. And yet, when the curtain rises and the ridiculous caricatures of men and women on the stage put their machine in motion once again, the faces relax into dull-witted gaiety and the atmosphere of bestiality increases and grows heavy. One stupidity follows another, piling up into huge rubbish heaps, gawkily overflowing. Boorishness triumphs absolutely over intelligence, it spreads in the applause, and deepens in satisfied tittering. It continues to haunt our steps in the putrid vapours of the evening, in the fogginess of approaching autumn.[9]

Despite generations of critique and postBrechtian effects we are still haunted by such behavior on and off Broadway, and in boulevard theaters all over the world, though we are more likely to find similar descriptions today of audiences watching the soaps and game shows on the tube, not only in the putrid vapours of the evening.

If both descriptions are full of emotions contemptuous of the torpor or, around the laughter, the imbecilic emotions displayed, Gramsci's sense of it may be more distressing and, to the degree that the condition persists, more germane: "They are moved, they are able to be moved. . . . " But the curious thing is the sadness which unspeakably veils their eyes and which suggests, in the residual humanism, something more mortifyingly difficult to assimilate than, in the victimized spectators of Brecht, drugged and helpless as they are, the unchecked lurchings of their emotions. They are moved, they are able to be moved, and as any theater director can tell you (with more or less candor about his or her collusion) that can happen with the most vacuous dialogue or makeshift business, or by emotions often embarrassing to the actors themselves – not because they are intimate or touch a nerve or reveal what should not be shown, but merely because they are embarrassing, as everybody in the theater knows, except at times the audience.

Of course, with the benefit of long critique and recycling through the media of every image, emotion, and reflex, a postmodern audience might be expected to know better. But now that the audience knows almost everything except why, through the persisting myth of community, it almost doesn't exist, there is likely to be a strange discomfiture, not only in its own dulled or lurching capacities – on the massive scale of the media – for something like canned response, but also (if no longer the expression of seriousness) the only too easy propensity amidst the huge accumulating rubbish heaps of history for the unchecked evasions of parody, with almost nothing more dependable than the readiness to laugh. Everybody loves a good laugh, and there are obvious virtues to a sense of humor, as there were in the period from the Watergate plumbers to leveraged buyouts in the levelling powers of parody, which is both attentive to and adept at conspiracy theory – as much as deconstruction the major theory of the time. (For a paradigm of the genre at the outset of the period, see Thomas Pynchon's *The Crying of Lot 49*; for an up-to-date media model of the ethos of conspiracy theory on the stylishly protracted and occulted edge of parody, see David Lynch's *Twin Peaks*.) But as parody may be in the bottoming out of suspicion a function of paranoia, the readiness to laugh may not be an emotional ripeness: thus the gawky regime of spectatorship that seems to have arisen, with a repertoire of kitsch and camp, out of the (dis)enchantments of the sixties, and the sometimes willfully brainless, other times artfully cunning, but mostly boorish effluvium of the theater of the absurd.

What we may see at midnight in the movies at the Rocky Horror Show may occur as well at a Beckett play. And if it has, in the anticipatory guffaws and tittering satisfaction, a generational appeal – that is, to post-adolescent audiences – there are some susceptible spectators who are rather like Beckett groupies whose guffaws and titters are tenured. Yet, as Gramsci perceived in the noxious bursts of laughter from the gleaming eyes at the Alfieri, there remains the capacity to understand pain, without which there has never been much substance to theater, and not wholly in tragic form. That, of course, is what Beckett understood through every hilarious non sequitur and vaudeville routine of his metaphysical farce. How delighted we were to discover through the recursive boredom of *Waiting for Godot* that it restored us through the annals of theater, and all its ruined conventions, to the brainy endurance and burlesque and festive cruelty of ancient comedy – with a kind of elegiac strain, however, in all its diminishing returns: "The air is full of our cries . . . " (58), even with Gogo sleeping like a member of the audience while Didi pronounces

133

banalities about the human condition that are, unfortunately, only too palpably true.

These are not, after all, merely ridiculous caricatures on the stage, with the automated reflexes of a broken-down desiring machine. And it may very well be that the platitudes are really painful not merely because they're repeated, but repeated and repeated because painfully in touch with the truth, like the mythology of the media, imbedded so deeply in our spontaneously lived life, and being so avidly studied today (not merely as mystifications) by quite responsive scholars and critical theorists who don't always have their alienation in effect. (As criticism shifts its focus to cultural studies, it seems that while we may still be aware, as Hannah Arendt once was, of the banality of evil, we're no longer sure of the evil of banality, as Gramsci and Adorno were, neither of whom could quite make his peace with certain aspects of popular culture.) These spectators are not, after all, mere crude lumps of flesh and blood wrapped in skin, though they may be watching something like the equivalent of what Gramsci saw at the Alfieri. They are moved, they are able to be moved . . . and the deeper sadness may be that we have to think of it now, with no aversions privileged, through the changing scale and expectations of postmodern culture, in which "the rummage sale of values" once announced by Kierkegaard has been extended to include – in the circuitry of simulacra, the sale that never ends – all the name brands of ready-to-wear emotions.

BRECHT AND LUKÁCS: COLLISION AND HEAT

Meanwhile, that the question of emotion in the theater is never simple Brecht himself suggests, through an estranging distance, in the early dispute with Lukács. The issue amounts, in fact, to a difference over the allowable lurchings of emotion in what, for Lukács, were the apparently grotesque and stochastic ventures of expressionism, with which the earliest plays of Brecht had certain affinities. Refusing to let Lukács claim realism for himself, Brecht won't concede that the works of Kaiser, Sternberg, and Toller are by any means "embarrassing business," nor merely "a deviation" ("Formalistic Character," *A&P* 74). He is actually making a defense of what Lukács considered the ruptured consciousness and decadence of formalist technique.

Brecht's counterargument amounts eventually to a claim (worked out in various essays and through the *Short Organum*) that by improving the apparatus of production even effects of incoherence may be progressive, a salutary deposit of political content. Moreover, as there are degrees of formalism with variable social effects, so there are "very precise measures" by means of which a technique, such as Joyce's interior monologue, may be seen as reproducing or falsifying reality, "that is to say the totality of thought or association" (73). So, too, with the expressionist techniques of "simultaneous registration, bold abstraction, or swift combination" (75) that he himself deployed in *Baal*, or the modernist strategy of surgical narrativity that in the emergent strategy of epic theater displaced causation in plotting with the anatomizing of the event. That was already more than apparent, almost literalized, in the boxing ring of *In the Jungle of Cities*: there are moments in that text (one can't speak for particular productions) that are like the opening up of a wound and, instead of suturing it with plot, cutting out the emotion. The knives that come at the end for the dying Shlink are, though arrested by Mary at the sticking point (of the gaze), no mere emblematic measure of an unmoving formalism.

"However often it is repeated," wrote Walter Benjamin in his dissertation on the panoramatic disjunctures and emblematic naturalism of the baroque, "it will never be true that the task of the dramatist is to exhibit the causal necessity of a sequence of events on the stage" (*Origin* 129). Brecht pretty much took that for granted as he began his career in the theater. Within the perversely (un)gendered perspective of *Baal*, Brechtian theory crosses Freud, who wrote in his essay on a case of homosexuality in a woman: "Linear presentation is not a very adequate means of describing complicated mental processes going on in different layers of the mind."[10] Despite his later distrust and attempted extrusion of the unruly behavior of the subconscious, Brecht never wavered in his view of what was required for the representation of complicated mental processes. He was willing to appraise the social efficacy of certain formal properties or, as he saw them in the Moscow performance of Mei Lan-fang, the "transportable techniques" of Chinese acting, whose (magical) social matrix was repugnant. He was willing to entertain contradictory propositions, whether or not at a cultural distance, but he was simply not going to debate the issue of realism on what he considered the unqualified formalist ground staked out by Lukács. That was rejected as merely aesthetic.

The distance from Lukács is marked, however, not only by the expected stress upon social functions from which, according to Brecht, the theater's powers and propagation cannot be separated, but by the degree to which a certain emotional charge is taken for granted: "the drama (force of collision), the passion (degree of heat)" ("Remarks," *A&P* 78). As for Balzac and Tolstoy – the indispensable standards of realism for Lukács – they were for Brecht, as he put it, "part of [his] own flesh and blood," but perhaps too forbiddingly or anachronistically so; given his own needs, difficult to learn from: "They had to master other problems" ("Formalistic Character" 74–5). As diversity of aims may require in any praxis strategic leaps and discrepancies of style that can only be adjudicated case by case, a useful definition of realism will inevitably move beyond aesthetic or literary guidelines: "Realism is an issue not only for literature: it is a

135

major political, philosophical and practical issue and must be handled and explained as such – as a matter of general human interest" (76). And as a matter of general human interest it was repeatedly focused by Brecht in terms of *emotion* – drama and passion, collision and heat – as with the quite remarkable passage where he explains the (unavoidable) liability of failure in experimental work: "One man will fall silent because of lack of feeling; another because his emotion chokes him."

To be sure, "the world is not required to be sentimental" (74), as it was with some apocalyptic frequency in expressionist drama, from which, nevertheless, Brecht felt that realists had much to learn. As silence is not golden, choking is not burning, but what exactly the theater should be at the level of *affect* – when? how? why? *how much emotion?* – one almost never reliably learns. Or at least it remained an issue for Brecht through his most exemplary productions, and in the last revisions of the *Short Organum*, as it does in the apparently non-theatrical practices of postmodern performance.

FAMILIAR BEHAVIOR IN ALTERNATIVE PRACTICES

Even where the practices are theatrical they have tended to keep their distance from realism or psychological process or naturalistic behavior until, with the desire for better acting, they could hardly do without them. This was the case to begin with in the performances of Spalding Gray or Eric Bogosian who, with a critical awareness informed by Brecht, have the skills of conventional actors and have been using techniques once deployed on building a character to develop, as Bogosian did (while improving his acting), a manic medley of social types or, in Gray's accretions of autobiography, a self-effacing but solipsistic persona (now moving with other accretions from his journals to cassette and film, and *then* recycled into live performance, which more or less accepts mass-mediatization, in a relation of reciprocity, as the condition of its being[11]).

With or without acting skills, the practices of realism were also germane to begin with in feminist performance based on the principle that the personal is political. Overlaid as they may have been with allegory, archetype, or creation myth (e.g., Nina Wise's *Glacier*, Spiderwoman, Norma Jean Deak) such performances were also derived from the overlooked commonplaces of women's lives, as with some of the earliest of them done in the seventies at Womanhouse in Los Angeles. It is not at all surprising that a theater of dissidence had to depend, in the task of consciousness-raising, upon what actors would recognize as the most basic experiential exercises, out of which came a series of nuclear or paradigmatic events in the repetitive form of a ritualized naturalism: Chris Rush kneeling to clean the floor in a piece called *Scrubbing*; or Sandra Orgel ironing a tablecloth with obsessive devotion; or in her litany of diurnal waiting – characterizing the experience of women from birth to death – Faith Wilding waiting to be diapered herself; or with the empowering rage of the Feminist Art Program she started in Fresno and brought to Cal Arts, Judy Chicago's *Cock and Cunt*, which starts with an argument over dishwashing and ends with a castration. There was in the visual art at Womanhouse more abstraction from the outset, but in performance the access to repressed experience depended for the most part, through encounter groups and psychodrama, on the conventional or realistic acting out of roles. If the performance events were, however, experimental in no other way they were, according to the ethos of Womanhouse (with its kitchen of sculptured breasts turned into fried eggs), sufficiently so in validating experienced emotions.

There was much talk at the time of alternative practices, and we have seen since far more sophisticated, escalated, and outrageous strategies. But where the politics draws upon the personal, the emotions are almost inescapably derived with ambivalent feelings and unpurged vestiges of realistic behavior from the ideological repertoire of bourgeois drama and the psychological framework of the oedipal family romance. No matter what we do with behavior – mask it, frame it, freeze it, laminate it with ritual borrowings, or deconstruct it in theory as the mask of logocentrism – the oedipal vocabulary of emotions is, as we know, not easily displaced. Not when the emotions *are* experienced, and particularly by *inexperienced* actors, who more often than not and quite naturally borrow their emotions. Actually, there is no acting that doesn't borrow emotions (and other cultures worry about that less), but with inexperience the borrowing is more conspicuous.

There was of course the famous experiment when Stanislavski, wanting the freshest emotion and "real" behavior on stage, brought in people from off the street. It was apparently effective in Moscow for its historical moment, as it has been recently in New York, with a sort of reverse methodology whereby participants in the theater event are moved around the city, to the Bowery or darkest Brooklyn, to see the indigence and misery in their unmediated state. Not even fresh contingents, however, of the worldwide supply of street people would guarantee in all their lifelike resemblance a spontaneous continuum of artless emotion. Abjects of mediation, they are under surveillance too, with cardboard shelters per- haps, but with the global processing of contemporary behavior – and batteries of television in department store windows – even the outcast or dispossessed may be watching themselves on the evening news. As for the emergent groups of inexperienced performers the personal may be political, but without exceptional disciplines or the extremist measures of camp or carnivalesque they will tend to reflect the deepest feelings through an established repertoire of behavioral images and emotional forms. So far as a political theater is concerned it may very well be, as sometimes argued, all the more effective for that.

EMPATHY'S DOUBLE BIND

The ideology of this aesthetic may be stated thus: who cares if you've seen it as long as you *see* it. Nor do I mean anything so subtly specular as the desperate tautology in the ingenuousness of Ophelia, unknowing agent of an invisible power, brutalized by Hamlet in the nunnery speech, but not yet mummified by Heiner Müller in the *Hamletmachine*: "T'have seen what I have seen, see what I see!" (*Ham.* 3.1.161). The line was once taken as a talismanic description of the rigorous practice demanded by the New Criticism, but the urgency of a political theater is likely to be more than a little impatient with that, as with the long-suffered canonical pathos of Ophelia, wrapped up by Müller, turning her into Electra, and in the words of Squeaky Fromme delivering a death threat to the whole oppressive phallocratic order, in a virtual piece of performance art. What mostly changes, however, in a gendered or ethnic performance unaware of or renouncing avant-garde strategies (and more often than not even when adapting them) is the specific materiality or experienced content of emotions seen before, including the historical pathos that sticks to victimization and, with empathy and mimesis, won't be exorcized at all. This raises the question, at any rate, of whether there would be any social or political efficacy to the emotions if they *hadn't* been seen before, that is, were without the capacity to arouse precisely the forms of identification, *across difference*, that the critique of empathy might forbid.

Here we encounter another double bind. That empathy crosses distance – and even, to his chagrin, the distancing measures of Brecht – turns out to be a problem for those who in art or politics insist on empowering difference as one of the prerogatives of dispossession. This insistence may be, in the dramaturgy of a radical politics, a provisional strategy. But whether or not it occurs with more or less provocation or fear of appropriation, the enforcement of distance by adamant difference is something quite other than the Brechtian A-effect. When empathy backs off under these circumstances, it's not always because it is convinced about the inaccessible experience of an essentialized other. One may have, in fact, serious misgivings about the new doxology of cultural otherness, and yet defer in policy to what both theory and the emotions resist. Whether or not theory knows better the contradictions involved may be, for the time being, warranted by history, as with any form of affirmative action, which comes unavoidably with a threshold of longevity and a quotient of mixed emotions, even from some of those who are the justifiable beneficiaries.

That was apparent recently in the controversy over bringing the musical *Miss Saigon* from London to New York with a white actor in an Asian (or, as modified for its star, Eurasian) role. When Actors Equity took a stand against it, later rescinded after numerous members objected, the action merely focused the contradictions that have long been manifest in the debates on integrated casting. There are few in the theater who would be any longer (at least in a public posture) dead set against integrated casting, but whether or not you are for it, or partially for it, the issue hinges on the problematic of difference: first of all the claim that difference speaks, and then that it makes no difference. Who speaks? While opinion in the matter may be more or less muted, it should be apparent that for an actor of any range and imagination, disciplined in the speaking of difference, it can't make much of a difference; that is, there is certainly going to be more than a little resistance to the ideology of otherness so far as it suggests, in the psychology of character, an uncrossable breach.

Nor does that imply – though often assumed in the linkage of psychological acting to bourgeois realism – an unthinking assent to a mythology of "human nature" or a sentimental attachment to a "common humanity" or the old liberal dream of "the family of man." (The actor may very well continue to speak in humanistic terms, the horizon of which may be, however, a certain solidarity of mutual needs that comes, with cultural variations, from the shared conditions and dangers of material life, particularly as they must be acknowledged in the body, along with the desire for identity itself.) Nor is it possible for an actor to have very much range without any view of history, or if history is thought of, indifferently, as no more than the shape of desire. There is no doubt something misguided in approaching Shakespeare as merely our contemporary, but you can hardly approach him at all if you can't think with some sense of distinction, in the synchronous crease of historical space, across the difference in time. Meanwhile, we tend to forget in the critique of realism that it developed *as* critique, a "ruthless critique of everything existing" which is exactly what might be said of Ibsen in the ineluctable words of Marx.[12]

THE DOUBLE AGENCY OF REALISM AND THE HEGEMONY OF IAGO

The drama of realism has been seen in somewhat misleading retrospect as an agency of bourgeois power, but it can also be argued that in its subtlest forms the drama was playing the role of a double agent. Which is just about what Ibsen had in mind when he brought the trolls down from the fjords, hid them under the cushions of the bourgeois parlor, and shifted from poetry to prose. What was particularly subversive in the drama of realism was that it depended on the analytical mechanisms of an acute subjectivity, given over to processes of *identification*, so that the critique in its emergence took place *from within*.[13] As for the acting in that tradition, if it has any sustaining virtue at all it is the virtue of transformation: not the masquerade or mimicry now theorized as transgressive, but *in its interiority* the most responsive accord, seeing it feelingly, becoming the other, the credibility of the becoming inseparable from the finest, most harrowing, tremulous distinctions, like the cloudiness in a drop of longing, which is what Rilke perceived in both the drama of Ibsen and the acting of Duse. The actor may not, after all, contain multitudes, but there are some for whom the powers of empathy are such, or the sympathetic imagination, that it can register not only the minutest behavioral forms of an apparently foreign psychology, but also the nuances, shadows, vagaries, the particle physics of difference, including its *illusions*, as they are grounded in (or ungrounding) the ideological categories of race, class, gender, or age. Or for that matter, the self, which the better actors know as the most elusive, unattainable, or illusory difference of all.[14]

This transformative capacity of the actor, impelled by empathy across difference, is for those who perceive it an empowering principle. Nurtured by history, it would seem to be a necessity of historical materialism, so long as there *is* difference. This is not the view, however, of certain new historicists who think of empathy as a preemptive power. Difference, it seems, can also do without it (which may also mean, in a circle of insularity, that it can do without difference). "There are periods and cultures," writes Stephen Greenblatt in *Renaissance Self-Fashioning*, "in which the ability to insert oneself into the consciousness of another is of relatively slight importance, the object of limited concern; others in which it is a major preoccupation, the object of cultivation and fear."[15] Inserting oneself into the consciousness of another could occur, we might suppose, with quite variable designs upon the other, and qualities of feeling as well, which might take the clinical edge off the insertion even if it's not, truly, an act of love. We have dreamt in the mythology of modernism, and even before, a disturbing array of shadows, doubles, and secret sharers, but there is no incontestable reason why the imaginative projection of a subjective state must be looked upon as a form of psychic invasion or body snatching or, at worst, like Saddam Hussein's occupation of Kuwait.

Since Greenblatt is more concerned, however, with its being an agency of bourgeois imperialism, his critique of empathy focuses upon a text that, in its well-intentioned humanism, might be considered "orientalist": Daniel Lerner's *The Passing of Traditional Society*, a once-influential study of modernization in the Middle East, which attributes the modernization to the breaking down of rigid structures by the transportable sensibility of the West, the global dispersion of its adaptability to change. The sociologist is a strawman in the new historicist argument about the operations of power. Although the notion of a "constrictive personality" in traditional societies is not quite so naïve as Greenblatt makes it out to be, there is something almost callow in Lerner's enthusiasm for the accelerating diffusion of a sympathetic or identifying power – "the capacity to feel oneself in the other fellow's situation" – from the Age of Exploration to satellite transmission, with *The Goldbergs* and *I Love Lucy* (the book was first published in 1958) representing abroad, at sustained and intimate levels, the diversity of our common experience that can also be shared by others. Not at all sanguine about that, Greenblatt lays out some of the abundant evidence (ubiquitous in such critique) that the Age of Exploration was exploitative and brutal, then shifts the ground from the zaniness of *I Love Lucy* to the duplicities of *Othello* "in order to demonstrate that what Professor Lerner calls 'empathy,' Shakespeare calls 'Iago' " (*Renaissance Self-Fashioning* 225).

In this metonymic shift Greenblatt links the empathic principle with improvisational behavior, pointing out quite rightly that improvisation, of which Iago is a master, is by no means purely random, its aleatory impulse being inseparable from calculation or premeditation. If anything, then, has been diffused on a geopolitical scale it is an appropriative economy in the mode of improvisation, by means of which we insinuate ourselves into existing structures (political, religious, even psychic) in order to take them over, a process "as familiar to us by now as the most tawdry business fraud" (227). Thus, if empathy is spreading around the world, as Lerner complacently says, it must be understood, according to Greenblatt, as another familiar process, "the exercise of Western power, power that is creative as well as destructive, but that is scarcely ever wholly disinterested and benign" (228).

This, of course, is hardly to be denied. Scarcely is merely hedging. Datum: *no* form of power is ever *wholly* disinterested. Thus, the critical problem remains to perceive *when* creative, *where* benign, the limits thereof, the variable mixtures of the creative *with* the destructive, the moral dilemma of their inseparability, before the usually precipitous weighting, in the predictable scales of the new historicism, toward the malign. If absolute power corrupts absolutely (and even that, with variable forms of absoluteness, requires further documentation) we are still not very adept at taking the measure of relative or *partial* power that may, in the disorientations of history, find itself improvising, no doubt inadequately, over unfamiliar ground, with admixtures of self-interest, mission, confusion, accident, dismay: the worst of motives, surely, and conceivably some of the best. Should there be anything too ameliorative in what I am saying here, let me add that my own disposition is sufficiently skeptical as to feel – given the evidence of this century alone – that the worst to be imagined is more likely to happen than not; but that appears not to be a privileged symptom of any specific form of power.

There's no such thing as impartial power, but whatever the power it's always *seeming*. That's where the figure of Iago is especially germane: not merely because he improvises (there are, in the theatricalization of power, various forms of improvisation) but because the appearance of impartiality comes from the masterful deployment of the subtleties of appearance. It comes, moreover, with the endorsement of spontaneity. What appears to happen by chance – and the aleatory impulse itself – is only further evidence of the heartfelt truth of emotion, which is itself a certification of an interior authenticity. Yet if Iago is, in the control of appearance, the outside danger or insidious prospect of the most exploitative inner drive, he is hardly the whole story of the exercise of western power, except in being so overdetermined – as suffused with seeming as the society of the spectacle itself – that we can hardly interpret him at all. Coleridge was probably wrong in speaking of his malignancy as "motiveless," though the productions that try to psych out or attribute motives in some quasi-case history or ideologically focused way are likely to feel reductive when referred again to the indeterminacies or ultimate silence of the text: "Demand me nothing. What you know, you know./From this time forth I never will speak word" (*Oth.* 5.2.302–3). There is a haunting malignancy here that is, after all, part of the perverse pleasure of the text. Whatever the case may be, it is hardly a case against empathy, so long as the concept is not merely understood as the power – pitiless, without compassion, an abortion of human feeling – to enter another consciousness and repossess it as the Same.

THE COMMISERABLE FORM OF EMOTION

While Lerner was still using the term empathy somewhat in the way the eighteenth century thought of *sympathy*, he is by no means as sophisticated as Greenblatt in thinking about its relation to theatricality and the art of acting. What Greenblatt does, however, by naming empathy Iago is to extrude from the concept any semblance of authenticity in the commiserable form of emotion that was more or less taken for granted from Diderot and Rousseau to William Godwin and Mary Shelley.[16] To the degree that it became sentimental such emotion was, in the hermeneutics of suspicion and the distancing mechanisms of modernism, looked at askance, as an impediment to perception and a political liability: what appeared to be social conscience might be, in its most maudlin form, the ideological leakage of a bleeding heart. But if there was in the epistemology of sympathy a particular sensitivity to human suffering, it was not without an anxious sense of unapproachable difference, while the symptoms of that anxiety showed up, as in the tableaux of Diderot, in a reserve of beholding or critical distance; or, in the theater of Marivaux, the unsettling exuberance of a witty desolation, as the heart played vainly through the impasse of distance – male and female, servants and masters, the menial body and the authoritative voice – producing thereby a proportionate indeterminacy, a "lack of certainty about a real and just perspective which is the mark of the ideological."[17]

The concept of sympathy, with its sensitivity to human suffering, developed through the Enlightenment with equal sensitivity to what we can never know of each other, particularly at the extremities of the body in pain. There was, moreover, a not unexamined sense of the relation of sympathy to the problem of representation.[18] It developed subsequently with the critique of representation, the relation always under pressure from the proliferous expanse of suffering beings, *how* to represent them in any judicial sense, not to mention something intolerable, unrepresentable in the human condition itself. This was so despite any rationalizing cover up in the optimism of the Enlightenment. It's hard to say when exactly sympathy outdid itself, but it was surely complicated in our century by the unassuageable dimensions of two world wars, the Holocaust, the Gulag, and with the multitudes of misery petitioning everywhere, the double inadequacy of feeling too much or, in the self-mortifications of a defensive screening out, never enough, numbed, or nothing at all. "The place is crawling with them!" The felt intensity of this condition is in the most pitiless moments of Beckett what remains unutterably moving: "Use your head, can't you, use your head, you're on earth, there's no cure for that! (*Pause.*) Get out of here and love one another! Lick your neighbor as your self!" (*Endgame* 68). Here we have the mordantly thwarted measure of hyperextended empathy that comes, in the improvisations of Hamm, from the very insidiousness with which he inserts himself not only into the consciousness of Clov, but that of anyone (I do not say the audience as a whole: there is no such audience) who has through protective laughter been paying sufficient attention.

Is there a vanity in such feeling? I don't know. Nor did Beckett, for whom life itself was a certain vanity. Nor would I be laboring the issue of empathy were it not for the tendency, in the ongoing critique of the uses and abuses of history, to conflate the uses and abuses of historically developed value. Some cultures may have done without the capacity to enter the consciousness of others, and there may be future periods in which it is, again, of relatively slight importance. I suspect that will be unfortunate. Vanity of vanities. On whatever ideological grounds, the empathic power is surely abandoned at risk, as with the emotion of pity excoriated by Nietzsche and, though later lamented in the Pisan cantos, also by Ezra Pound.

It may very well be that, as in the conscience-stricken compensations of sentimental liberalism, empathy can be misguided, or that in the warmth of responsive sameness there is, instead of the active forgetfulness of Nietzsche, a narcissistic turn. "You fill my heart with emotion," says the song "Unconditional Love," though in the empathic embrace of actor and character, or the solicitation of the spectator by the actor – a more or less open clandestinity in the assignation of the gaze – the love may be self-love. In working out an ethics for the theater, Stanislavski was aware of

143

that: he warned the actor about the difference between loving the art in oneself and loving oneself in art, which is, despite the emphasis on psychological process, not altogether different from Brecht's warnings about the excesses of that process, where the identification with character may indeed be a pretext for the self-enamored self loving itself in art, making over the character in its image. Brecht pointed to the liability in the process that the actor may be carried away, but as with Eliot's view of depersonalization (that only those would understand it who have some personality to begin with), there is nothing to alienate if, emotionally, the liability isn't there.

Drama and passion, collision and heat. There may be, *then*, degrees of identification in a combinatorial play of emotion which may be more or less analytical. The power of transformation may be modulated for critical purposes in any given performance, but if it can be shaped and articulated, or arrested in judgment, as in the pregnant seizure of a Brechtian *gestus*, it may also serve as an exemplary instance of a yielding to otherness, which is in the subtlest naturalism the paradox of authenticity. (The yielding may be, it should be said, quite as provisional as the arbitrary insistence of questionable difference on otherness itself.) If there is still, in this becoming, a form of appropriation involved, it is hardly hegemonic, at worst, or best, a kind of surrender, and would that most of us *could* identify like that: not only through relatively familiar difference, but when the appearances of otherness are really remote, strange, repellent, perverse, or at their extremities revolting. If an actor with such capacity believes s/he can play almost anything, there should nevertheless be no problem in that actor's understanding why, ideologically, blacks, Hispanics, lesbians, gays, or in the case of *Miss Saigon*, Asian actors, don't want anybody else speaking for them, or having their roles appropriated, while claiming at the same time that they can do the roles, across difference, that they very rarely get.

As a matter of equity, in the economy of our theater, the insistence on difference is a different story.

MIXED CASTING, MIXED FEELINGS: TRANSFORMATIVE GRAMMAR

Some years ago liberals were left hanging on this issue when, after they had argued strenuously in favor of mixed casting, Black Power came on the scene and, in theory at least, said you can keep those honky roles. Danger winks on opportunity. As blacks had (however inadequately) somewhat more, they had mixed feelings, and theorized less, taking the roles, and if they could get them in classical drama (particularly Shakespeare) often preferring them to characters in plays written by blacks. Now, on television, we see blacks performing scripts that may be written by blacks but are, in their forms of behavior and structural emotion, "essentially white." (This is not particularly surprising or venal in a profession where almost all actors, indiscriminately, do things in order to survive that violate their intelligence with their identity.) Whites are likely to be confused about essential whiteness, but where the issue is race the pressing question remains as to whether we should be color blind or, as an articulation of value, color conscious. In either case we are left with various unresolved questions about the specificity of history: just how material we want it to be in the theater's signifying practice, *when*, and *in what way*, for it is surely of material consequence to insist that the color we're seeing is not what we're seeing.

This assumes, of course, no onerous whiting out of, say, a black man's face. I say onerous only on the further assumption that the whiting is not *intended* as a mask. Which leads to this sort of conventional question within the casting practices of conventional theater: can a really undisguised black play, for instance, the munitions maker Undershaft in Shaw's *Major Barbara*? Certainly he can (or she), so long as you have a conception of the play to go along with it which is not diminished by your pretending *not* to see what you clearly do. There is nothing wrong with the pretending, since we do that in the theater even when we're pretending we're not, except in so far as it diminishes the seeing. Whether or not you're specifically attentive to historical setting and social class, blackness on stage is there to *be seen*, like any other occurrence or value, although it may be deployed (and/or responded to) in a convention of avoidance, in which case we'd have an aesthetic statement of the ethos of color blindness. Or assuming it will be seen – differentially seen depending on *where* it's seen, and *by whom* – the blackness itself may be interrogated, like gender or Jewishness, as a historical construct, a function of language or social production, whose identifying borders are blurred. Any way you look at it the issue is emotionally charged, although the ground rules are such today that it very rarely carries over into the structure of performance as something to be examined, as it was with insidious intent in Genet's *The Blacks*, where black actors *are* instructed to wear white masks, "in such a way that the audience sees a wide black band all around it, and even the actor's kinky hair."[19] (One can easily imagine in a Genetic scene that if the hair weren't kinky it might be treated to make it so.)

What is the status of the phenomenological evidence? There is no way of separating that question from the ideological subject of performance, no more than the residues of mimesis or the irruption of empathy from the politics of performance. In recent years the emotional complexity of these issues has been complicated by theoretical insistence that race, gender, and age are linguistic categories, historically constructed. There is a potential richness to the complication in the conceiving of a performance, though there are few productions as yet which articulate the various shades, gradations, and codings of such constructs, so that instead of forgetting that s/he seems black we might ask of a particular actor in a given context that implies s/he is something else: *is* s/he black? *how* black? what is *black*? and (overlooking for the moment the problematic of the conflated *s/he*) if the perception of blackness persists through its counterillusory absence, what, then, does the seeming mean? There is, it would seem, a destabilizing politics in all this, as there is in the question that might have been asked to begin with about what is an undisguised black, precisely the sort of question raised by Genet in a prefatory note to his play: "One evening an actor asked me to write a play for an all-black cast. But what exactly is a black? First of all, what's his color?"

This might appear to be the last word – if there were any such thing in Genet – were it not for history's habit of not keeping pace with its subversions of value, while confusing one issue with another. We may relativize it in our minds, or disperse it in performance, but so long as color is still perceived it may be that, even in an apparently liberated context, the construction put upon it is not what we might have wished. This was the case with the politically sensitive and aesthetically sophisticated production of *'Tis Pity She's a Whore*, staged (in the spring of 1990) by Joanne Akalaitis at the Goodman Theater in Chicago. About a year or so before, Akalaitis had done a version of Genet's *The Screens* at the Guthrie in Minneapolis, and there was every reason to assume from this, and her previous work with the Mabou Mines, that she had thought past the erratic historical pitfalls of interracial casting. As it turned out, however, the acute sexual politics of the performance of *'Tis Pity She's a Whore* was sending somewhat fuzzier signals about race. For the unavoidable liability of mixed casting (ethnic as well as racial) in the psychosexual morass of the drama was that certain characters inevitably aroused emotions divided between the assumption of color blindness (out of approval of the casting) and the inability to sustain it, not at least without the risk of an invidious identification. If we're specifically attentive to the local siting of perception, this was all the more true, I suppose, for a predominantly white audience seeing the play amidst the charged racial politics of Chicago, which has not quite relinquished the concept of blackness either to deconstruction or the illusion of indifference. When the misogynist Soranzo was savagely beating his pregnant wife, beyond the manifest measure of the Jacobean text – a scene whose dimensions of brutishness took on, in this production, the emblematic proportions of absolute male dominion over the woman's body – one might have preferred not to notice that the actor was (or should I say appeared to be?) black. As there were probably few in the audience who really overlooked it, there were also no doubt those who might have preferred that this particular actor were unambiguously white.

If we turn, however, from the appearance of blackness to the "colorless all-color" that dazzled Melville in the metaphysics of the whale, and from this blinding whiteness to the historically unstable constructs of gender and sexuality, we may imagine other productions where social value and aesthetic value could support each other or clash, with quite unsettling emotions, depending on where you stand in the shifting field. There is, to be sure, the potential erasure of the semantic barrier in s/he, with its restrictive legacy of an ego psychology in which the ego leans as an effect of power to the predominantly male. We have had much precedent for this erasure in the theatrical experiments of the last generation, with a falling away from mimesis, which showed up first in role-playing games and character "transformations," then shared, serial, or fractured roles, or none, then purer image, or the ideograph, or other variable functions of a sensed disjuncture in experience, a dissolution of the ego or break in being, with the adhesive trace of what was breaking under Derridean *sous rature*. If the actors could exchange roles, they could also exchange genders, a commonplace of studio improvisations (after Genet's *The Maids*) that eventually showed up in such plays as Caryl Churchill's *Cloud Nine* or, more recently, Timberlake Wertenbaker's *Our Country's Good*; and even on television (aside from pop icons and MTV) in the double cross(ing) of race and gender – the doubly inscrutable mustached Oriental revealed as the missing woman – in *Twin Peaks*.

What we see in such plays still tends to be – as compared to the threat to identity in Genet, or various subcultural forms – rather surface masquerade, without much jeopardy to gender beyond impersonation or makeup. There were, nevertheless, rather astonishing exercises and occasional performances that were something more than a mock exchange, and in the transformative grammar of modern acting the actor could increasingly say, like Lady Macbeth, unsex me here. In the same way performance might, but not merely in a convention of blindness, become indifferent to color. This became increasingly possible with the emergence of theater forms that were diffracted, hieroglyphic, atemporal, abstracted. The more abstract, the more miscegenated. This has implications for an aesthetic that resists the aesthesis with the paradox of an otherness wanting more of the same. Thus: in one of his last books Roland Barthes used the homosexualization of experience as a programmatic (he might have denied the word) metaphor for the erotic plurality of thought and fantasy which he preferred to the double violence of mimesis and finite meaning. Yet if things were coming semiotically out of the closet, they seemed to swerve, if not quickly into fashion, back into the structure of the mimetic, or both, with other finite meanings, familiar emotions, and through all the free-basing libido and "selves in alterity" the subject positions of emulable identities. So it was, after the death of Charles Ludlam, in the warmly empathic responses to the canonical variations on his transvestite roles, like Marguerite Gautier in *Camille*. Whatever the sexual politics, we are moved, we want to be moved, and sometimes by emotions that are, with whatever estranging devices, not so remote from the crudest of culinary desires or, with "the uneasiness of being a subject torn between two languages, one expressive, the other critical," like Barthes himself in the doubly inverted camera obscura of his *Camera Lucida*.[20]

BARTHES' *PUNCTUM*,
AND THE CHASTITY OF ROBERT WILSON

"Affectivity is banal, or, if you prefer, typical," Barthes wrote in the preface to the early *Critical Essays*, in which writing is seen as "merely the constellation of several persistent figures" (the impoverished power of naming) and form is acceded to as that which "permits us to escape the parody of feelings" that repeats itself endlessly in "an absurdly restricted number of functions: *I desire, I suffer, I am angry, I contest, I love, I want to be loved, I am afraid to die . . .* " (xvi–xvii). What is "original" about these functions, *as revealed*, is the infinite repeatability of their essential indiscretion, which accounts for the cautionary semiology of Barthes' early work, guarded as it was against a falsifying pathos: the experiential vanities and ideological duplicities of bourgeois emotion. It was the death of his mother, however, that caused Barthes to confront the possibility that there is no way out of the dilemma of pathos and experience, with its desire to sustain or recover originary feeling, the substance of authenticity. There were intimations already among the choreographic figures and performative utterances of *A Lover's Discourse*, but in *Camera Lucida* it was as if he had taken upon himself, with a kind of solipsistic excess, the once-disreputable figure of Empathy itself, confessing to "oddly old-fashioned" emotions like *grief* and *pity*, and to a total identification with the figure of loss itself, "entering crazily into the spectacle, into the image," taking the dead into his arms (116–17), giving himself over to the power of affect that his phenomenology had denied.

Nor was this anything like a surface of random intensities as described by Lyotard in his conception of a libidinal economy. Or the mutation of it in the *theatrum philosophicum* of Foucault, actually based on the phantasma-physics of Deleuze, the "epidermic play of perversity" that is the prickly heat of libidinal flow. In the postmodern ethos of surfaces, Barthes' *punctum* is a seizure, the rip, the tear, the wound that on the flat surface of the photograph confirms an interior *depth*. For this master of demystification there is fetishism besides, as he dismisses everything except the charismatic *detail* that rises "of its own accord into affective consciousness" (55), though sometimes – as in Mapplethorpe's photograph of Bob Wilson (a diptych with Philip Glass) – Barthes is touched, inwardly and acutely, but does not know why: "is it the eyes, the skin, the position of the hands, the track shoes?" (51). I will return in the next chapter to the delirium of the *punctum* and the idea of theater in Barthes' view of the photograph, but for the moment we are a long way from the political consciousness of the *Mythologies*, where Barthes in his Brechtian mode tracks the ideological abuses of the bourgeois ego with its mystifying delusions of affect. Or the essay on the Bunraku puppets, where he speaks with distaste of the fetish, and the space of deceit in the western theater where the empathic link between character and actor "is always conceived . . . as the expressive channel of an interiority" (*I-M-T* 173).

There's obviously more to be said, along this channel, about the *political* resources of empathy, whether we are dealing with sympathetic *or* estranging emotions, though there is an apolitical strain of the non-conventional spectacle that I'd like to speak of now, in which the emotions are a good deal stranger than those of Brechtian alienation. The work of Robert Wilson, who also admires the Bunraku, is hardly without fetishism, but whatever the allure of the track shoes they are not likely to move, with the belated pathos of Barthes, in the overheated channel of an expressive interiority. As for the oneiric images of Wilson's productions, they may be *sui generis*, but ideologically, and psychosexually, they are also supremely chaste, and if there is a politics in it nevertheless – in the filamenting profusion of image and drawn-out sediments of time – it remains at a cool and pristine distance, even when the text is Heiner Müller's.

The argument made by Brecht, about formalism as a realism, so far as it improves the apparatus of production, might be advanced in this regard, and Wilson's techniques have also been adapted in the theater to more specifically political content. (It was, by the way, Louis Aragon who, before Wilson's eminence here, praised *Deafman's Glance* in Paris for bringing at last to its consummation the ideals of surrealism that, in the dream-thought of Aragon, were inseparable from socialism.) There is obviously a trickle-down economy in the usages of technique, but what I am referring to in Wilson, and in other postmodern forms, would seem to be a radical departure from either the meaning of affect or the validity of emotion, or what might be thought of as validating emotions, the kind invoked by Gramsci in which you can "feel humanity." Not merely, then – in the absence of validation – a rummage sale of values, but something like a warp of value, the very *concept* of value, as if through the refracted planes of recursive sound in Philip Glass or the precisionist lighting of Wilson in *Einstein on the Beach*, whose impeccable kilowatts do not come entirely, however, from the general theory of relativity in the infinite curvature of space. Aside from the obvious ideological paradox of the high-priced presentation of this avant-garde work at the Metropolitan Opera, or the ready accommodation of Wilson's most ambitious projects with extensive subsidy in the state theaters of Germany, there are insistent questions of value and valuation that arise from the operatic scope and extravagant spectacle of the productions, the attenuated indeterminacy of their emotions.

SOMETHING TO BE DESIRED (HOW GERMAN IS IT?)

If in what follows I seem to be taking Wilson to task for that tenuous, and no doubt beguiling, aspect of his work, it is with considerable admiration for his achievement (even the managerial achievement), which restores to the stage certain qualities too long forgotten, like surprise and wonder, produced with the most incisive naïveté by the elements of stagecraft itself, including the incantatory appearances of protracted motion that constitute, remarkably, an altered sense of time: disbelief suspended because belief is no issue at all. What is simply undeniable – amidst the ubiquity of aimless image in the quotidian spectacle – is the astonishing visual beauty of this singular theater practice. All that is well known. There is something exotic about it, and surely auratic, but there is overall a peculiar stringency in the copiousness of the form. Or to put it another way: Wilson is one of the few practitioners with anything like an "accuracy of abundance," a phrase actually used by Wallace Stevens about the acting of Sarah Bernhardt. There is, indeed, a certain majesty to the work, which has within the ecological imagination and communitarian ethos of its origins the arcane and sumptuous features of a royal masque. If that in itself is something of an ideological paradox, there may be some reason to ask why, when the plenitude leaves us speechless, it is not necessarily because – in the sense invoked by Gramsci – we are *moved*.

Or moved inexplicably by what, if examined, might trouble us more. But then, what "us" are we talking about? for there are some who are, apparently, not troubled at all by the proposition that you're not supposed to be asking questions about Wilson's images, as if we're back again with Coleridge and, in the orders of imagination, the notion of a primary power whose plasticity is such that it resists examination. That, according to Wilson himself, is the encrypted intention of his theater of images, accepted at face value by almost all of those who write about his work,[21] some of whom might in the political sphere be worried about the arcane, as with the logistics of opacity and absence in the principle of sovereignty itself. The masques of Wilson may suggest as a cautionary inflection of the discourse of power that not all forms of sovereignty are alike, though its mechanisms may be. To this possibility let me add that while I have, like Yeats or Walter Benjamin, a rather high modernist disposition to difficulty and even obscurity – on the assumption that some things, as Benjamin said, are more intelligible when obscure, or can't be said at all without a certain *dérèglément* of meaning – there is still the issue in the indeterminacy, the attenuated magic of Wilson's stagecraft, that if not exactly wanting at the level of emotions does leave something to be desired.

This raises the question, rather ignored in theory, as to what kind of emotion *is* desire, which seems in reality (not to mention other traditions, from metaphysical poetry to eastern lore) much less univocal than its recent discourse, or for that matter – with the rather mixed feelings that blur an emotion – considerably more perplexed about the "claims of desire," even when linked to difference. Meanwhile, there has developed through the upped ante of the ideology of desire the surrogate notion of *affective intensities* that, with energy flying in all directions, may give us the impression that it all feels alike, including the widely divergent species of postmodern performance. On that radial axis of the postmodern it is not Wilson that I am mainly concerned with, though it is precisely his distinction that may focus the ideological questions involved, which are no less than ever wrapped up in emotion.

Or to put it another way, related to Marx's view of the constitution of the five senses: the complex state or elusive status of emotion is drawn and quartered by, reformed, imbued with and impelling the movement of history itself, the ever-present sensation and material burden of its indeterminacy. Sometimes an artistic practice will attempt to reflect exactly that, like the recent paintings of Gerhardt Richter, *18 Oktober 1977*, on the still-mysterious deaths in Stammhein Prison of members of the Baader-Meinhof group. There are serialist affinities, across forms, between Richter and Wilson, though the indeterminacy in Wilson, precisely in its allure, is not similarly burdened. Nor do the quasi-historical accretions, the virtual antiquing process, in the sculptured properties exhibited from his theater productions, suggest anything like the grievous pressure of history or the gravity of distressed emotions in the reliefs and installations of Anselm Kiefer.

True enough, Wilson is Texan and not German, but Germany is now the inaugural space of much of his work, and we are dealing, moreover, with an aesthetic that in the ceaseless itinerary of the director, also flying off in all directions, seems to exemplify the widespreading desire for the "planetization" of culture, along with the new fascinations of difference that are part of the logic of advanced capitalism. As with the global conception of *the CIVIL warS*, organized at first for the Los Angeles Olympics (at projected costs for the completed work approaching $6.5 million), this is not in Wilson's case altogether separable from the imperial ambition that has haunted the history of modernism. That does not, however, appear to be the thematic of the production of *King Lear* in Frankfurt, whose focal concern according to Wilson is primarily with aging. But to see feelingly almost any aspect of what, at the end of the twentieth century, still cuts to the brain in that play would seem to require some tangible sense – across any cultural difference materialized in the event – of the audience, the financing, the by no means cancelled history that is unavoidably its context, all the more at the historical moment when the Wall has fallen down.

THE ANTIOEDIPAL PROJECT
AND THE IDEOLOGY OF AFFECTS

Let us shift back, however, from the comparison with other visual artists to theater practice itself, and more specifically to other practitioners with a high priority on spectacle and a proliferous quotient of image. What I want to say more about, in that context, is the apparent change in the status of emotion alluded to before: the displacement of the felt, shared, or validating emotions of a presumably discredited humanism by an altogether different, indeterminate notion of affect. This is part of the antioedipal project of undoing the mimetic and, at the chiliastic extremity of poststructuralist desire, destroying not only the image-repertoire of bourgeois representation, but the repressive structure of representation itself. What emerged through the sixties as a theater of images did not necessarily theorize such ideas, but they were with more or less messianic urgency a good part of its agenda. The antimimetic bias remains in those modes of performance where the images still prevail, with more or less desperation trying to outperform or short circuit the demon of analogy, up to its old tricks in falsifying emotions. Where the emotions, however, are not simply extirpated they may be virtually upended and swept along by the sheer radical *velocity* of affect, though that would seem to be a contradiction in the long suspended dynamics or radical *viscosity* of Wilson's productions.

As if the slow motion were an index of emotional differences, those productions – even with political figures in the title, like *The Life and Times of Joseph Stalin* – would seem to be at the other end of the spectrum of postmodern performance from, say, the almost frenzied invention in the Choreographisches Theater of Johann Kresnick. I am thinking particularly of Kresnick's *Ulrike Meinhof*, with its vast momentum of exhaustive image in the defensive elegy on the terrorist heroine, who is if anything – through the high-tech menace of the dazzling scenography – the remorselessly terrorized subject of abuse.[22] To turn to the work of a more familiar figure, Pina Bausch: the spectacular elegance of Wilson is still a far cry from the equally extravagant stagings of the Bochum Tanztheater, with its neo-expressionist energy and epidermic play of perversity and, with an elegance of its own that is corrosively witty, the explosive assault on the sensibilities of the viewer. At its most elemental level the performances of Kresnick and Bausch would seem to differ from Wilson's in the ensemble sweat of the performers, *labor value*, the basic investment of bodies (whatever you think of the aesthetic) in undeniably exhausting work. Yet as we position such performances in the scene of the postmodern, with its orbiting surplus of image, and think of the spectacle moving through the atmosphere with the speed of light, we come in another Doppler effect, the accelerating recession of motion in space, to an *ideology of affects*, in the sense addressed by Deleuze and Guattari. These relate "only to the moving body itself, to speeds and compositions of speed among elements." Here the retardation of Wilson, its formal austerity and psychosexual cool, and the autoerotic discharges of Bausch, the swift projectile force or (repetitively) random topography of the dance, *intersect*, and we can see them as part of the same ideological dispensation or "passional regime" or "machinic assemblage," to use the curious terms of schizoanalysis on nomadology and the war machine.[23]

This is obviously lightyears from the "machine in motion" that increased the bestiality at the Alfieri, making Gramsci sick at heart. Nor is it quite the passional regime of Meyerhold's biomechanics, still attached to an empathic tradition of felt humanity for all the machinic assemblage of its furious passion. What we have is an energetics rather than a poetics of performance, in which all forms of energy cross as in the phantasmaphysical version (Eleatic not Eliotic) of the still point of the turning world. "From this standpoint," write Deleuze and Guattari of the newer domain of affects, "the most absolute immobility, pure catatonia, is part of the speed vector, is carried by this vector, which links the petrification of the act to the precipitation of movement" (*Plateaus* 400). It's as if in an inversion like the production of ideology itself – or rather, perhaps, the manifestation of a fetish – the state of catatonia described by Brecht *in the audience* becomes, at first, a description of the behavior *on stage* in Beckett's *Waiting for Godot*, and then the soporific principle out of which Wilson made performances, with something like the somnambulant aesthetic of a waking dream. It is a curious aesthetic, however, in which for all the moving bodies it is a kind of bodiless presence that links the petrification of the act to the precipitation of movement. That may be what, as with a fetish, makes it alluring.

FETISHISM AND SEDUCTION: WHERE'S THE BLOODY HORSE?

Yet the affect of this bodiless presence is for all the appearance of a compelling stasis something more than seductive, the mere fetishistic shadow of an entrancing thing. As already suggested, one of the most imposing aspects of Wilson's early work was the emergence of an idea of performance, its virtual structure, from apparently unmediated or retarded behavior, in the other clinically diagnosed sense. Or the sense, rather, of the excluded other: the deafman's glance or the autism of Christopher Knowles, as in *A Letter to Queen Victoria*. I have written elsewhere about the therapeutic achievement inseparable from the aesthetic,[24] but as we can see in the recent productions of Wilson – and his increasing desire to work with more highly trained and experienced actors – there has been a suspension, at least, of his own particular fascination with these alien figures of the presumably unmediated, aside from the quick liability of its aestheticizing today, despite the disposition of theory against the aesthetic. What is of residual consequence in Wilson's earliest experiments is that they raised, contemporaneously with the critique of origins, issues of primacy and authenticity, and despite his own aestheticizing tendencies a distrust of mediations.

Which is not the case, however, in another highly visual theater with a specific energetics of the body, like Martha Clarke's, where fetishism has been, as in *Vienna Lusthaus*, as much the subject matter as the outcome of performance. With the body itself as a fetish, the performance is imbued with all the illicit sensation and emotional values that we might expect from *fin-de-siècle* nostalgia, the curvilinear sensuosity of *Jugendstil*, autoerotic and polysexual experiment, and a palette of cross-gendered movement ranging from the ironic tonality of Schnitzler to the iconography of Klimt to an annotative choreography of what, in its perverse figurations, was once shocking to Krafft-Ebing and Freud, from masturbation and pederasty to necrophilia and child abuse. Here the body seems to be caught, however, between the historical *representation* of highly charged, and not unattractive, sadomasochistic emotions that, up through the *Anschluss*, become politically menacing, and the *generative activity* itself – the production of images in the (im)mediacy of the dance – by means of which even the most repellent sensation, the expense of spirit in a waste of shame, may become eroticized in such a way as to be seductive, so that precisely what is distasteful is the specular bait of desire. Thus it is in *Vienna Lusthaus* with various images in which, with the delicacy of a butterfly, copulation thrives, and then, in the libidinal economy of the performance, turns ghastly or bestial, or in the exchange of handsome bodies has the arousing brutality of a runaway horse.

What happens in all this to the emotion of love itself? I ask the question because, in the midst of writing the passage above, I broke off for a walk on the rue de la Roquette in Paris, off the Bastille, and went into a gallery where I saw a series of theatrical tableaux by the relatively young artist Françoise Quardon. In the voluptuous poverty or Monoprix luxury of these bewitching installations with specifically translated or bilingual titles – *Adieu, L'Amour Est Doux (Mais Dangereux)*, *The Fire of Love (Désir)*, *Caldo Sangue (Hot Blood)*, *Trop Tard (Too Late)*, *Requiem für Ein Traum* – the horse again is a recurring image, the pop art insignia of a Mobil gas station flying horse, which has (for me, at least) more affective substance in Quardon's modest *mise-en-scène* than the real stallion in Chéreau's *Hamlet* on the vast stage at Avignon. If there is also some nostalgic allusion to Bouchardon or the equestrian statue of Louis XV, there is in the panoply of affects a devolution of hot blood in the veins that, with the scratchy background noise (waves? a merry-go-round? a drum or washing machine? the deep-bubbling oil for *frites*?), also suggests the film on marathon dancing with Jane Fonda, *They Shoot Horses, Don't They?*

As the catalogue suggests, the art and literature of the twentieth century has not exactly been hospitable to either the staying power or "the energy of the sentiment of love,"[25] nor tried to capture it in performance. Emotion. Sentiment. Passion. This psychosomatic spectrum of interwoven words takes on a considerable range of nuances in France, and if one had to choose among them for the art of Françoise Quardon one might be tempted to say that she wants, like Baudelaire, to be passionately in love with passion. But this is still, even with a summer's testaments to de Gaulle, the simulated Paris of Jean Baudrillard, and as in *Vienna Lusthaus* the operative word is *seduction*. As it were the debased and rusted counterfeit of the Great Chain of Being, seduction may be thought of as the bejeweled and cynical offering to our capacity for deception, the merest persuasive replica of reciprocal desire, as in several coincident versions of *Les Liaisons dangereuses* (by Stephen Frears, Milos Foreman, Heiner Müller) at the theaters and movies of Paris. But in the flooded circuitries of exchange with not even the remotest electronic measure of a true center of being, it seems natural enough to be carried away by seduction: what happens to love not in the expertise of appearance but at the (purported) end of representation. (Where seduction operates and prevails we're never quite sure of the order of things in the scheme of affect, whether the petrification of the act linked to the precipitation of movement, or vice versa.) To be carried away from the center of being is what seduction classically is, but it's not only the fire of love which is at stake, its thrills and fevers, the vertiginous speed of love that exhausts itself in a seizure of the heart, but a sort of coronary bypass of language itself, of which seduction appears to be, in the world of simulacra, its terminal collapse.

With Quardon, of course, the spectacle is intimate, the scale is small – and no actors to speak of, no actors at all – but this is the emotional environment of her tableaux. Though not entirely. Suffused with the idea of performance, there are other sentiments as well, and hints of remembered passion. There is also a lingering sense – in the warm colors, the domestic signs (the ardency of a *fleur de lis* out of crimson strands of pepperoni), and the dialectical embrace of the polyglot titles by the murmuring static of unhearable words – that we love, still, in the idea of loving. This idea would seem to be very French, but the affect is more (or so it seems to me) like a rather bemused declension of Shakespeare's sonnets, of which, coincidentally, I saw last year a theater piece on the same rue de la Roquette.[26] Whether in the (juridical) sessions of sweet silent thought or the furious winter's rages, the sonnets speak of love through every diminuendo of feeling and inevitable failing as an ever-fixèd mark that, shivering and shaking through an ether of indeterminacy, could hardly be imagined without the metonymic bonding in the words of love ("every word doth almost tell my name" (Sonnet 76)) and the nuanced mediations of the figures of representation.

155

5

THE STRUGGLE TO APPEAR

THE BASELESS FABRIC

As compared to the lyrical installations in a small gallery near the Bastille, the spectacles of Robert Wilson might very well be on the stage of the space-age structure that now dominates the *quartier*, with the ambivalent ostentation of a "people's opera." (Which is the virtual oxymoron used by the Ministry of Culture when the building was designed.) Wilson has worked in minor dimensions, but as prefaces to major projects or as interludes to productions that are magisterial in scale. Whatever the scale may be, the substance of appearance, as opposed to its *manifestations*, is not for him a haunted or grievous problem, as it is in the oedipal dramaturgy of our metaphysical theater, which has been critiqued as a refuge of invisible power. That it remains, at least, an arresting problem can be seen in recent productions of *The Tempest* by other masterful directors with a propensity for scale, Giorgio Strehler and Peter Brook, whose ideological differences converge, as if under the spell of Prospero, in the bewildering, yet indemnifying powers of illusion. Or the blurring of illusion with theater magic, with more or less implication that theatricality is the real. If Brook finds grounds for this, after early experiments with the cruelty of Artaud, in a multilingual company with the experience of other cultures, Strehler's long-standing commitment to Brecht has managed to absorb a return to Pirandello and (with some dissipation of an alienating distance in the consciousness of mortality that comes with age) a continued fascination with the play of appearance. As we find it in Pirandello, an indecipherable play, shaped by desire, and all the more maddening for that.

With Wilson, however, there is nothing to decipher in the play within the play, because the play is of another order, the images there before you with, apparently, nothing standing behind. Always, of course, the apparency is the rub, to the degree that it's not transparent or entirely legible; but if there is a residual hermeneutic in the fascination effect, it seems cast upon doubt by perception itself, like the shadow of a magnitude that appears to have disappeared. Wherever the doubt comes from, the theater

157

event is not conceived around the ontology, or conundrums, of appearance. The manifestations may be mystifying, but we are not confronted with a dialectical exercise over illusion and reality, nor an implied hypothesis about the seeming laminations of a possibly anterior truth that, in the calculus of specularity, must be strenuously explored by the actors during the course of performance. This would seem unavoidable in approaching classical plays, as Wilson has recently done, but the effect remains the same: the texture of performance is such, its attenuation, that we may think of all appearances as "the baseless fabric" of a vision in which the actors have melted into air, thin air, even before the revels have ended (*Temp.* 4.1.148–56), since they have assumed from the beginning – without that fractiousness of will which is a figure of the drama and its paradox of necessity – the function of a sign.

It is not quite a matter, however, of constructing meanings from empty signifiers. What Jameson has called "signatures of the visible" are, as a virtual aesthetic in Wilson, more protean and elusive than that, as if the hegemony of the gaze were no competition at all, but simply mastered by "the illimitable richness of the visual object." Signs are taken for wonders, we would see a sign, even as we worry about their existence as signs. Such is the vanity of signifying practice that, in the society of the spectacle, it seems to have caved in to the energy of the visible. This is alarming to Jameson, who combines, as the opening assumption of a new book, Debord's argument about the spectacle, which is itself the apotheosis of commodification, with Baudrillard's notion of the visible as obscene: "The visual," says Jameson, "is *essentially* pornographic, which is to say it has its end in rapt, mindless fascination; thinking about its attributes becomes an adjunct to that, if it is unwilling to betray its object."[1] He is about to talk of film, but he could be writing of Wilson, whose work might also be thought of in terms of postmodern pastiche as a function of the logic of consumer capitalism. But that would betray, in the reign of reifications, the singularity of the object by a simplified account of how it processes its materials, which is in Wilson something other than bricolage.

There are now and then in the productions elements of kitsch or camp, and aspects of pastiche, but occulted somehow in the alembic of performance, "a commodius vicus of recirculation"[2] that seems to occur in a different world from this, its objects antiqued with the absence of history; or, with a sort of hieratic minimalism, cut, zoned, or diffused by light, as if interrupting their existence as commodities. While the specific gravity of circulation may lead, through the viscous flow of the fascination effect, to the same old economy of exchange, there is nevertheless the beautifully managed illusion of a *suspension of value*. Or, with blazons of shattered myth and intimations of primordiality, it would seem that the most intimately archaic experience is being projected and densely mediated by the autistic floating fantasy of the dreamlike ruins of time, with the human figure itself as an increment of eternity, without a story or a psychology because it is merely figuration, denatured, cybernetic, the autochthonous element of an origin that is nowhere to be found.

As he turned to dramatic texts – particularly *King Lear*, obsessed as it is with origins – Wilson could not quite avoid dealing with story and psychology, and I shall say more about that later in this chapter, as well as his relation to the marketplace of signs. Meanwhile, there is an aesthetic and historical irony in the mesmerizing repetitions that, as they seem to erase value at the edge of trance, are the incantatory index of Wilson's distrust of mediations; for the distrust was shared at the other end of the spectrum of theatricality by the search for the originary truth of emotion in realistic acting. As we have seen, that was also – to the point of a compulsive introspection that resembled autism – concerned with authenticity.

BEING AUTHENTIC: PATHOLOGY AND PRAXIS

Here we encounter the mode of appearance that is the surfacing of a depth, which is, however, reluctant to appear. Here we encounter, too, as the dynamics of visibility is factored into the psyche of the profession, the relationship in acting between pathology and praxis, itself occulted by the absorption of the pathology into acting technique. That was complicated a generation ago by growing ambivalence among actors about the power of authority (producers, directors, the apparatus itself) and the authority of the text, including the primacy of character, though in the restricted economy of the American theater they were still desperately competing for roles. There was, however, a new demography in the theater, and if there were emerging critical differences in purpose and ideology, there were also differences in the *quality* of acting, between those experienced in the commercial theater or the developing regional theaters, and those in the sprouting countercultural workshops who could hardly, yet, be considered experienced actors, and many of whom – despite new regimens of training, and whatever else they might do proficiently in the alternative theater – could never perform adequately in a conventional play.

Some of these actors might very well have been in the early Wilson productions, as under the long skirts of the imposing figures of the Bread and Puppet Theater, where the imaginative vision and principles of execution were essentially Peter Schumann's, and the inexperienced performers, with less time perhaps to have developed obtrusive egos, suffered less from invisibility than more experienced actors with professional investments. As for some of the actors who developed reputations in the experimental theater of a generation ago, and still win Obie awards, to this day they are by no means as convincing in the character roles they now want to play as were the actors of the previous generation, trained in the techniques of realism and, in the participatory mystique of the sixties, scorned for their ego psychology. As the experimental groups acquired more skills from diverse sources, or at a sort of degree zero of technique invented exercises for particular needs, the ideological differences were actually focused by the use of the term "performer" instead of the opprobrious "actor" with a self-indulgent inner life and deluded truth of emotion, which was the same old tired truth of an exhausted bourgeois drama. Meanwhile, being authentic was a criterion in both camps, and charges of inauthenticity inevitably came back, however circuitously, to some idea of the self. This was especially true (and remains so) with another cadre of inexperienced performers who, in the politics of marginality, were yet to assume that an autonomous self is an exhausted proposition.

At the time when Clifford Odets was denouncing the self that was printed on dollar bills, the Group Theater was developing a legacy of internal technique that has been indelibly associated (not always correctly: witness Franchot Tone) with the activist politics of the thirties. A generation later there was a shying away from anything like an explicit politics in the introspection of the Actors Studio, though it could be safely assumed that the majority of its members were attached to liberal causes or residually on the Left. If that was symptomatic of the tranquilized period in which the Studio emerged, it was best symbolized by the embittered split between Arthur Miller and Elia Kazan, after the latter's testimony before the House UnAmerican Activities Committee. The breach was not entirely healed even after the production, by Kazan, of Miller's autobiographical *After the Fall* at the Repertory Theater of Lincoln Center, which opened in temporary quarters downtown at Washington Square, at just about the time an alternative theater practice was developing in the vicinity. If the authenticity sought for during the course of this history had been blurred in the aberrations of method between the `claims of self, character, and experienced emotions (was the character in some sense *more* experienced?), it soon turned in the alternative workshops to the displaced subject of politics, and with residues of commitment to *existential* authenticity, a theatricalized politics at that. It was a politics of performance not quite imagined, however, by Clurman and Strasberg in the formation of the Group, whose orientation, after all, was always the commodity system of the Broadway theater.

In the fervent years of the sixties performance became a sign of protest whose lessons were very widely absorbed all over the political spectrum (as we can see today at abortion clinics in the strategies of the militant Right). With images moving so fast in the society of the spectacle nobody much noticed that, if signifying practice was in disarray, the models of theater were also confused. Brecht had pointed out, as long ago as his notes to *The Threepenny Opera*, that there was in the economic priorities of the theater a systemic danger of theatering it all down (*Brecht* 43), but it wasn't until the excitements of the sixties had subsided that we began to realize the degree to which theatricality had been absorbed into the logic of advanced capitalism as an instrumental asset of the apparatus of production. Critique itself, it seemed for a while, could only be homeopathic, infused as it was with notions of play and performance. It is perhaps another historical irony that just as theory has come, in refusing the existential, to accept the inevitability of mediations, we may see more than a residue of a theatricalized politics not only in various types of postmodern performance, but also, through the hegemony of the media, in the service of quite conventional forms of power indifferent to authenticity. Or in the muddle of method, wanting the *look* of authenticity, which in a mediated politics is the essence of appearance.

Which leaves us with a critical practice that, in rejecting or wobbling on the notion of the authentic (attached as it is to origins), is itself without any method for contending with appearance, since even the correctest politics is subject to that, like ideology itself.

SURFACE TENSION

It follows, of course, that we now have an extensive discourse looking for a conceptual model not dominated by the dialectic of appearance and essence: latent/manifest, surface/depth, authentic/inauthentic. Actually, most of the alternatives seem to play it close to the surface, though nobody quite knows how to get rid of the feeling of something deeper, elsewhere, undercover, or, in the culinary thematics of broken immediacy, something raw even if it seems cooked.

Or is it the other way around? So far as the nature/culture controversy is itself a function of power, there are good political reasons for wanting to resolve it or dissolve it, along with questions of primacy, into a heterogeneous discursive field such as that described by Ernesto Laclau and Chantal Mouffe in their rethinking of hegemony and a radical democratic politics. By deconstructing the various discursive surfaces of evolutionary Marxism, they discover a logic of the social that in turn provides them "with an *anchorage* from which contemporary social struggles are *thinkable* in their specificity." From this anchorage, where the real is never thought without mediations, subjugated voices may be viewed, with agencies and strategies of their own, as occupying the same plane as the voices of established power. They may be thought of thus, and desirably so, but if we can imagine such a heterogeneity, or its anchorage, it was discovered by Laclau and Mouffe – as their "principal conclusion" – hidden *behind* the transformations of the concept of hegemony itself.[3]

Whatever, then, the multiplicity of voices in a plurality of spaces, or "the open, unsutured character" (*Hegemony* 192) of this social logic, it hardly needs saying that the binaries are tenacious in the hegemony of appearance. Or if they seem to dissolve for the moment in some meltdown of power, we can hardly blink our eyes before they seem to be there again. The paradigm was in Genet, but we've now seen it in Eastern Europe, where the unsubjugated voices are, with long-repressed emotions, summoning up old divisions, and no more so than with claims to being authentic. Where pragmatic necessity intersects the politics of inexperience (or inexperienced politicians), as in Poland and Czechoslovakia, there are other divisions brought on by having to include in the discursive field, however selectively, the suspect voices of formerly established power.

Around these occurrences the discourse on postmodernism continues, with its heterogenous attitudes about the ideology of the aesthetic, though there are views of the relationship between social and artistic strategies that correspond to the notion of a democratic politics on a radically levelled plane. Jameson has spoken elsewhere, for instance, of "a new kind of flatness or depthlessness."[4] For good reasons of its own, beginning with cubism, modernist art had long anticipated that. And while it is true that the metastases of postmodernism can be thought of as a self-conscious appropriation of an earlier aesthetic for non-aesthetic purposes, or in the form of an antiaesthetic, the historical materialism of Jameson does not pursue in this case the lesson of history that rubs ideologically against the grain. The master narratives may be gone, but thereby hangs a tale:

The projection of the myth of flatness (for it was surely that: a myth) onto the premised flatness of the picture plane gave us a membrane that, as a law unto itself, was obliged to represent without representing, since it could not (ostensibly) count on illusionary depth or its conventions to support an expressive function. But the picture plane never could just leave it at that, as a kind of conceptual dust gathered on its surface, clotting it with adhesions or sediments of the extrusions, as if even the drawn shadow of a depth reproduced it, or as if history weighed upon the surface that dared to deny it, laminating it with lost or lasting illusion. (The entire process can be summed up, along with the tenaciousness of specularity and adhesions of the gaze, in the successive titles over the course of half a century of a "work" by Man Ray, with an image of a metronome and a photographic eye: *The Object to Be Destroyed* (1923), *Object of Destruction* (1932), *Lost Object* (1945), *Indestructible Object* (1958), *Last Object* (1966), *Perpetual Motif* (1972).) In the resistance to illusion, the notion of flatness has been incessantly rethought, in relation to the instabilities of the picture plane, or the liability of the proscenium stage, even when the frame was apparently broken – the field stretched beyond endurance by abstract expressionism – and the art came off the wall into happenings and environments and the hegemony of performance, from whence it has since returned onto the canvas again, along with the figuration that seemed to have been abolished. If that seems flat and depthless as compared to what it was before the figure was erased – particularly the human figure – by non-objective art, the struggle to appear continues, as if inherited from the theater (its immaterial substance or ghostly presences longing for human form) or the humanistic thrust in the performative energies of action painting itself. These were hardly dissipated, though variously dispersed, in the discursive fields of minimalism or conceptual art.

It was during the period of minimalism and conceptualism, or in fiction the *nouvelle vague*, that we had a particular intensification of the dialectic of depth and surface, by emphasis upon the self-referential validity of the culturally made thing, which seemed for the historical moment to rule out illusory depth, and with it the factitious panoply of motivating, myopic, appropriative emotions. What Robbe-Grillet called "the myth of depth" was in every instance "a continuous fringe of culture (psychology, ethics, metaphysics, etc.)" merely superimposed upon things, "giving them a less alien aspect, one that is more comprehensible, more reassuring. Sometimes the camouflage is complete: a gesture vanishes from our mind, supplanted by emotions which supposedly produced it, and we remember a landscape as *austere* or *calm* without being able to evoke a single outline, a single determining element."[5] In his resistance to "this systematic appropriation of the visual" by the bourgeois legacy of romantic sentiment, Robbe-Grillet refused as well, as another interpretative screen, what was then, at least, the "convenient category of the absurd" (*New Novel* 19). The world, he insisted, is neither significant nor absurd, but just *there*, as if in a holding pattern or still frame of phenomenology, to be seen as it is.

Not wholly objectivist nor totally impersonal, since such impersonality "is all too obviously an illusion" (18), Robbe-Grillet directs us, however, to the surface as evidence and sanction, a virtual sanctuary from the falsification of depth. With more or less illusion of objectivity or impersonal rigor, an ethos of surface ran through the phenomenological bias of the period, with the latency of a psychologism that seemed to return like the repressed, along with tabooed emotions, in the activity of perception itself. "What you see is what you see," said the painter Frank Stella, in a gnomic pronouncement associated with minimalism, and (in unpurged formalist practice) with affinities to Robbe-Grillet. What we may see after all, however, is that both painter and novelist may have suffered from what Whitehead defined as "the fallacy of misplaced concreteness." If we read *The Erasers* or *The Voyeur* today – or see Resnais' *Last Year at Marienbad*, scripted by Robbe-Grillet – we may discern a pathos secreted in the most fastidious contours of the objects established by their prevailing "*presence*" (21). And even at the time it was not entirely clear in Stella's tautology whether what you see is what it *is* or what, as if with the eyes rolling inward, you *want* to see, thus opening up vision to the ideology of desire, which may take us, recessively and regressively, back to the depths:

"Yet something is added to my interpretation," wrote Virginia Woolf in *The Waves*, with the perspective from another part of the psyche than that of *A Room of One's Own*: "Something lies deeply buried. For one moment I thought to grasp it. But bury it, bury it; let it breed, hidden in the depths of my mind some day to fructify. After a long lifetime, loosely, in a moment of revelation, I may lay hands on it, but now the idea breaks in my hand."[6] Almost everything in that passage is anathema to the demystifying tendencies of current theory, which is with ideological variations still very much committed to seeing as it is, or if not that, as a matter of praxis signifying otherwise. In either case, with no waiting around for a revelation from the nurturing depths that, even if it appeared, couldn't be grasped – leaving us empty-handed except for a useless pathos, which even the severest minimalist reduction never escaped.

We could see that once, in the vanguard of modernist art, in the null structures and surfaces of Malevich's suprematist void, which seems to evacuate a previous history of abundantly expressive and emotive means (the range of which can be verified in the early paintings now released from the underground of Soviet museums). And we could see it again, with the emergence of minimalism, in the nullifications and entropic cleansing of Robert Smithson's view of space, where all representations of action have – or so it seems for the historical moment – passed into oblivion: "Space is the remains, or corpse, of time, it has dimensions. 'Objects' are 'sham space,' the excrement of thought and language. . . . Objects are phantoms of the mind, as false as angels."[7] If these objects are familiar, it's because they are defined as Marx defines ideology, though there is an emotive resonance in those angels like a ring around the moon, which would seem to be topographically – cold, blank, disused, vapid as it is – a site-specific realization of minimalist desire. Only commodities, Smithson has said, can afford illusionistic values, but if the objects of minimalism, or the eroding magnitude of the *Spiral Jetty*, were not commodities destined for "consumer oblivion" (*Writings* 12), they were in their splendid desolation, or in proportion to the reduction, emotionally overcharged – no less than, when it appeared on the scene of undeterrable progress and capitalist accumulation, the second law of thermodynamics itself.

CERTIFYING CHARACTER

Let us rehearse these issues – and the relation between the ethos of surface and the ethos of suspicion – by shifting back to the theater of a generation ago. Wanting to see it on the surface, no cover up, was the aesthetic counterpart of political demystification. If there had been, in the course of modernist painting, a critique of perspective that pushed reality up front, fastening image to the picture plane, there had been in the theater a similar move, linking falsifying perspective to the naturalistic techniques of objectivity, as the culpable resources of an illusory truth.

There is always a kind of evasion about those who claim to objectify reality by putting things in perspective, like the demoralized *raisonneurs* of Pirandello's plays. As Brecht advised us with an alienated eye, take things out of perspective, and look again, restoring them to history. Nor did he much like actors who were receding into the unconscious. In our theater there was a similar attitude about the psychology of behavior when – in the jargon of authenticity left over from the sixties – we preferred people who were "up front" and "all there," although in the bodily presence of the theater that is something of a problem, as it is not with stretched canvas and acrylic paint. We have all seen the actor who is, so far as we can tell, all there and up front too, though he may not be very much. Or there may be more than appears on stage, but he has no idea as to why he's there. Or he insists he knows why – like the actors who are playing the characters who are searching for the Author – though we may continue to have our doubts, which makes the actor nervous, so he overacts, believing the compensation – and that would have been very irritating to Brecht, who'd have thought it too much there, and not in history. And, meanwhile, psychologically, s/he keeps receding, even with the gender shift.

The issue became particularly troublesome in those years when some of us directing in the theater, prompted by a tendency toward deconstruction running from Pirandello to Brecht, began to subvert, discard, or renovate the dramatic text, displacing the anchoring support of character in favor of the prerogatives or the self-validating presence of the "unmediated actor." It was something more than Brecht intended, but it was the doubleness he encouraged in the historicizing process which reminded us that character, as we see it in the classics, is a victimizing mechanism, serving the gods, the plot, the author, and therefore inhibiting to an alteration of reality. What degraded the actor was an unthinking acceptance of character in the authorized or unexamined text. If you couldn't believe what the character said – or preferred that s/he didn't say it – you either had to take a stand against it or, rather than violate your own convictions, get out from under the text. It was only the actor who had nothing to say, or was afraid to say it, who would – pretending to a "personal truth" imposed by a duplicitous convention – retreat into the psychology of character.

It was a psychology distributed through the infrastructure of power. As theatrical fact the entire reproductive apparatus was ideologically suspect. What we wanted on the surface was a liberated figure, self-creating, without the fraudulent disguise of a familiar role in the repertoire of marketable fantasies. These fantasies were, as we've since heard from theory, derived with predictable emotions from the old oedipal narrative, as perversely as the character of Hedda Gabler from her father's pistols. I do not want to be Hedda Gabler, but Judith Malina, said Judith Malina playing Hedda Gabler. She would not, however, *be* the role but *show* us its illusions, what

Hedda Gabler *is* or, given Judith Malina's strong convictions, *should* be – providing the theater with a model of signifying practice by stripping the mechanism of character as the real story is told. But that's easier said than done. The old plot is in the deep structure and, like atomic waste, not easily disposed of. Repeated dismantlings of the mechanism are required, and even then . . . the dismantlings continue after the (Reichian) character armor is off. Thus, when he was still with the Performance Group, we saw the actor Spalding Gray, in a dismantled version of Brecht's *Mother Courage*, going in and out of the character of Swiss Cheese, who has next to no identity, and then insisting he's his own man, "Original," as the rock star Hoss in Sam Shepard's *The Tooth of Crime*, yet finding it hard to shake off the Image, the pictures, the entire repertoire of fantasy, not only of the character but of the actor, the empty outside of a desperately performing self, which leads to the real Spalding Gray as the original Spalding Gray in *Sakonnet Point*, his own confessional drama (about the suicide of his mother, his actual mother), which led to his current mode of diaristic performance. (Later in this chapter I shall say more about the modulation of the idea of acting in Gray's evolution as a performer.) Putting aside the technological recycling spoken of before, we have here the semblance of another problem:

Actually, the picture plane doubly flattened with paint was always trickier than meets the eye, partially because of the eye meeting the picture plane. So, too, the unmediated actor, thoroughly exposed, is an immediately recessive surface, there and not-there, through personal frailty, forgetfulness, moorlessness, stage fright or – in the most presumptive bravado of fully confessed exposure – the delinquency of a presence that is always passing out of sight. That occurs not only in the eye of the beholder but in the Freudian unconscious, which no method can keep in its place, accessible, or throw out of the theater entirely – though some methods tried hard. In his Ontological-Hysteric Theater, Richard Foreman had, for instance, the actress Kate Mannheim playing a figure named Rhoda in a series of plays, not as a character with whom you can identify, or critically divided as in Brecht, but as an atomized unit in the projected activities of the author's reflected body, warding off emotional involvement in a relational structure of performing energies. The real flesh-and-blood Rhoda is the author's memory, a mere echo of his consciousness, through the real flesh-and-blood actress, who is merely an echo of herself. She is scripted in an entirely different way, as a register of serial excitations, not the emotive arc of her own desires. It is a kind of phenomenological self-effacement that – even for actresses aware of the delusive ego-gratifications of the old character – might make them want to play Hedda Gabler again, with her own aggressive purposes matching the actress' own. But even the relatively non-existent Rhoda is an accretion of behavior(s) and, if not a character, something *other than* Kate Mannheim, about whose displaced gratifications one may think, as she nevertheless became identified, through time and repetition, with whatever it is that *is*, in Mannheim's absence, metabolically there.

The extremity of the experiments that broke down character into serial roles or molecular behavior or a medley of tasks or a set of variable functions within a structure brought the issue of character back into focus through what was actually a critique of the art of acting. It is a critique that may have been initiated by Hamlet, but was certainly exacerbated by Pirandello, always subsiding into conventional dramaturgy before it started up again, as it did in the sixties, out of political motives. When it started we were asking very elemental questions of the actor, so self-evident they were unbalancing. Like: *what are you doing here? and what do you want?* Within the purview of the Stanislavski Superobjective, the actor used to ask such questions, not of him/herself, however, but of the character. Now we're likely to say, never mind the character, what about *you?* (In the various kinds of participatory theater, the same questions were more or less asked of the audience.) Or, like the earlier Foreman, we may not care what the actor wants, thinking of her or him as an impersonal object among things, in order to minimize the claims of the unconscious with the claims of character.

In this perspective, acting is not what it presumably was in realistic theater, case history, but an agency of a structural rhythm, ideogrammatic, disjunct, whether improvised or intensely scored, as in the Laboratory Theater of Grotowski or in my own work with the KRAKEN group. As I've already implied, it was much easier to tell untrained actors who had never played anything of consequence before (like Kate Mannheim) to go easy on the ego with its false continuities than it was to tell those who had already become professional in the powerlust of the great roles: a Clytemnestra or a Coriolanus, with their notions of Destiny, or the accomplished narcissism of a Blanche DuBois, preserving herself as a subject by the allure of lies. Even a Willie Loman might balk at being no more than an object. But whatever you ask of the actors, even if you just ask them to stand around and wait, like the tramps in Beckett's play, there are always issues of identity at stake. To ask an actress, say, to be more or less feminine as Lady Macbeth as she speaks about being unsexed is to make a stipulation about presence that is probably more demanding, or at least confusing, than asking her to play at sleepwalking with her eyes open and sense shut, rubbing out the damned spot. In our experiments we also ran the gamut of more-or-less acting, after a generation of less is more, an orthodoxy in which the actor was, while resisting indication, considered best when she played herself. As the concept of the self was itself confounded by history – disappearing into the shifting subject of language – we were left with something like dispossessed performance, in which our standards of credibility also shifted.

167

WHAT BLOODY MAN IS THAT? (A BEGUILING THOUGHT)

In due time we confirmed about acting what we always really knew: that if it's impossible to keep oneself out of a role, even when there is no role, it is harder to be oneself on stage, and probably more artificial, than to be a character – which is what the most liberated figure of the self quickly became, though it might be a character with the actor's name. (I am not talking here of the movies where, among the stars, it was the same invariant actor with a character's name.) That doesn't mean, however, that character was therefore absolved of the ideological charges made against it, and could be restored to the stage just as it was, as if nothing had ever happened. I should say too, before going any further, that in the ordinary theater none of this is very much of an issue at all – no more than narrative is a problem in the ordinary novel – and we continue to see the old reliable character played imperturbably in the old reliable way through the same unreconstructed plot.

"What bloody man is that?" It's as if the question asked in the fouled air of the opening of *Macbeth* has left the issue entirely open in the troubled state of our theater – to self-conception, perception, time, and thought. The important thing was to understand through all the hurlyburly about deconstruction, "of the revolt/The newest state" (*Mac.* 1.2.1–3), and the powers of theatrical framing, the affective force of artifice itself. What we are playing with now are the nuances of a beleaguered convention, even when – as in the characterization of time on stage, or the temporal dimension of character, or the relations of time, character, and the language of the self – one convention bleeds abstractly into another.

What some of us learned from the disruptive speculations on the idea of character, and the (seeming) breakdown of the convention, is that the actor's presence is in-and-of-itself a beguiling *thought*, with a multitude of possible articulations or *degrees* of presence, a virtual scale of value in a valuing structure. In the depreciation of character we have discovered the discriminating powers of performance, *as* thought, with character at one end of a Moebius spectrum of possibility that, however, recedes into the history of the convention as it does into the psyche of the actor. Everything asked of the actor by performance is in some degree mediated, the shading of a convention – which is the *idea* of acting itself, hardly a natural occupation for a *person* who has been taught, in the apparent truth of an interiorizing craft, to think of the self as undisguised. That truth is now subject, of course, to the proposition that there may be no self without a disguise. So: character actor person self. These are but declensions of the name for the unformulable act, the act of interpretation, not of character but of the play of thought, which is doubled over in performance by affinities and projections of thought, the indeterminable subject, persona mask double and the double's shadow – haunted by the faulty memory of an unforgettable act.

If there was reason to distrust the duplicity of character, there is something even more perverse about the notion of the (dis)appearance of the self in this pure unmediated act. Some of us worked terribly hard to achieve something like that (e.g., the Living Theater), but none of us has ever really seen it – in or out of the theater. What we have seen, however, in the theater is the reimagining of performance through the permutations of character actor person and self, the combinatorial possibilities of the fictions, playing the nuances of behavior off against each other; as with the permutations of gender or race, so with the construct or construction of a self, the actor acting in his or her own name, reaching for character or alluding to it, letting it drop provisionally or artificially putting it on, sometimes moving through a solipsistic withdrawal, or in the sediments of appearance leaving scarcely a sign – in a further refinement of the act of perception, with a subtler interplay of the watching and the watched, eliciting here another fiction, its unaccountable character, the semblance of an *audience*, summoned up.

AUTHENTICITY AND ACCOMPLISHMENT: MORE WOMAN THAN WOMAN

Something there is that wants to appear. With all the critique of a recessive presence, the traces of that struggle are still there, and with it the telltale signs of an ineliminable sense of depth that, however rescored as surface, comes from the refractory presence of the actual body in performance. The body may have been assigned the role of a function or carrier of signs, but there is something restive about it, unsurpassed, as in the transformations of hegemony itself – not a social logic, however, but the logic of an unquenchable longing to *be* there in its unmediated presence: authentic. To show how refractory it is the same may also be true, across ideology and on other aesthetic grounds, when it is assigned the function of a character, where the authenticity of the acting is the authenticity of the role is the authenticity of the person, who is when all is said and done merely an avatar of the authentic body. And that's true not only of realistic acting but, as I learned some years ago in an exchange of techniques with one of Japan's greatest actors, a National Treasure, it is also true of a Japanese Noh performer who happens to be a Shinto priest who in fact believes, as this actor did, that the role he plays cannot be truly performed without being, authentically, a Shinto priest.

The word Noh does not quite mean authentic, but rather an *accomplishment*, a fruition, the untarnished perfection of a form, which would seem to depend, however, on an authenticity in the performer that is, in its embodied consummation, almost absolute. The Kabuki theater is not quite

169

so pristine as the Noh, having developed through the seventeenth century as the preferred form of an urbanized middle class, which contributed to the incomes of the actors – there were women at the time – by enjoying some prostitution on the side. This is what caused the Tokugawa shogunate to prohibit women from appearing on the stage, a banishment that persists in the Kabuki to this day. What is apparent in their absence, however, is that the idea of accomplishment taken over from the Noh has become, in one performer at least, no less authentic or absolute. "He is more a real woman on stage than a real woman can be. He creates a woman, he does not imitate."[8] That is the Polish filmmaker Andrzej Wajda speaking of Tomasaburo Bando V, the superstar *onnegata* (a male performer who does women's roles), whom Wajda directed several years ago in a little theater in Tokyo as the tragic heroine Nastasya *and* her epileptic lover Prince Myshkin, in a version of Dostoyevsky's *The Idiot*. As he was inexperienced in playing male characters, never having done one before, Tomasaburo apparently found Prince Myshkin the more demanding role: "It is easier to play a character much different from myself," he said, "such as a woman" – an observation perhaps troubling to the politics of difference, though even women concede in Japan that he does it supremely; as Wajda said, more woman than woman.

One might assume that the transformation is made possible primarily by the ritual conventions of the Kabuki theater, which like the hieratic Noh passes on family names, roles, and practices from generation to generation. Yet when Tomasaburo, who was not born into a Kabuki family, was adopted by the famous actor Kanya Morita XIV and his wife, a dancer of traditional forms, he was given intensive training in the gestural repertoire of the Kabuki, its vocalizing and music, and the intricacies of makeup and costume. All of this seems intensely, ornately artificial; yet as Kanya groomed the male heir – starting when the child was 6 – to become his own leading lady, the regimen of training and behavior in family life were kept inseparable, for the sake of authenticity. The canons of Kabuki, formulated in the eighteenth century, require that an apprentice *onnegata* must live his everyday life as a woman in order to act with unimpeachable naturalness on the stage. The form is abstract, the effect real, and if certified thus as realer than real, authentically so in the deportment of the body. In another culture, at another time, this might have been thought of as building (a) character.

THE ILLUSION OF DEPTH AND THE BURDEN OF PATHOS

While the aspiration to the authentic is, across cultural difference, almost unavoidable in acting, it has not had a very good press in critical theory. When I pointed earlier, however, to the seeming concurrence of critical theorists and network politicians on the dubious value of authenticity, or its illusory status, I was not saying, of course, that across the full field of the historical the motives of one are the same as the other. That would be somewhat like Greenblatt's treatment of empathy, which can indeed be converted to self-serving or nefarious ends, an arousal of affect by the appearance of authenticity, whose most cynical figuration is that of Iago (in whom at times, if the truth were known, I hear my own voice: don't we all?). One may be cynical about being authentic, another may be authentic in refusing to believe s/he can be. Or since the difference does not sustain itself in a flat field, I suppose in theory we'd better examine again our relation to *depth*, which is almost ontologically second nature in performance, even when we try to extrude, mask, design away, or technologically displace the human figure, whose outside danger is always *pathos*, whether or not blamed on the illusion of depth.

So far as the substance of theater is concerned, which may be thought of as the shadow of performance (a shadow's shadow?), all its ideological battles have to do with soliciting or minimizing that danger, which may be, still, the greatest illusion of all. This seems to be the conclusion, after years of demystifying practice, of one of the more versatile directors of our time, Giorgio Strehler, who has since the brilliant staging of *The Tempest* put that illusion as a matter of consciousness in the unmoored center of the stage. The series of productions, including Corneille's *The Comic Illusion* and Eduardo de Filippo's *The Great Magician*, has become for Strehler something of a last will and testament to the illusory power of theater or its power *as illusion*. If that represents to a still-faithful Brechtian something of an ideological danger as well, it is a conceptual risk not likely to be very exorbitant in American productions of *The Comic Illusion*, a play that would hardly be known if it weren't for Strehler's prestige, and the quick currency today of any international success.

Surprisingly, then, Tony Kushner's adaptation for Mark Lamos' production at the Hartford Stage Company does have an attitude toward the play's history, excising as it does Corneille's final tribute, shared by Strehler, to the power of illusion itself as constituting the value of theater. In that sense, it is a darker if not more cynical version of the play, and the institution of theater, which fails the intelligence of this production in not offering (in the United States, at least) any dialectical context for the bleaker emotion at the end. To the degree that the play *is* known, and taken seriously through the "caprice" (what Corneille called it), we are back again at the impasse that haunted Pirandello, about the reality of appearance and the appearance of reality, and the anguished circle of its ceaseless pain. That's what Strehler returns to through the egregious charm of the comic illusion – the pain so unbearable its laughter is maniac – at the end of the staging of *The Great Magician*, where to all appearances there is no relief, only the pathos, which some postmodern forms thought they could muffle by parody or, as if grief were noise, filter out. Or, as in the mixed media events by the young director John Jesurun, who seems influenced by Pirandello but grew up with television ("I know a little more than a little," says one of his switchover figures, "but not much else"), the unbearably strong emotions are, like the tortuous old drama itself, dissipated in verbal play and visual translations, siphoned from stage to screen or, in an array of video monitors, imaged out.

What do we do with the pathos? Mediate it more or less. Since its earliest annunciations of unassuageable pain, that's what the theater has always been about, though the representations of pain may have been over the years more or less mercifully, or more or less cruelly, sublimated. Even cruelty is sublimation, as Artaud painfully understood, because the rupture out of which the theater came – "already *disposed* and *divided*," and with more or less struggle against it, *disposed to its division* (*T&D* 50) – can't be represented. Which only increases the pathos, though that has been over the years deflected, diluted, variously disguised.

It was, indeed, as if this issue were being addressed in a return to the drama of ancient Greece by the Théâtre du Soleil, with an openly affective content unusual today in most sophisticated forms of theater, whose alienating devices are likely to be reflexively at work. This would seem especially true of a theater born from the politics of May 1968 under the sign of Brecht and, in recent years, drawing freely upon a wide range of distancing techniques from the multicultural apparatus of a postmodern world. (The devices of Indian, Japanese, Malaysian, or African theater – once so unknown, inaccessible, or seemingly arcane – are now seen everywhere, and though the Théâtre du Soleil does things on an informed and formidable scale at the Cartoucherie in a suburb of Paris, one wonders even there whether the current uses of oriental techniques aren't, if not orientalist, part of the same repertoire of surfaces as postmodern pastiche. But putting that aside:) As part of its program for the recent work on the House of Atreus (*Les Atrides*), there was a glossary of terms both misleading and foundational ("Mots Trompeurs et Fondateurs") to an understanding of the Greek theater. Under "Pathos," there is an entry from Littré, defining it as a term of rhetoric, concerned with a certain emotional movement, or appropriate figures that strongly touch the soul of the auditors. There is another entry from Bailly, who defines it, first, as what one feels or experiences (in the sense of a trial or being put to the proof) as opposed to what one does; and then, as all that which affects the body or soul, whether for good or bad, but above all bad – though it's still not entirely clear whether catharsis (which also has an entry in the program) makes up somehow for that.

As directed by Ariane Mnouchkine, the production takes on the burden of pathos by restoring the full-scale dramatization of what is only reported, in a powerful if asphyxiated image, in the marvellous choral ode that follows the awakening of The Watchman at the opening of the *Oresteia*.

What appears with the voice of the prophet Calchas out of the vast imaginings of this chorus, ranging with laser vision over a space of myth and history, is the sacrifice of Iphigeneia, which even at the establishment of the Areopagus is, if not entirely forgotten, never sufficiently redeemed. That issue – abstracted by the appearance of the Furies and receding into the political compromise worked out by Athena at the trial of Orestes – seems to be the emotional datum of the Théâtre du Soleil's conception of the Aeschylean trilogy, though the whole of it (announced on the program) was not being performed when I saw it, and Orestes never appeared, except (as a doll) in swaddling bands. What was being shown, rather, is the first play of the trilogy, the *Agamemnon*, preceded by Euripides' *Iphigeneia at Aulis*, that is, the better-known tragedy with its neglected but poignant preface. It's as if the pathos had to be wholly constituted, wholly remembered, before asking anything more about what, cathartically or otherwise, the whole etiological drama could conceivably mean.[9]

There are slight elements of satire, as in the whininess of Agamemnon, with black braids and whited face, defending the necessity of the sacrifice; but the drama is nevertheless deeply moving when Iphigeneia herself – so long unrepresented, it seems, even by Clytemnestra – finally appears. Yet even when the pathos is restored, in the barely pubescent, imploringly vibrant figure of Iphigeneia (performed by Nirupama Nityanandan, who also dances with a baffled delicacy her terror and assent), it seems only to be a sign of a greater pathos behind, whose memory is so mediated it can hardly be recalled. When we come to the *Agamemnon*, we hear once more of the feast of Thyestes, though it seems – as we may gather, too, from the great mantic ode that speaks of Iphigeneia – to be only another horrific figure of the originary division (a virtual rape of nature?) to which the theater in its inception seemed already disposed: what Artaud saw clairvoyantly, like another Cassandra.

MEDIATION AND NEGATION: THE DISSOCIATED EYE

There are times when it seems, as in the tremendous expanse of receding images in the timewarp of the *Oresteia*, that the necessity of tragedy is not so much, as figured, in the operations of fate, its predictable dramaturgy, but in the silent blessing of its condition of amnesia. Which is to say that at some protective level of unfathomable remembrance – division contained, forgotten, vaguely recalled (*why should we remember? and how could we forget?*), as indelibly as a dream blurring in daylight – the necessity of the drama is the necessity of mediation. As for mediation itself it is not, as sometimes thought, inevitably evasive or negative, and never was, for how would we know of the division except for the mediation that permits us to bear it.

Which was hardly enough for Artaud, who could not himself bear the proxy and substitution that was inescapably a *negation*. Few of us are prepared for the primal energies or intensities that Artaud sought, with no mediation at all, but we recoil at mediation when it confounds our capacity to *feel* or to believe that what we are experiencing is anything like a real experience, but rather the experience of the mediation itself. As we shift, however, the planes of consciousness from the ancient world to the postmodern, from the primal to the electronic scene, there is a liability in speaking for what others will feel, particularly when there's a generational difference at stake. It's a long distance, of course, from Iphigeneia at Aulis to Jesurun in Soho, where it may be taken for granted – as with the precipitant figures shuttling from stage to screen – that there is no other experience but mediation. Or that may be, in the *paideia* of the postmodern, the preferred experience, which with the more or less reflexive mimicry of transgression has the requisite look of life as a dream. As with Madonna's autoportraits on MTV, the resemblance is rather arbitrary. If not as remunerative, there is a similar arbitrariness in Jesurun's *Deep Sleep* or *White Water*, though he seems intelligent enough to realize that there is a significant difference between a traumatic specularity that produces the unconscious and a commodified spectacle that reproduces itself. He is also young enough to be touched, in the occasional abatement of programmed effects, by experience that can't be displaced, filmically, into the dismissable facsimile of a dream.

That returns us, I suppose – perhaps as a generational piety – to the resistance to mediation when, as facsimile or proxy, it seems to divest us of anything like a real experience. (The resistance is important, I think, even when we find ourselves theorizing – since the restoration of structuralism on the critical scene – the questionable claims of experience by the phenomenological subject. But back to that in a moment.) The problem with the proxy – what Artaud detested; in Derridean terms: surrogate or supplement – is that it inevitably *absents* us or leaves us *in absentia*, not as observant bodies, but rather in subservience of the other senses to the dissociated Eye, with the body then reduced to a mere spectatorial presence. It's as if the Eye and the spectator – as distantiated agencies of the actual body of desire – check out what has lapsed or defaulted in identity, as if they were mere conventions by means of which we ascertain what's missing in the self, which should have known it was a fiction in the first place. This, of course, cannot be said of Madonna, who seems to have known it from birth, and is therefore constructed (by whom?) as a facsimile of a self, which seems especially captivating to those who haven't thought much, or couldn't care less, about the commodification of the self (having the right attitudes about sex, AIDS, censorship makes up for that), or the quality of the fiction dispersed into the spectacle.

This is by no means true of Robert Wilson, who was also remarkably thoughtful in a specific case of (apparently) lapsed or defaulted identity: that of Christopher Knowles. In this case, it was the normalization of the fiction, or its vain appearance in previous therapies, that Wilson put off, or bracketed – including the idea of its being a case. What had been seen as painfully estranging was, in an aesthetic context, magically transformed. The autism was treated not as an impediment but as a sort of invitation, around which the other performers might articulate themselves, as if the disabled figure were the genius of the performance, its structural rhythm or genetic code. While Christopher Knowles might have been used as a confirming agency of the repetitive patterns already engrailed in Wilson's theater (some said at the time that he was merely used) his acceptance as a virtual incarnation of the principle of repetition apparently made for him a life in art. That should be justification enough for any artistic practice, but it provides another complication to our theme.

THE PURE PHENOMENON

There is a sense in which Christopher Knowles, as the determining element of a Wilson composition, was not a historical or phenomenological subject. He was, rather, what both Artaud and Brecht were aware of in quite different ways: Artaud, by remembering himself Plato's remembrance of the Orphic mysteries (*T&D* 52); Brecht, in the atomized energies of the industrial world, where "the continuity of the ego is a myth" and man himself no more than an atom that "perpetually breaks up and forms anew" (*Brecht* 15). It could be said that these two notions come together in Wilson's *Einstein on the Beach*, but what appears in either case – as if before history or in the throes of history – is the streaming sonorous presence of the thing itself, a field of force or *pure phenomenon* (*Brecht* 30), to be witnessed perhaps, or registered, but neither empathized with (certainly not to be pitied) nor (for Artaud) interpreted.

By *whom*, if there were such an inclination? and within the illusion of a felt humanity in what register of emotion? As the observer watched the revolving figure that structured *A Letter to Queen Victoria*, it was hard to tell what the emotion was, or whether there was anything in the "performer" that corresponded to emotions as we normally confront them on stage, and, despite the whirling reference to Sufism, even in the stylized performances of other cultures. With crisscrossing satellites and a worldwide network of innumerable festivals, it's hard to tell how culturally specific those emotions are anymore, or whether the remotest of them are now as available in the marketplace of signs as the exchangeable surplus of transportable techniques.[10] If that whirling figure is nevertheless, even as a pure phenomenon, an extraordinary instance of a life in art, there has been through the history of the theater, again and again, the desire to return art to life, as in the work of Stanislavski himself, who used the other phrase, however, as the title of his autobiography.

What is meant by that return is itself a historical problem of a tautological kind. We may think immediately of Chekov. If that example is more complicated, however, than Stanislavski's naturalism made it appear, or *less*, since Chekov himself apparently thought there was too much naturalism, it may still serve as a referent for the vicissitudes of emotion in the give-and-take dynamics of art and life. Of course, we are mostly conscious of that dynamics in the domain still thought of as *art*, particularly when we think of life as distinguished from what it is *not*. To the point of periodic declarations of the death of art, the following is a mnemonic abbreviation of a repeated historical pattern: *more life, less art; more art, less life*. With more or less drama and passion, force of collision, degrees of heat.[11]

HYSTERICA PASSIO

Unexpectedly enough, these have become the issues for Wilson as he came eventually to Chekov through his engagement with classical texts. His recent production in Munich of Chekov's one-act play *Swan Song*, with its aging actor (that is, the *character*) playing Lear, was a sort of preface to his confrontation in Frankfurt with the overwhelming magnitudes of the thing itself. Lear is the theater's maximum challenge, perhaps, not only in the perils of pathos, but in distinguishing the pathos from its passion and, wracked upon the wheel of fire, the passion from its pretense. With a kind of poetic justice, one of the theater's greatest roles presents what is, in theory and performance, the greatest of acting problems. While Diderot remains the classical text on this issue, Meyerhold took it, in his citation of Oscar Wilde, to another pitch of emotion, about which he seemed to have at the time an absolute conviction, though I'm restating it as a question: if you can mimic a passion you do not feel, what do you do when it burns you like a fire?

You *don't*, even if you feel it, according to Wilson, one of the postmodern exemplars of a non-mimetic art. None of this is to say that Wilson is wrong in what remains a formalist approach to acting, or to any other aspect or mode of performance. In recent years, formalist detachment has been the target of much critical abuse, to which there are, however, certain honored exceptions, particularly when there's passion that burns like a fire. Despite Trotsky's irony over the furious idealism of his experiments, Meyerhold is one of these, and Eisenstein; and with an elegiac modulation, Beckett in our time; and even in her nineties, Martha Graham. According to Christine Dakin, Graham never wavered in her belief "that you should be able to write your shopping list while dancing a role," and yet "be ravaged by it." At the same time wanting the audience to be ravaged too. Or to find itself feeling guilty. Or even, with emotions so deeply experienced they might have come from classical drama, "to feel pity and horror." Dakin was actually speaking of her own performance as the

Chosen Victim in Graham's *Rite of Spring*, to which she brought memories of her fellow dancers who had died of AIDS.[12]

How much emotion should be allowed to surface, more or less inflamed, may be provisionally suggested by a self-reflexive moment in the hyperrealistic cultural critique of the itinerant theater Squat. What I am referring to occurred in a theater piece completed after Squat lost its storefront theater (next to the Chelsea Hotel in New York), where an onstage fire used to be the emblematic signature of the group. An earlier work was entitled *Pig, Child, Fire!*, and *Mr. Dead and Mrs. Free* concludes with a woman rejected by her lover stabbing her vagina with a fiery shish kebab. The images may be grotesque, wild, campy, or bizarre, but there is a quite traditional feeling for form within the aesthetics of the classical avant-garde, and for all the outrageousness of the effects a sophisticated ethos of emotional distance. This can take, however, a bewildering turn. In a recent piece, *"L" Train to Eldorado*, which moves on stage and in film through decoy sequences of aroused empathy, the spectators come to realize not only that the characters are caricatures – effects of Eva Buchmuller's extraordinary *trompe-l'oeil* – but that they have also been, emotionally, suckered in. There is something more, however, than a distancing formalism or Alienation-effect in the scene where the Director has his film crew fan the flames as a visual correlative of aroused passion, and then suddenly stops them, leaving the burning in abeyance: "Never mind," he says, "smoke is enough."

But even smoke is suspect in Wilson, although part of the problem in *King Lear*, as we shall see, is that where there's smoke you may want some fire. In another recent, but earlier, approach to a classical text, the *Alcestis*, Wilson seemed to work with greater certitude, as if the presence of the Chorus and the severance of roles gave greater purchase to his imagistic techniques, as in the eloquently vivid passage where, with several Alcestis figures on stage, there is a collage of competing feelings about what she is constrained to do for her husband, as if the structural emotion of the Euripidean text were so distressed it required separate expressions. "Someone is touching me," one of the figures cries, "and I am afraid." There is the fluttering movement of a white curtain as fragile as the last and plaintive thought of life itself, as another Alcestis exclaims that she feels herself drawn to death.

Wilson uses in this sequence techniques that seem derived from the Japanese Noh or the Bunraku, along with the parsed out scenography that, whether scored or subject to chance, operates in our own tradition from Brecht to Cunningham to postmodern dance and performance: lights, music, rhythm, motion, all on their own distinctive tracks. This may be, in fact, a formalism without its metabolism, or what in critique is usually attributed to it: a quasi-organic ensemble of effects aspiring to aesthetic harmony, including the balancing act of structure, or convenient duplicity of paradox, that "resolves" ideological contradictions. If Wilson remains indifferent to ideology, contradictory or otherwise, his operatic structures are often described in terms of the Wagnerian *Gesamtkunstwerk*. If scale works wonders the radical differences are crossed, but there is a sequence in the *Alcestis* that is, if not a transfiguring crescendo of Wagnerian unity, something like its supremely poignant inversion, as the white curtain moves in silence and, aloft on the Delphic mount, a great boulder tilts and falls with all the mammoth silence of death. (The only thing I've seen of similar affect, not with the boulder but a similar curtain – moving silently through the sublimity of Racine – was in Klaus Michael Grüber's unorthodox staging of *Bérénice* at the Comédie-Française.) But so far as this production portended anything for *King Lear*, it was perhaps in the rather bungling caricature of a plexi-glassed Admetus, replete with intravenous tubes, so that it was hard to tell whether the father was simply being parodied, as he argues for a life that has already been too prolonged by medical technology, or whether he can be taken seriously at all in his own plain-tively self-justifying, aging fear of death.

Obviously, even the best of directors can be uneven in a series of ambitious productions, but with the approach to *King Lear* the ideological basis of the practice is more than subject to doubt. At the same time, the claims of an alternative practice are, in the hegemony of the postmodern, subject to review, each form theoretically having its own generic powers. As he has done with Heiner Müller, Wilson said of his approach to *King Lear* that his staging is intended to keep interpretation from getting in the way. As if he were stating it as an objective infinitive in Stanislavski's terms, the aim is simply "to make the text available," but without the sort of emotional interference that comes, with whatever stylization, from the naturalistic tradition. Yet this is easier said than done, even by so resourceful a theatrician as Wilson, since *King Lear* is a drama in which, whatever you do, it is as hard to suppress the solicitations of sympathetic emotion as for Lear himself to keep that mothering force, the "*hysterica passio*," down (2.3.57). Whatever it may be for the character, is it not the actor's passion? whose excess may destroy a character, but without which there'd be no character, and not much of a performance either, which is surely the case with Lear, who having been told that he was everything has aged into excess itself.

It is Lear, as we recall, who virtually inaugurates the text as a command performance that leads, disastrously, to something like an anti-Lear. But however you read the character, even as a semblance or shadow of itself (or on the great stage of fools, a shadow's shadow) there is going to be trouble with the *hysterica passio*, whether it's there or whether it's not, and it was barely there in Wilson's staging, though he had a matriarchal figure of the German theater, Marianne Hoppe (the wife of Gustav Gründgens), playing Lear. (I am not speaking here of the absence which is *there*, as in the execution of a Brechtian *gestus*, which by arresting a delinquency suggests what should have been done.) What I'm saying has nothing to do with ordinary reverence for the text, or some predisposition to the characterization of Lear, some more or less conventional notion of how he ought to be played. It's possible to imagine an even more radical production in which the text is made available (I hesitate to say explored, because of Wilson's resistance to interpretation) without any recourse to the convention of character at all, as Wilson has done with other materials. But so long as there was the semblance, there was a demoralization of affect or the sort of affectless imagism that, however masterful it may have been before, was simply unmastered by the language of the text, whose emotional power is such that, even if minimally spoken, the *drama* is still there, struggling to appear, like that "climbing sorrow [whose] element's below" (2.3.57–8) – what Wilson's earlier work had been able to do without.

This in turn affected the nature and requirements of the performance, in which the actors seemed confused. The double bind was that (outside the announcement of a plain uninflected reading, but why then in the theater?) there had to be sufficient acting, or *enough* acting (that is, mimesis) to verify the presence of the drama. But then we're dealing with a drama in which enough is never sufficient, as Lear's infinitely resonating nevers definitively suggest. The production might have moved in other directions, transposing, disrupting, decimating, or even abandoning the text, but once we were reminded, through the spoken words, of the potential capacities of the play, its expected dimensions were such that no irruption of spectacle, however momentarily imaginative, could overcome the fact that the enactment was rather feeble. Given the dimensions of its conception, that may be a liability of *King Lear* however you stage it, but to begin with, theatrically, a certain tribute has to be paid, against any aesthetic resistance, to the upped ante of its emotional demands. If not psychological realism, some ample and credible surrogate. I am not saying that it had to be realistic, but in the world as we know it now the connection is hard to sever, even in a departure with the symbolism of Kurasawa's *Ran*.

As I've already suggested, one might for any number of reasons move from Shakespeare's text to an altogether different work that is nevertheless derived from it. Unless they are thoroughly wiped out, however, none of the questions of ambition, family, authority, justice, sexuality and power, the barbarities of *Realpolitik*, or the intense inanity of the universe itself, are altogether separable from the psychological study of the nature of Lear's madness, which seems to confound interpretation with the concept of nature itself. As for our psychological concepts, the madness seems to escape them as Lear does the Gentleman and French soldiers who, sent to find him by Cordelia, approach him with the wrong therapy, indulging his delusions and trying to humor him on the heath. "Come, and you get

179

it, you shall get it by running. Sa, sa, sa, sa" (4.6.202–3). It may be that something like schizoanalysis, with its affinities for perversity, comes closer to the mark, but all of the symptoms are to be discerned, smelling of mortality, virtually taunting our apprehension in the available text. "Dost thou squiny at me?" What Lear says to Gloucester, with his "case of eyes," is like a devastating summary of the challenge of the text. "Read thou this challenge, mark but the penning of it" (4.6.136–44). But how do we mark it? "I see it feelingly," says Gloucester (4.6.149), when Lear describes the world as if Iago had been recorded through lesions in the brain. We have become very sophisticated about the perils of interpretation, and certainly so at the level of feeling, but given the penning of this text that may be, still, the only way to see it at all. And that includes the matter of aging that Wilson said was his major concern, though it's hard to say from the absence of affect what to think of it at all.

With equal moments of brilliance in the staging, there was far more emotional intensity in a recent production of *King Lear* by Tadashi Suzuki. Much of it, true, was also gratuitous, and grotesque to the point of parody, less derived from the atrocities of the play than, it seemed, the manneristic excesses of Japanese films. That may suggest only the short fertile life of any mode of behavior in the international traffic of images, which makes what was once strangely ceremonial or potentially estranging – that is, alien in the Brechtian sense – seem like the merest cliché. Even if I was missing something it was hardly nuanced or subtle. Here was a case, then, where large-scale capacities for emotion were far from adequate to the full range of issues in the drama, from its multiple views of nature to the great image of authority in the mordant equities of the storm. Or, in the collapse of any concept of the human, the deranged emergence of the thing itself. Yet there were, in this production, certain promising elements: a far more abstract and prismatic, consciously disintegrated treatment of the text, and a more complexly imaged approach to the dramatis personae. Men with beards were playing women and, in the demented frenzy of an atomized power, Lear was to begin with either a shattered codex of mere quotation or a mutilated figure of speech, and not, as with Marianne Hoppe, a single actor whose body suggested, for all the surrounding fracture of image, some beckoning measure of psychological coherence.

The inadequacy of Wilson's production was not so much that a woman was in the role of Lear, for she brought to it years of experience and her own almost mythic status in the German theater. Yet in being dutiful to the director's requirements for making the text available, hers was neither a particularly gendered performance (like Ruth Maleczech's in Lee Breuer's production, crude in other respects, with a *Mad* comics version of Faulkner, and a family like the Snopes) nor in any way amply responsive to the political dimensions of Lear's aging, no less the myriad views of the miserable king, "as full of grief as age, wretched in both" (2.4.273), about whom it could be said at the end: "Vex not his ghost. O let him pass, he hates him/That would upon the rack of this tough world/Stretch him out longer" (5.3.314–16).

There were, to be sure, extraordinary images through the production, but by Wilson's own standards unevenly so. There was at the opening a minimalist white inscription of a lightning bolt on the black field of the stage floor that seemed in one hard-edged elliptical stroke to bring the illimitable heavens down to a promising concept. It seemed a visual datum that might, indeed, bypass anything like the dramaturgical crescendo of emotion that would ordinarily mount with the *hysterica passio* into the cataracts and hurricanoes on the heath. But instead of being a provocative instance of conceptual art the storm when it came just about summed up, astonishingly, the conceptual problem. The astonishing thing was that in this great crux of staging – how to do the storm in *King Lear*? – Wilson's own vaunting imagination turned to high-fidelity cliché, and with no postmodern irony to be perceived. The storm was nothing but a very loud recording of a storm, neither a musical score nor a sound abstraction, but just such a storm as might have, in its prodigious mimesis, broken the speakers of another era. Without throwing light, or lightning, on the stupendous verbal image of the storm, it became a sign of what the actors couldn't conceivably live up to even if they were allowed to by the conception.

The theatrical fact is that any knowledge of the play, even through delinquent German, exceeds in expectation anything anybody can realize, no less when there is very little acting at all. Or, since the text couldn't do without any drama at all, the bombastic facsimile of it that some of the actors produced in older German fashion (not Marianne Hoppe, who was relatively subdued) when an image was not reining them in. The choral opening was a fine idea, silently resplendent, more powerful than the storm, a meditatively static ensemble out of which a feminine voice, not yet in the role of Lear, or identified with it, spoke some lines about aging, from the late poetry of William Carlos Williams. All the rest was, however, with some inflections of Wilson's visual wizardry – e.g., the impeccable birdlike cage that descended for the eye-gouging of Gloucester – simply insufficient.

THE THERAPEUTIC FUNCTION

"Insufficiency my heart doth sway," wrote Shakespeare in one of the sonnets, but that occurs through the teasing vulnerability of gradients of the gaze in the parlous regime of empathic emotions. More life? less art? Within that empathic regime, as it has come to possess the theater, it may be hard to distinguish when less is more, or whether at some limit of its therapeutic function we are still dealing with art at all. If Wilson's *King*

Lear, at least as I saw it, was a waste of considerable acting experience in a questionable aesthetic, there are times, in realistic acting, where the greater the experience of the performer the more it might seem like therapy. If there are certain performances that suffer through that, there are others that may be all the more impressive, particularly when we are astonished by what appear to be inadvertencies, things that merely surfaced, or were struggling to appear: emotions that might have been inaccessible, or a gesture we'd never have seen, "locked in the mind past all remonstrance."

A certain rigor is required to unlock it, which is not only an acting technique but also a poetics. The phrase is from the preface to *Paterson*, by William Carlos Williams, whom Wilson drew upon for the opening of *King Lear*. Not rigor alone, however, but "rigor of beauty is the quest" – an aim that Wilson might share. Despite his programmatic objectivism (and long ideological quarrel with T. S. Eliot), Williams sustains in the connotations of that re-*monstrance* a feeling for the sacramental in artistic practice, before he goes on, "To make a start/out of particulars/and make them general, rolling/up the sum, by defective means – "[13] Since much of our theater is still merely a grab-bag, and nothing within memory like a ritual tradition, there is a sense in which the means are always defective in American acting, and there may be, as a result, a failure of generalization in the private moment. But while I was somewhat critical earlier of the introspective legacy of American acting, its resistance to indication, only the ideologically naïve can really believe, in levelling judgments against that as a mere solipsistic vice of bourgeois realism, that acting anywhere is without the liabilities of a therapeutic function. There may be no concept of therapy, or it may be called something like meditation or healing, but we encounter it – with the foundational techniques of focus and concentration – in the spiritual disciplines of other cultures that are inseparable from the acting methods in their theatrical forms. As I said earlier, when we admire the results of these disciplines, it is often while ignoring the psychic and social costs, which is not quite what Brecht did when he appropriated the techniques of Chinese acting. The "accomplishment" of the Japanese Noh performer is not so generalized either, and remains arcane, since it was in its inception far from being a democratic or pluralistic form.

I have been concerned in these remarks with the possibility that, with experienced actors, the consummation of a performance may be inseparable from its therapeutic function, in that respect imbuing art with life, or restoring life with art. But let us turn from the prospect of an accomplishment back to the insufficiency: with very little experience whatever, in theater or in life, the inexperienced might perform, and might under given circumstances perform the better for their want of experience. If this is true of a certain (misguided?) naturalism where experience gets in the way, it was also true of the antinaturalism in which, out of games, tasks,

182

and transformations, very inadequate "actors" could seem to be quite experienced "performers," the two terms signifying at the time a considerable ideological difference about the functions of theater, and its relations to therapy, though eventually the better performers might want to become actors again, or something between the actor and the performer, like Spalding Gray, who makes much in his performances of being in and out of therapy, though the therapy seems to be as continuous and (in Freud's sense) interminable as the performance.

THE SAVED FIGURE

Some years ago Gray described his evolution as an actor as a movement away from the learned techniques of emotional memory. It was as if he'd been making a constant draft upon a stockpile of available emotions, so much so that it became "a kind of unspontaneous 'work.' "[14] That work could be, in a fine actor, a quite dignified and complicated labor, and the technique of searching one's own life to fill a role which seems objectively *out there* is still for the actor a challenge of rich dimensions, though it may also be in the art of acting a semantic option, or a manner of speaking about what is being enacted, or how it should be approached as the figurative limit of meaning itself. Putting stock feelings aside, Gray was experiencing in his career what I've talked about before: the shift of emphasis toward the desires of the actor rather than the privilege of the role as an authoritarian construct linked to the power of the author and other forms of (dubiously) objective value. Richard Schechner, with whom Gray worked then at the Performing Garage, would not speak of the character Hamlet but the series of actions named Hamlet that the performer would enact, on the assumption that acting in the old sense was somehow factitious, if not basically false.

The problem, however, was not only whether, as with Gray, the performer had the emotional resources perceived in the series of actions, but whether the series of actions could be accurately perceived. What happens in Hamlet? as the scholar J. Dover Wilson once asked, thinking he could discern it more or less, though he didn't quite have in mind anything so exorbitantly specific as what the actor must discern, that is, with its calculus of physical activity, the series of actions to be performed. Never mind what he's thinking or feeling, or the guesswork about meaning, but what exactly is Hamlet *doing*, moment by moment, when he speaks, say, "To be or not to be . . . "? (Sometimes the nature of this problem can be seen more precisely when it's not focused on Hamlet, nor even on a conspicuous minor role like the Gravedigger, but somebody like a spear carrier or miscellaneous courtier whose presence in the text is a vacancy usually filled, as in the duel scene, with stereotyped gasps and groans. The director will have an exasperated sense of the delicacy of the issue when the actor assigned to such a "walk on" turns out to be quite zealous, asking at every moment, as rehearsal time is running out, what am I doing now? Such productions are not likely to be done, however, within the egalitarian ethos that pretends it doesn't measure the size of a role, with equal time accorded to all.) In previous methodologies, the determination was made in respect to the text, as if the molecular code of performance were always precisely there. But as the priority was given to the performer over the questionable (or questioned) canonical text, Gray was able to speak of *using* the role of Swiss Cheese in *Mother Courage* not as Brecht may have wanted it, but as a referential structure for the expression of personal needs and obsessions, letting the audience integrate connections between the role and the text. In *Sakonnet Point*, part of his autobiographical trilogy, this led "to the desire to create an open narrative of personal actions" whose loose ends might be tied together by the audience. He wasn't sure this would happen, but the idea was to maintain "the same dialectic . . . dropping the text and allowing the mind of each audience member the chance to create its own text." This was Gray's variant of the idea of audience participation, but without the mission of collectivity from his days with the Performance Group.

In time the questions changed, and he began to ask was he acting all the time, "and was my acting in the theater the surface showing of that? Was my theater acting a confession of the constant state of feeling of my life as an act?" The old questions of identity surfaced with that, the idea of a life more substantial on the other side of the act – and with it the familiar implication of a lie intrinsic to the act of acting, the source of dramatic tension in classical theater, and of much, it could be said, of what happens in *Hamlet*. What Gray is rehearsing is also like a recapitulation of Stanislavski's modification of his method, away from the deciphered psychology of character toward a method of physical actions. For him, however, "The conflict between acting (active interpretation) and non-acting (just doing the actions) created a new thesis, a new 'act.' The separation I had experienced in the theater previous to this was transformed into a kind of Gestalt. It was closer to the bone. It was the dialectic between my life and theater rather than between role and text. The 'figure' became myself in the theater and the ground was the contingency of everyday time out of which this timeless, and therefore 'saved,' figure grew" ("3 Places" 33).

There are obvious therapeutic resonances in this account, as in the *Rhode Island Trilogy* itself, with its specific psychoanalytical content. The psychoanalytical component may become trickier and more self-reflexively focused in an experienced performer with the skills of an actor, which is what Gray has now become, with a lamination of celebrity besides, coming back to the theater from *Swimming to Cambodia* and his performances in other media, recordings and tapes. As for the inexperienced performer in this rather tautological circle of acting and non-acting, art and life, I want to make one more observation about the relation of theater and therapy, as if there were a spinoff from the circle, and with it a fine line between the mediated and the unmediated, though nothing like what we have seen in Wilson's collaboration with Christopher Knowles. It does have some relevance, however, to those forms of theater, more or less politicized, that came to begin with from consciousness-raising groups. Here there may be a tricky relationship between sincerity, authenticity, and the desire for power.

PROCESSING THE UNMEDIATED

Spalding Gray tells his stories and shapes them by retelling, as in the accumulating manuscript of the unfinished novel that is, in his most recent monologue, about the writing of the novel, which may be thought of as the text of the always-to-be-finished monologue itself – at which he has become so practiced over the years that everything he experiences seems to be spontaneously absorbed into it. That others who don't quite know what to do with their experience may become adept at processing what appeared, perhaps, as involuntary memory and unmediated emotion, I became especially aware of years ago – not only in the training of actors, but in workshops that I would give at various theater departments or gestalt institutes when consciousness-raising was in vogue.

One might see the same person in successive workshops, first struggling with the elements of what may have been deeply repressed, maybe even mortified to let it come out, then with growing confidence telling the same real life story that was so well and sympathetically received the first time round. In that "supportive" atmosphere – with embraces and hugs, and confirmation that the worst you can think of yourself had happened to others as well – it was told again and again, shaped up according to reception, the laugh that came here, the tear that fell there, perhaps this incident slightly modified, another introduced that maybe never happened, or not quite like that (but if it didn't it should have), the way you might tell a dream as (you think) the analyst might like to hear it, or, with the audience in mind, might doctor a play.

There are aspects of this practice that are easy enough, as here, to satirize, but there is also sufficient evidence in the whole syndrome of therapies from Esalen to EST that the naïveté of the narrativity (maybe enforced with other measures: meditation, massage, or sound/movement exercises) "worked," though very often ironically in the grain of an older psychology. There was much talk then, as there is in theory now, of undoing the acquisitiveness of the ego, or of the various forms of becoming, not as end-in-itself, or closure of being, but a ceaseless process; yet one might see with growing confidence in the process the emergence of a sturdier ego, or sense of self, through the building of a character which didn't exist before the narrative or had to be discovered there and when it did materialize, not easily abandoned: another figure to be saved.

Callow as some of this was, or indulgent, it became the ground of any number of practices in which the personal was political, and out of it came as well a new concern with subjectivity. I wrote in an earlier chapter on developments in theater practice, particular feminist performances, that were offshoots of consciousness-raising. There was also a good deal of talk at the time about getting in touch with your feelings, as well as considerable emotional investment in what I've referred to before as the intensities and flows of a libidinal economy, or at some lubricious pitch of the ideology of desire, the epidermic play of perversity. It should be chastening to certain tendencies in postmodern thought to recall that what became laughable in time was doubly sublimated and displaced into theory, though, as I say, it didn't entirely disappear from the theater. For these things showed up, too, not only in workshop exercises, but in the stagings of various groups, and still persist in multiple venues around the country which accommodate performance art or the more way-out practices of certain standup comedians, particularly women, who are, like the late Bob Carroll, or Spalding Gray, or Eric Bogosian, drawing on personal narratives. What we see in all of this, however, is a processing of the unmediated that hasn't been able to purge itself of the problematic of identity, and which, like theory, may talk as it will of deferring meaning and resisting closure but sooner or later closes around an identifiable persona whose narrative (not to mention behavior) resembles that of an autonomous ego. Which is no less demanding if only a fiction.

Nor did it entirely discredit the process that some of the stories told either seemed to be modeled upon, or were models for, narratives we had seen or would eventually see in the media, with undiminished feeling. Whether or not, then, there is something like an inevitable circuitry of registered emotions going back through the tube to the master narratives of the movies (derived in the recessions of history from the fictions of the ancient theater), one thing seems important enough to observe: the most discontinuous manifestations of spontaneous lifelike performance – the decentered subject itself – inevitably seem haunted by the psychology it disavowed, with its facsimile of an ego and fiction of character. And with more or less emotional distress, the fiction of their dissolution.

I have commented already on the issue of emotion as inevitably attached, through the unpurged recurrences of psychological realism, to the status of character in the drama. What I want to stress again, however, is the critical bearing of emotion on the character of performance, as if emotion were the measure – how much? what kind? at what imagined distance? – of the ideological status of performance, and not merely its affective result. In my own experience with psychological method we used to say to actors

186

(directors still do) don't play the result, *play the action*, meaning the action that produces the desired emotion; but that was before, in theory, emotion vanished into desire, or with the body itself into the ideology of desire. Nevertheless, if most ideological issues begin with emotion, or become distracted by it, they are eventually returned to it in theory, which for all the vicissitudes of subjectivity in the discourse of desire seemed to siphon out emotion in the interests of critique. As the careers of Meyerhold and Brecht suggest, that is, even with distancing techniques, somewhat harder to do in theater, which seems to arise out of pain and rupture, and seems to live in division while struggling to overcome it or, in the homeopathy of a double estrangement, is divided all over by the emotion of distance itself.

But let's follow this up again by returning for a moment to the theory and practice of Meyerhold, at a time when ideology had taken over his furious passion.

SUBJECTIVITY AND STRUCTURALIST ACTIVITY

Subjectivity itself, as a kind of false consciousness, was Meyerhold's major concern in his inaugural speech to the company of the Free Theater, renamed among the objectifying acronyms of the time, RSFSR Theater No. 1. On that occasion, filled with ideological zeal, he addressed the "psychologism" of the theater and the psychological makeup of the actor, both of which were inimical to the corporate mission of the theater as the revolution was consolidating itself. In this regard, Meyerhold was less like the futurists and more like the structuralists, his other contemporaries, who wanted to avert thinking of ideology as either free-floating desire or as pure speculation (what Marx had warned against in the theses on Feuerbach) and, in the short-lived *glasnost* of the period, to avoid the dispersion of revolutionary consciousness in the arbitrariness of individual psychology. That remains the importance of structuralism's emphasis on a substratum of material existence as prior to the subject, and which – if ideology is to be free of the vices of specular consciousness – must preclude the participation of the subject in its origin. If ideology is not necessarily deceitful, falsifying reality in its representation, then what must be posited at its origin is not the subject but material reality itself.

We've had an unexpected cognate to this in the rarely theorized practice of the American experimental theater, specifically in the plays and manifestos of Richard Foreman, whose early productions felt – through the stripped-down, iterative, unemotive play of words – like a silent movie accelerating into the structuration of structure or an exacerbated version of "structuralist activity" (probably familiar to Foreman in the early Brechtian Barthes). The clockwork mechanism of Foreman's autoperformances were marked, through the incessant repetitions of the manic obsessive figures, by a dematerialized subject in a method (also indebted to Brecht) that does think of material reality at its origin. It might be, however, a headache or a bill to pay, since Foreman's materiality, like that of Gertrude Stein, is always intensely personal, individualistic, and the work idiosyncratic; in its relation to actors, even imperious. It is a work subject to the charge made by Gramsci, in his prison notebooks, against "the arbitrary elucabration[s] of particular individuals." As they first appeared before very small audiences in his loft above lower Broadway, Foreman's elucabrations were a hermetic sideshow to the main action below, spilling into the streets, where there seemed to be the prospect of another revolutionary scene.

There the problem Meyerhold was addressing came up again, with the animus against psychology and the egotism of the actor, in the participatory theater of the sixties. The animus was shared by Foreman in his manifestos, though he could pretty much ignore it in practice, since his own splitting ego took center stage as the vociferous source and associative substance of his work, while the distributed play of thought was embodied by amateurs. (When he later moved out of the loft and began to work with professional actors, it was a somewhat different story.) With the emergence of a counterculture as the matrix of performance, the ego might dissolve into a mystique, as in the Living Theater's embodiment of "polymorphous perversity" or, as it was absorbed into the theatricalization of everyday life, the participatory utopianism of Norman O. Brown. The dissolution may have been facilitated by drug culture, but with or without drugs, mantras, nudity, and occultism, there was in the theater an ideological commitment to "collective creation" and a shift away from the ego psychology in the subjectivity of the Method to ideographs of the body (surpassing in another sense: Love's Body), abstract figuration, and the entire dispensation of play: the games, images, "transformations" referred to before, denaturalizing "tasks," or quasi-ritualistic gestures borrowed from the martial arts or the stylized disciplines of eastern forms.[15]

This was eventually, as we know, not merely a phenomenon localized in America, but one of our major cultural exports as well. If we've borrowed liberally from the theater forms of India or Japan, young directors in those countries are still doing exercises developed in the studios of our alternative theater, with recycled elements of their own disciplines. The Kathakali and the Noh are still preserved, too obdurately ritualized to be infiltrated, but this is not true of other ritual forms, nor the established theaters of Europe, even including the Comédie-Française. One may see the active inheritance of the alternative tradition, with its ethos of play and impulse toward collectivity, absorbed by the authoritarian structures of the most sophisticated German theaters and *Tanztheaters*, or the powerful personalities of their major directors and choreographers, sustained by the subsidies we couldn't dream of. Thus, in Reinhild Hoffmann's choreography for *Kings and Queens*, the ensemble appeared with "silver" orbs (more like lead) with the heft of bowling balls that were rolled in various figurations over the stage, or deployed for other than kingly purposes, or kicked about in aleatory fashion, while the most imposing and solitary figure of massive royalty was revealed as a trio of male dancers (two short, one like a stilt) in a capacious transformation of the king's mantle that, dipping and tilting on its single wing, soared over the stage as a giant bird. As in the work of Pina Bausch there were impulses toward stylization even in the most obsessive compulsive emotionally charged indeterminacies, but not in any event to distance emotion; if anything, to exacerbate it. In a later sequence, however, there was the serial image of a royal marriage that in its declensions from a force of "nature" – and for all the style and preceding mythifications – reminded me of the domestic improvisations in the exercises of the Open Theater or, more exactly – with the King as a sort of biomechanical *nebbush* directed by Paul Sills – Second City.

With Meyerhold, strategies of stylization occurred early in his career, in the avoidance of psychologism never quite keeping its emotion at a distance. For like Stanislavski, whose techniques he could never entirely disavow, Meyerhold was not really liberated from the rhetoric and sentiments of European romanticism, which made it possible for him to think of a structuralist activity that burned like a fire. Both stylization and naturalism, he said, were grounded "in the heart"; and, in his conception of the Theater of the Straight Line, all technique was to vanish in that encounter with the spectator, face to face, where the actor "*freely* reveals his soul." In working through this process of revelation the question inevitably arose as to which comes first, the activity or the fire, the play of emotion or its form. In a footnote to a commentary on his work with Maeterlinck, where "the expression of the tragic sorrows of the soul" (an expression inconceivable, except with mordancy, in Brecht) was dictated by its content, Meyerhold remarked: "At the time we adopted the procedure of restraining the emotions until the form was mastered, and that still seems to me the correct order. People will object that this only leads to the form fathering the emotions. This is not so" (*Meyerhold* 52).

This is an old conflict, or conundrum, of acting that I won't rehearse any further here, that is, the question of which comes first, the emotion or its constitutive form, the objective correlative of which can be found in other doctrines of modern art, like imagism, vorticism, Hemingway's "sequence of emotion and fact," the Brechtian *gestus*, or for that matter the objective correlative itself. There are quite other purposes today in what Meyerhold called "the search for new forms," and it may seem amidst the precession of simulacra of a cybernetic age, with new technologies of the theater, anachronistic to mention it at all, no less determine the priority of feeling or form. Practitioners have their biases in this matter, as they

189

do in the relation between the body and emotion: feeling the action before doing it, or doing it so it can be felt. In Grotowski's "poor theater," for instance, the body was the datum with the physical action coming first (which was apparently true in Stanislavski's method at the end). Yet as we rediscover affect again, through the redundant distantiations of ideological critique, it may be well to remember that it never occurred to Meyerhold, nor to Grotowski later (doubly enflamed by Meyerhold and Artaud), that so far as you are doing theater there is anything more urgent than emotions at stake – even if, through the collisions and heat in Brecht, the emotions at stake are thought to get in the way.

SPONTANEOUSLY LIVED LIFE: THE MARROW'S DELICACY

In Meyerhold, for all the stylization, the psychological processes of the Moscow Art School were never forgotten: "Our teachers, the actors of the old naturalistic school, used to say: if you do not want to ruin the part, start by reading it over to yourself, and do not read it aloud until it sounds right in your heart" (55). I've been calling attention to a period when the part, and the texts themselves, seemed extraneous to the theater. But as we saw in the murderous outcome of Meyerhold's career, and his extinction for many years from the Soviet encyclopedia (he was eventually restored), the rightness of the heart was a problem, ideologically, even for one who dedicated himself so scrupulously to serving the Party. And so it remains in the spontaneously lived life of the *individual* artist – now that we're using the term again, ratified in Eastern Europe – within the spontaneously lived life that, according to Althusser, *is* ideology.

This is obviously not the conception of ideology that Vaclev Havel has in mind when, speaking of the first performance he saw by the *Semafor* theater, at a festival in Karlovy Vary, he remembers "being overwhelmed by how completely beyond everything ideological it was," and how all ideological debates in the literary magazines "were suddenly rendered ridiculous by this performance." What he admires, however, as he goes on to describe what the work of *Semafor* came to mean for his generation, is its feeling for something very much akin to the spontaneously lived life of which his generation had been deprived:

The performances were not about anything. They were just a series of songs, one after another, and the songs themselves were about nothing in particular, but it was the delight in performance, the rhythm, the pure fun, that seemed to make all those learned ideological debates seem fundamentally inappropriate, without much in common with real life. It was a manifestation of uncensored life, life that spits on all ideology and all that lofty world of babble; a life that

190

intrinsically resisted all forms of violence, all interpretations, all direc-
tives. Suddenly, against the world of appearance and interpretation,
here stood truth – the truth of young people who couldn't care less
about any of that, who wanted only to live in their own way, to dance
the way they wanted to dance, simply to be in harmony with their
own nature.

(*Disturbing* 49)

Havel has testified elsewhere that the American counterculture of the
sixties – its dissident lifestyle, dancing to its own music – was of considerable importance to him and the intellectuals of his generation. It is
apparent, moreover, from the passage above that if there were any conceptual model for the spontaneously lived life it would be closer to Bakhtin's
carnival than Althusser's ideology.

What Althusser had in mind, however, when he *identified* it with ideology
is obviously something other than an oppressive regime of thought or sticky
doxology or even, as Lukács thought of it in *History and Class Consciousness*,
the generic base of tangible struggle. Althusser was articulating his view
of ideology in relation to Freud's principle of overdetermination – with its
symbolic dimension and multiple meanings. What that brought him to is
the concept of ideology as an organically specific formation, or secretion
of representations, that is "the very element and atmosphere" indispensable
to the "historical respiration and life" of a society, without which "it can't
imagine the utopian idea of a world without ideology" (*For Marx* 232). If
this relieves ideology of its more onerous connotations, there would appear
to be no assumption, so far as I can see, that the spontaneously lived life
is exempt from contradictions.

To go back, then, to that other, less velvet revolution: if Meyerhold was
distrustful of the inner life of experienced emotions, he was certainly not
inclined to dogma either, or subservience to the commissars, though it was
hard not to take seriously the criticism of a Trotsky. If it was impossible,
then, to be indifferent to ideology, it was for Meyerhold something like
Althusser's conception, the identification of ideology with the spontaneity
of an "inner synthesis." There is an energy in that synthesis that, with
the respiration of history, must struggle to appear, before it is available
for tangible struggle. And it arises from the "hidden features" of a period
(*Meyerhold* 43n) or – revealed as it may be by whatever external gesture
or evocation – an "inner dialogue" that should be overheard, "not as
words but as pauses, not as cries but as silences" (36). Meyerhold is
speaking here with something like the "marrow's delicacy" in the mania
of Artaud, or with Rilke's fine attunement to a drop of longing in the
dialogue of Ibsen, its contoured silence, or as if (with remarkable prescience) he were describing the Beckettian resonance in the space between

191

words: "the complex inner emotions conveyed by a rustle, a pause, a break in the voice, or a tear which clouds the eye of the actor" (36).

Although Meyerhold deplored, like any artist of imaginative force, the passive experiencing of emotions that reduced the creative intensity of the performer, or the critical responsiveness of the spectator, there is a troubling subjectivity in the clouded eye of the actor that would seem to bring us, inevitably, back to psychological process, though it may go in the methods of other cultures by other names. As Brecht remarked in that early debate with Lukács, the world is not obliged to be sentimental, but because it is, or inclines to be, certain theorists and practitioners – from Kleist and Gordon Craig to Oskar Schlemmer to Wilson and Foreman and Kantor to the lesser-known Adrian Boon or Joseph Dunn or, collectively, Soon 3 – have felt obliged to use actors simply as moving vehicles of abstraction, or even not to use actors at all. Given the way of the world this may have a powerful but not enduring efficacy.

Meanwhile, the dominance of realism has been such that it's still hard to bypass the issue that, with the question of ideology, Meyerhold couldn't avoid: what to do with emotion without psychology, or the psychology worked through by Stanislavski in the mood swings of Chekov's plays? That remains an open question. So far as Chekov himself was concerned the psychology was impaired by the obtrusive naturalism and emotional excess of Stanislavki's productions. Yet the question is no less open in our theater, where we can hardly put emotion in its place, and with it subjectivity, by interdiction, structuralist activity, or any privileged technique. Nor the fiction of egoless process that postmodernism inherited from the communitarian idealism of the sixties.

THE REVERSED LENS

For Roland Barthes, the impasse of this fiction, and estranged emotion, came with the death of his mother and the writing of *Camera Lucida*. A far cry from the semiological disposition of the early Brechtianism, the insistence in the later work was on the singularity of his grief, and the privileged intentionality of emotion. Determined to be guided by what had been for theoretical purposes bracketed, deferred, defrayed, alienated – the consciousness of personal feeling – his "phenomenology agreed to compromise" with the power of *affect*. What makes it powerful is its irreducibility. So far as this book was a study of photography, he wanted affect there as well, but with an extremity of feeling out of emulsified difference: it may not have been the full-scale majestic dismemberment of the tragic *sparagmos*, but he wanted the lesion in the surface, the rip, the tear, the wound: the *punctum*.

It was, however, a daunting project, for he wondered whether he was up to the imperative of reducing the photograph to something at the furthest selvedge of the camera obscura, "a view of the object which was immediately steeped in desire, repulsion, nostalgia, euphoria" (*CL* 21). It is through such emotions that the photograph moves – as if through the reversed lens of Marx's figure of ideology – closer to theater. "We know," Barthes writes, "the original relation of theater and the cult of the Dead." That relation as origin is still being argued in the anthropology of theater, but its symbolic manifestations – "the whitened bust of the totemic theater, the man with the painted face in the Chinese theater, the rice-paste makeup of the Indian Katha-Kali, the Japanese No[h] mask" – define for him the nature of photography. All the more "in its frenzy to be lifelike," photography reveals itself as "a kind of primitive theater, a kind of *Tableau Vivant*, a figure of the motionless and made-up face beneath which we see the dead" (31-2).[16]

In Meyerhold's technical use of the stopframe, and his own affinity for the Japanese mask, there is something like this (photographic) theater of the dead. So, too, in his feeling for the decorative eloquence of the grotesque, its arresting status. But even more, there is his early desire for a "static theater" – the model of which was the suspended abstractions and silences of Maeterlinck – where he seems to be returning through the hooded backside of the camera obscura to the troubled subject at the heart of theater who/which seems to be staring into the grave. Or does the stare actually come from the grave? (I may be inordinately conscious of that possibility, here in Paris, with Beckett dead – who always suggested it – and having just seen Tadeusz Kantor's *Aujourd'hui c'est mon anniversaire*, the last rehearsal of which took place the day he died. It was customary for him to be on stage during performance, arranging props, correcting a gesture, looking grieved over the impossibility of ever telling it all. But his Theater of the Dead continues, at least for now, with a surrogate figure in his place, as if he were somehow observing from the grave.) This leaves us, however, as death invariably does, with the recurring question of authentic emotion, distressed perhaps by stylization, but not necessarily abolished from a work that "justifies its existence if it springs from an inner necessity" (*Meyerhold* 171). The material nature of this inner necessity must be forever ideologically suspect, as are the properties of emotion itself, whether as affective intentionality or the claims of the heart, inevitably swayed by insufficiency, or – as Yeats would have it in the ritual delirium of his born-again drama – *excess*.

I suggested earlier that, for all the wariness of an ideological disposition, there remained in my own sense of performance an unpurged affinity for the claims of the heart: "Go to your bosom,/Knock there, and ask your heart what it doth know" (*MM* 2.2.136-7). There may be, as with Isabella petitioning Angelo, an element of self-deception in the purest of hearts, and which of us wouldn't blush to claim that for our own. Yet if we can barely remember a lost innocence because it maybe never was, there may also be the moment when – as Meyerhold wanted it in the theater, or Artaud, or even Brecht – the passion burns you like a fire and, bereft of reason, you can almost make the claim. To be sure, it's only the moment, but it's surely the moment we want in the theater. I take for granted in all this that if the heart has reasons that reason doesn't know they are not infallibly the best of reasons. Which is why, as I suggested earlier, we may have to run an ideological check. There is a point at which one understands only too well that the claims of the heart are not to be construed, as they are *not* in *Measure for Measure*, as if they were exempt from the claims of ideology, even at the place where prayers cross. No matter. The vanity of our frailty occurs as it does for Angelo when the word of the law, or the correctness of our politics, is once again, as ever, baffled by desire.

GHOSTING: AN INTERIOR DISTANCE

This is not, then, a recidivist longing for what Barthes, in his demythicizing phase, had once called "the romantic heart of things." It is, rather, a response to the specific promptings of a felt interior. The notion of such an interior may be scanned with a jaundiced eye, and the promptings explained in ideological terms, but they came here, as to the opening pages of this book, from long experience in the theater itself: a concrete praxis, gradually theorized, but invariably tested by the always surprising, immensely rewarding, if often unsettling work with actors. There was always a certain ambivalence in this work, to which I've pointed now and then, as to the ideological critique of the social institution within which it occurred. I have worked with actors who would seem to be models of what the critique is about, bourgeois actors with predictable reflexes, but this is not necessarily a function of reputation or method, and actors in offbeat theaters a thousand miles from Broadway can be as predictable as any. I have known remarkable actors over the full spectrum of our theater, but the ambivalence remained even when the work moved quite radically to the margins in its most experimental forms, and with actors whom I had trained myself. I have also pointed to the tendency – not wholly theorized, but a correlative of the critique – to displace the actor in favor of the performer, whether in the theater or with indifference to the theater, in the theatricalization of the other arts. Yet it was next to impossible to work with actors – regardless of their methodological bias – and believe as you might do with steel or paint or plastic or videotape, or even the more clinically disposed bodies of body art, that the materials of art are mute or neutral, with an entirely unquestioning surface and no recessive depth.

I know that this reliance on my experience in the arguments over surface and depth can still be considered theoretically unsound, but there are times at the limit of difference when still another experience comes to mind:

194

I was standing beside the most esteemed theorist of theater technology in the country at what was then the most advanced lighting switchboard in the world. After many years of thinking about it, he had the chance to design and build it. It was during the dress rehearsal of a production I was directing, the board was state of the art, but when the lights were dimmed out they always kept "ghosting," that is, there was always in blackout a residue of light. I would point to it, and he would not see it. Or refuse to see it. He would explain, moreover, why it couldn't be so. I won't invoke other witnesses who saw what I saw, because they may have been seeing unsoundly with similarly untutored eyes. Let us call it a critical standoff: the light was minimal, crepuscular, but I believe what I saw, though it was surely not what I wanted to see. With the actor, however, it was precisely that element of ghostliness, inexplicable, that always seemed to me, beyond any other conviction in the acting, the actor's wisdom, a residue of light, what s/he knew without knowing it that no one else did. I looked for it, I always looked for it, though I was never quite sure where it came from, or if it would come at all. Nor, indeed, did the actor, who might have been troubled by that as well, as something recessive or inaccessible, and certainly not ideologically accountable, even if the actor wished.

Which is to say that, for the actor, the malediction of an interior distance, a humanized substance at the uncertain core of things, is unavoidable, whatever the ideologized proscription against it, and despite the actor's own assent. There may be reason for the proscription that may in practice move a performance toward a more useful and critical objectivity; yet when the actor looks askance it is more often than not to find a way *in*, and I'm not convinced at all, having worked with and observed actors from other cultures, that this is true only of actors in the West, and mainly those emburdened by naturalistic method. The world is made of the substance of the performer. I'm not sure that's really true, but I'm reasonably sure that at the empyrean of performance the best actors believe it, again regardless of the disposition of method. (It is a belief, by the way, which the traditions of the East have no trouble with at all. Thinking of particular actors, I've already referred to Duse as a virtual index of that idea. You'd expect assent here from, say, Marlon Brando, but it seemed to me markedly true of someone who thought of himself as a political actor, Ekkehard Schall at the height of his powers with the Berliner Ensemble, when he was performing Arturo Ui, or later Coriolanus.) So far as the actor's power is in the lure or the quest or the necessity of otherness, s/he is committed to what Robbe-Grillet disdained as a "*traged-ified* universe," and to the final recuperation of "all failures, of all solitudes, of all contradictions" (*New Novel* 67). It may be deluded, but it is an undeniably moving mission. Of course, whatever the resources of the actor,

195

whatever endowments of memory or desire, s/he is bound to lose, which is doubly tragic.

As for what that *means*, what can it mean except that the loss is utterly palpable, and yet the meaning hidden, as if it were buried in the heart of the world. In the heartless way of the world it may very well be that there is nothing whatever hidden, no meaning but the world, which taunts us with its appearance. But if so, what is the meaning of our persistence in questioning behind it or beyond it, whether or not with an impulse toward transcendence? Which may be, in this late phase of advanced capitalism, no more than what moved Jean-François Lyotard through Marx and Freud and Heidegger back to Kant, and the perhaps impossible articulation of something imbedded that was maybe once but probably never transcendent, which he describes as a materialist sublime. To call it delusion is too facile. The persistence is as natural as breathing (which is not to launch a full-scale argument for the "human nature" that has also been demythologized). At the extremes of demystification we are still suffused with appearance, as if demystification itself were producing appearance, with no solution yet to that contradiction. Or to the possibility that the mystifications are themselves a mystery – not their accretions, as from an economic base, but what causes them to accrete whatever the base.

SURPLUS VALUE: NOTHING *BUT* . . .

It may seem absurd to talk of the heart as having an economic base, without invalidating the claims of the heart, but that was just about accomplished, if not by Marx, by Dostoyevsky – perhaps the profoundest dramatist of the nineteenth century – when he opened the great metaphysical inquisition of *The Brothers Karamazov* with 1,800 rubles concealed on Mitya's chest. It's as if he were literalizing Shakespeare's proposition: go to your bosom, knock there . . . the passionate Mitya virtually knocks, as if at the nurturing bosom of ideology itself. It may seem even more anomalous to pursue the epistemology of the heart in the context of classical Marxist thought, but what we've learned from that other great figure of the nineteenth century, as in other ways from Freud, is that what is seen on the surface as *real* is not only different from but the reverse of concealed essential relations and, as Marx points out in *Capital*, the conception which corresponds to them. This involves the double inversion I mentioned earlier (in connection with the camera obscura): the "real" one at the level of essence accounting for the inversion experienced, because produced, at the level of appearances. The reproductive process of the bourgeois mode of production not only inverts, like the image on the retina, but imprints the inversion on consciousness, which remains attached as ideological consciousness to the appearances that disguise the inverted social relations.

Ideology, then, is neither an invention nor a negation of reality. "Yet the ideological representation is not," as Jorge Larrain observes, "an immanent attribute of reality which deceives a passive consciousness, but the projection into consciousness of petrified appearances produced by men's practice. Ideology negates the inverted character of social relations; it takes an aspect of reality, the appearances, and gives them an autonomy and independence which they do not actually have. In this sense ideology fetishizes the world of appearances, separates it from its real connections" (*Concept* 58). Since Brecht, we have tried in the theater to become conscious of the real connections, but to the extent that theater also fetishizes the world of appearances – an unavoidable aspect of what it is, even when not disguising but specifically conscious of what it is – it is nothing but ideology.

To the extent that it is nothing *but*, and therefore sponsors illusion, the theater is the practice that is, and will forever be, a failure of practice. For Marx, that is what ideology is: a distorted solution in the mind to contradictions unresolvable in practice, including the contradiction which is *theater*, the nothing that comes of nothing, which is also a projection in consciousness of *practical* inabilities. The greatest drama is a discouraging record of such inabilities, though it has taken over the centuries a remarkable histrionic competence to keep that record, which in the inversions of performance is equally remarkable for its ability to be inspiriting. There is another peculiarly negative capability in theater: one may perform in fantasy what cannot be accomplished in practice, as actors can be what they couldn't dream of being in life, and be that too with incredible spontaneity, as if it were in fact a spontaneously lived life. Although this image of ideology has been ideologically opposed, it is also possible in performance to negate and conceal the contradictions by which it is made, resuscitating on an imaginary plane a coherence not sustainable, or in any way materializable, off the stage or outside the perimeters of performance. One might also perform in fantasy, as in tragedy, *conscious* fantasy, what *might* be accomplished in practice if such fantasy didn't prevail, in its *image* of powerlessness, to make us powerless. Amidst the complexities and contradictions of these possibilities, arising from its (inevitable) failure as a practice, the theater remains self-conscious about being theater, which perhaps wouldn't be true if it hadn't failed.

That it has always been self-conscious in this way seems to be part of what it is, *even before* the specific (or supplementary) consciousness urged upon us by the historicizing theory of Brecht. To repeat: all one has to do is to read through the canonical drama, as the historical textualization of performance, to feel the almost unabating intensity with which the theater has always questioned what it fetishizes, distrusting the very appearances from which it is made. There are periods and forms of theater which, in turn, have attempted to mitigate or minimize the distrust, which is only to say, as Brecht and Artaud have said, that they betray the theater as well, though there may be something like an urge to betrayal at the very heart of theater. Or, as the theater suggests, at the very heart of things.

This is one of the mystifications that may remain a mystery. As disturbing to the theater as the possibility that there is no hidden meaning but the world is the equal and opposite possibility that there is nothing but hidden meaning, and the additional possibility – also recorded in tragic drama – that the meaning may not be so good. If we are somehow empowered to act against it that may or may not be spurred on, or only provisionally so, by any particular method or strategy. It does seem to me, however, to be inseparable from the persistent questioning that may, with empathy or alienation, have brought us to that impasse: beyond, behind, or where we were to begin with, precisely where we are. If all of this reasoning is circular, that's no doubt because it has to do with the theater, more theater, less theater, which is inescapably tautological. But no sooner do we think of it, *because we think* (nothing either good or bad but thinking makes it so), the same appears to be true of the world. Whether there is any margin for doubt – about the impasse, about the mutable glass of the theater of the world – has to do with what, and how, we think of the world. The world may be mirrored or made out of language for all we know, though nowadays it seems as if that is all we know.

Whatever the case may be (for Wittgenstein, the world is all that is the case) the play of appearances can hardly be denied. To all appearances there *is* an abstract world in our heads, there *is* illusion in our hearts, there *is* a concrete world out there, and they continue to inform and rehearse each other, despite the intensified historical pressure of recurring exorcisms. I have said that the persisting ideological problem is the incessant struggle over the future of illusion, and that's because the most ingenious deconstruction or stringent materialism contains the fatty tissue of surplus value which is, with its temporal index, always a matter of appearance. If, then, my intention here has not been – while asserting that ideology suffuses and is suffused with theatrical fact – to advance an ideological position, what I have been suggesting is that in the approach to meaning any such position is necessarily an illusion. What else would anybody think after spending so many years aging in the theater, where one fears, like Lear trying to undo the button, not being in one's perfect mind.

Here, unquestionably, the distressed emotion is mine. What I have been trying to do, so far as I can grasp my intention, is to open up a discourse that may have been active elsewhere but has been virtually absent, until recently, from the American theater. (Some preliminary versions of these ideas have helped, I think, to get things started among younger theorists, but there is still a large culture gap between theory and practice.) That

THE STRUGGLE TO APPEAR

in itself is probably something like an ideological position, which amounts to saying that so long as we are in the theater there is some point in improving the quality of our illusions, out of which – if I can believe the theater – the theater seems to be made: a somewhat utopian illusion on which I will stand my ground.

NOTES

1 STATUTES OF LIMITATIONS

1 Bertolt Brecht, "Alienation Effects in Chinese Acting," *Brecht on Theater*, trans. John Willett (New York: Hill & Wang, 1964) 94; this volume will be abbreviated hereafter as *Brecht*.

2 Stuart Hall, "The Toad in the Garden: Thatcherism among the Theorists," *Marxism and the Interpretation of Culture*, ed. and intro. Cary Nelson and Lawrence Grossberg (Urbana, Ill.: University of Illinois Press, 1988) 35.

3 Terry Eagleton, *Criticism and Ideology: A Study in Marxist Literary Theory* (London: NLB/Verso, 1976) 95–6. Eagleton is quite aware of the undergrowth of value, largely concealed, which determines what we think of as fact, but he is not particularly concerned with the void that cannot be explained, nor the merger of ideology with the structure of the unconscious. He is more likely to be attentive to that aspect of ideology in which what we say and think is linked to the structure and relations of power, invariably the form of power that reproduces itself. (For Eagleton that power is preeminently bourgeois, though one may wonder whether there is any form of power that doesn't, so far as it can, reproduce itself.) Within this conception of the ideological we are meant to realize that local and individual, subjective variations of perception occur as effects of history and socially conditioned or structured ways of perceiving. I will, of course, be talking of ideology in this sense as well.

4 Louis Althusser, *Lenin and Philosophy and Other Essays*, trans. Ben Brewster (New York: Monthly Review Press, 1971) 161; abbreviated hereafter as *Lenin*.

5 Jean Baptiste Poquelin de Molière, *The Misanthrope* (and *Tartuffe*), trans. Richard Wilbur (New York: Harcourt Brace, 1965) 117.

6 What was powerful in *The German Ideology* was the negative concept of the ideological, the imputation of an inversion of consciousness that, "so long as it remains unrecognized," as Engels said, "forms what we call *ideological outlook*" (quoted by Jorge Larrain, *The Concept of Ideology* (Athens, Ga.: University of Georgia Press, 1979) 76, abbreviated hereafter as *Concept*). In this concept the base/superstructure formulation is no guide to inverted or non-inverted forms of consciousness. For Marx, the ideological always involved a distortion in favor of the dominant class, no matter what class. The implication was, too, that some intellectual production could escape the ideological. Not so with Lenin, and later Lukács and Gramsci, in whose thought ideologies were distinguished by class as expressive of particular interests, but thereby detached from the concept of a necessary inversion, the ideology of the proletariat being

200

preferred on the grounds of truth or cognitive validity, as against the distortions of bourgeois ideology.

7 Sometimes ideology is taken to mean all forms of consciousness as biased – theoretical predilections, structures of belief, mental representations – usually with a partisan objective, whether open or veiled, although the more sinister aspect of the ideological is associated with what in expressed conviction presents itself as objective or is merely disguised. The ideological is what, presumably, gets in the way of seeing reality "as it is," though what it is is invariably – in the other meaning of ideology – the result of ideological difference. Depending on the degree of consciousness in its disguises, ideology consists of illusions and other distorted sediments that belong to what Marx considered an *idealistic* (he rarely or never spoke of an *ideological*) *superstructure*, reflecting the social contradictions it conceals. Consciousness may historically outlast the contradictions, but ideology exists only in their reproduction, and not without them. According to Marx, ideology manifests itself as the effort to sustain the legitimacy of a mode of production when it is about to disappear. There is no basis for ideology when contradictions in social reality are not yet tangible but only latent. When, however, contradictions surface and intensify until they are almost intolerable, ideology grasps at straws, for it is an aspect of ideological consciousness (not the whole of it) to grow hysterical or hypocritical when it has no grounds at all. Whether or not ideological consciousness always, at some level, disguises the truth from itself remains an issue. But then, the same might be asked of any form of consciousness.

8 The concept of the inversion was developed by Marx from *The German Ideology* through the *Grundrisse* into *Capital*. It was constantly being reworked, but it was the specific analysis of social relations and relations of production that led him to believe that what appeared to be a distortion of reality by ideas, so that reality seemed inverted, came about rather because reality *is* inverted. He was eventually convinced, moreover, that what mediates between inverted consciousness and the inverted reality is a system of appearances which is a projection of the system of circulation and exchange.

9 Jacques Lacan, *Écrits: A Selection*, ed. Jacques Alain-Miller, trans. Alan Sheridan (New York: Norton, 1977) 236–7.

10 Jacques Derrida, "Violence and Metaphysics: An Essay on the Thought of Emmanuel Levinas," *Writing and Difference*, trans. and intro. Alan Bass (Chicago: University of Chicago Press, 1978) 80; abbreviated hereafter as *W&D*.

11 Louis Althusser, *For Marx*, trans. Ben Brewster (London: NLB/Verso, 1977) 150.

12 Charles Olson, *Charles Olson and Ezra Pound: An Encounter at St. Elizabeth's*, ed. Catherine Seelye (New York: Viking, 1975) 53.

13 Antonio Gramsci, *Selections from Cultural Writings*, ed. David Forgacs and Geoffrey Nowell-Smith, trans. William Boelhower (Cambridge, Mass.: Harvard University Press, 1985) 51.

14 Fredric Jameson, *The Political Unconscious: Narrative as a Socially Symbolic Act* (Ithaca, N.Y.: Cornell University Press, 1981) 9.

15 Gramsci is perhaps the paragon of Marxist thinkers who at some limit of their identification with the masses – as what he called "organic intellectuals" or "collective individuals" – can't quite manage their aversion to the cultural expression of the underclass and, against ideological commitment, turn out to be organic elitists. While he anticipated the ideological analysis of mass culture by the questions he asked of popular novels, there is a reflexive distaste for any expressive form, whatever its origins in the lower classes, if it is inimical

201

to the growth of rational and analytical powers. Thus his aversion to the "grafting of Asiatic idolatry onto the stock of European Christianity," and even more to the fanatic addiction to Negro music, its incessant repetitions, that cannot be without ideological effects. As he hears it, the effects are bound to be deleterious, especially for the young (*Letters from Prison*, ed. and trans. Lynne Lawner (New York: Harper & Row, 1973) 122–3).

16 Guy Debord, *Society of the Spectacle* (Detroit, Mich.: Black & Red, 1983) note 34.

17 The touchstone of a debate on this issue was Michael Fried's essay "Art and Objecthood," first published in *Artforum* (June 1967) and reprinted in *Minimal Art: A Critical Anthology*, ed. Gregory Battock (New York: Dutton, 1968) 116–47. For a sample of the ongoing debate, see the section on "Theories of Art after Minimalism and Pop," in *Discussions in Contemporary Culture*, no. 1, ed. Hal Foster (Seattle, Wash.: Bay Press, 1987) 55–87.

18 Rainer Maria Rilke, *The Notebooks of Malte Laurids Brigge*, trans. M. D. Herter Norton (New York: Norton, 1964) 196–7.

19 Quoted in *Libération* 25 July 1990: 16; my translation.

20 Jacques Lacan, *The Four Fundamental Concepts of Psychoanalysis*, ed. Jacques-Alain Miller, trans. Alan Sheridan (New York: Norton, 1978) 129–30.

21 Samuel Beckett, *Endgame* (New York: Grove, 1958) 1.

22 Which is not to say that the insistence *achieves* an absolute music, even when Beckett directed. Does such music require the most dutiful of actors? Billie Whitelaw could perform in and for Beckett with an accomplishment that outdid unquestioning acquiescence – letting him hear for her – but there are other actors who might do better if they trusted their own ears. Now, of course, there's no alternative.

23 " . . . not dead yet, yes, dead, good, imagination dead imagine" (Samuel Beckett, *Imagination Dead Imagine*, in *First Love and Other Shorts* (New York: Grove, 1974) 63).

24 See the chapter "Origin of the Species," in Herbert Blau, *Take Up the Bodies: Theater at the Vanishing Point* (Urbana, Ill.: University of Illinois Press, 1982) 78–144.

25 Walter Benjamin, *Illuminations*, ed. and intro. Hannah Arendt, trans. Harry Zohn (New York: Schocken, 1969) 257.

26 *The Marx–Engels Reader*, ed. Robert C. Tucker (New York: Norton, 1978) 143; abbreviated hereafter as *Marx–Engels*.

27 What Brecht says here of practice was suggested by my colleague Roswitha Mueller, in *Bertolt Brecht and the Theory of Media* (Lincoln, Nebr.: University of Nebraska Press, 1989) 20, though I've quoted an additional sentence and the translation differs. The passage occurs in the long chapter on film, including *The Threepenny Opera* trial, in Brecht's *Gesammelte Werke*, vol. 18 (Frankfurt: Suhrkamp, 1967) 193.

28 Karl Marx and Friedrich Engels, *The German Ideology*, ed. C. Arthur (London: Lawrence & Wishart, 1970) 54.

29 Sophocles, *Oedipus at Colonus*, ll. 1135–7, trans. Robert Fitzgerald, *Greek Tragedies: volume 3,* ed. David Grene and Richmond Lattimore (Chicago: University of Chicago Press, 1960) 162.

30 Jerzy Grotowski, interviewed by Richard Schechner, "Third Theater," *Village Voice* 1 May 1984: 103.

31 See the opening chapters of *The Impossible Theater: A Manifesto* (New York: Macmillan, 1964).

32 See chapter 2 of Blau, *Take Up the Bodies* 29–77, entitled "The Power Structure."

33 These remarks on Fugard's play, and the ideological shift from outcast status

to international eminence, were prompted by Jeanne Colleran of John Carroll University. Her concern for the problematic politics of Fugard, and the ways in which performance may ratify ideology, are aspects of a book on his work, now in progress.

34 Quoted in *Libération* 26/7 January 1991: 38; my translation.

35 The phrase is Eric Bentley's, from a note to me after the collapse of the DDR.

36 Even revisionist Marxists, amidst the debris of history and the recurring evidence of historical failures, including Marxism itself, will hesitate to acknowledge illusion (or use the word) while speaking of the utopian. This is particularly marked in the conclusion of Jameson's *The Political Unconscious* 298–9.

37 Derrida, "Structure, Sign and Play in the Discourse of the Human Sciences," *W&D* 279–80.

38 Lawrence Grossman, "Putting the Pop Back into Postmodernism," in *Universal Abandon*, ed. Andrew Ross (New York/London: Routledge, 1988) 181.

39 See the chapter with that title in Havel, *Disturbing the Peace: A Conversation with Karel Hvížďala*, trans. and intro. Paul Wilson (New York: Knopf, 1990); abbreviated hereafter as *Disturbing*.

40 Anders Stephenson and Daniela Salvioni, "A Short Interview with Dario Fo," *Social Text* 16 (1986/7): 167.

41 Alfred de Musset, *Lorenzaccio* (act 5, scene 2), trans. Renaud C. Bruce, in *The Modern Theatre: volume 6*, ed. Eric Bentley (New York: Doubleday/Anchor, 1960) 88.

42 John Jesurun, an interview with Michael Feingold, "Pulling the Image Apart," *Village Voice* 11 February 1986: 49.

43 Antonio Gramsci, *Selections from the Prison Notebooks*, ed. and trans. Quintin Hoare and Geoffrey Nowell Smith (New York: International Publishers, 1971) 168.

2 THE THEATRICAL FACT

1 An important figure, obviously, in the move toward signifying practice was Michel Foucault, who understood with considerable subtlety both the desire to banish representation and the inability to function in thought without some residual space of representation, which also serves in the archaeology of thought to keep the severely questionable notion of human nature alive: "if we follow," he wrote, "the archaeological network that provides classical thought with its laws, we see quite clearly that human nature resides in that narrow overlap of representation which permits it to represent itself to itself (all human nature is there: just enough outside representation for it to present itself again, in the blank space that separates the presence of representation and the 're-' of its repetition); and that nature is nothing but the impalpable confusion within representation that makes the resemblance there perceptible before the order of identities is visible" (*The Order of Things: An Archaeology of the Human Sciences* (New York: Vintage, 1973) 71; this volume will be abbreviated hereafter as *Order*).

2 The move toward professionalism is also true of the use of technology in performance, which has had to be rationalized if not theorized. In this respect, the success of Laurie Anderson has raised a pivotal question in performance art, aside from the discomfiting issue of the success itself, which is being rationalized by theorists of mass culture. What I am referring to, however, is the allover technical excellence, and the resources that go with it, which were in the marginal years of performance art – in the galleries, lofts, and storefronts

of the seventies – a sign of ideological privilege, if not conceptual emptiness. Here the issue was drawn within the artistic community itself, before Anderson achieved a wider popularity. When she started her work in performance, it was politically advisable to disguise her natural gifts and/or cultivated abilities in the mode of the amateur, a strategy she eventually abandoned as a deceit, accepting the artist's power to seduce and control, as well as the long-enduring desire, repressed in modernism as a matter of principle, to connect with a larger audience in a more acceptably public space. What we have in Anderson's performances now is not only a new economics, underwriting the technology, but something of an old-fashioned stage show with avant-garde content, designed for a mediatized era where everybody mixes the media, even in the bourgeois living room. When, in an earlier piece, she wore a T-shirt with the inscription TALK NORMAL, she was suggesting what is reality principle for most of the present generation of performers (there are still primitivists among them), that a voice modified or synthesized by high tech is no longer out of this world, but something like second nature. And to prove that it is not ideologically embarrassing, with all the amplifiers up at once.

3 This is a concept developed in my work with KRAKEN (see Herbert Blau, *Take Up the Bodies: Theater at the Vanishing Point* (Urbana, Ill.: University of Illinois Press, 1982) 116).

4 Harold Pinter, intro. to *Complete Works: Four* (New York: Grove, 1981) x; subsequent quotations from Pinter will be from this volume, abbreviated hereafter as *Works*. The prize was awarded in 1970.

5 Antonin Artaud, *The Theater and Its Double*, trans. Mary Caroline Richards (New York: Grove, 1958) 51; abbreviated hereafter as *T&D*.

6 Samuel Beckett, *What Where*, in *Collected Shorter Plays* (London: Faber & Faber, 1984) 316. Further references to Beckett's shorter plays will be from this volume, abbreviated hereafter as *Shorter Plays*.

7 Roland Barthes, *Critical Essays*, trans. Richard Howard (Evanston, Ill.: Northwestern University Press, 1972) 73. A quarter of a century ago I wrote similarly about the American scene, in Herbert Blau, *The Impossible Theater: A Manifesto* (New York: Macmillan, 1964), and that book is still capable of producing rage. Subsequent references to Barthes' *Critical Essays* will be abbreviated in the text as *CE*.

8 Walter Benjamin, *Understanding Brecht*, trans. Anna Bostock, intro. Stanley Mitchell (London: NLB/Verso, 1983) 11.

9 To the degree that the audience sees itself *as mirrored*, it succumbs to the lure of emulation, that relation which, as Foucault describes its operation in the classical order, frees similitude from "the law of place" so that it is able to function, "without motion, from a distance." In this accord across space, matter and spirit reflecting each other, things may also imitate each other "from one end of the universe to the other without connection or proximity: by duplicating itself in a mirror the world abolishes the distance proper to it; in this way it overcomes the place allotted to each thing." Foucault doesn't speak of it thus, but the place allotted to each thing, particularly the human being, was known in Greek thought as *Moira*, and there is a sense in which emulation in the drama, gathered into catharsis, did try to overcome, or at least emotionally relieve, that originary image of fate derived from the strict and deadly limits of tribal law. In the diaspora of modern life we are more likely to ask, as Foucault does in his following sentence: "But which of these reflections coursing through space are the original images?" (*Order* 19).

10 Cornelius Castoriades, *L'Institution imaginaire de la société* (Paris: Seuil, 1975) 203.

11 In the age of simulacra and recombinant DNA, symptoms of the overdose, ideology would appear to be a function of confused signals or mere seduction, both of which lead, as in other dangerous liaisons, to no semantic conclusion. Once we move beyond the mirror of production, we are no longer talking of false consciousness, no less systematic doctrine, but something like an instantaneous incursion of flashbulbs, like some inverted or spastic radiance from the camera obscura, the bright obscure, all the film exposed and doubly obscure. What this amounts to, as Arthur Kroker and David Cook suggest, upping the ante on Baudrillard, is a kind of baffled illumination or "seduction by a skeptical freedom," with ideological discourse promising "the return of *vertical* being; the recovery, that is, of a real difference between the centripetal (dispersion) and the centrifugal (immanence) tendencies in experience" (*The Postmodern Scene: Excremental Culture and Hyper-Aesthetics* [New York: St Martin's, 1986] 89). I'm not sure that's what is being promised, but as it is more than can be delivered, the skeptical freedom may turn in its dream of power into a fantasy of transgression. As seen by Kroker and Cook, postmodern ideology "is a parody on the high seriousness of the 'flash'. . . . This would also suggest that the only serious 'ideology' today is parody" (90). Or – to carry this mode of thought to its hyperconclusion – that the inclination to parody, if not ideology itself, is bankrupt.

12 Fredric Jameson, "Architecture and the Critique of Ideology," in *The Ideologies of Theory, Essays 1971–86*, vol. 2: *The Syntax of History* (Minneapolis, Minn.: University of Minnesota Press, 1988) 45.

13 Walter Benjamin, *Origin of German Tragic Drama*, trans. John Osborne, intro. George Steiner (London: NLB/Verso, 1977) 84; abbreviated hereafter as *Origin*.

14 Students for a Democratic Society.

15 Dick Hebdige, *Subculture: The Meaning of Style* (New York: Methuen, 1979).

16 Roland Barthes, "*Le Balcon*. Mise en scène de Peter Brook au Théâtre du Gymnase," *Obliques* 2 (1972): 38.

17 Roland Barthes, "Diderot, Brecht, Eisenstein," in *Image-Music-Text*, trans. Stephen Heath (New York: Hill & Wang, 1977) 73. The term was borrowed by Barthes from Lessing's *Laocoön*. This volume by Barthes will be abbreviated hereafter as *I-M-T*.

18 "Objects have no future," wrote Sartre, "while the future surrounds faces like a muff" ("Faces, Preceded by Official Portraits," trans. Anne P. Jones, *Essays in Phenomenology*, ed. Maurice Natanson (The Hague: Martinus Nijhoff, 1966) 162).

19 Karen Finley, *The Constant State of Desire*, in *The Drama Review: A Journal of Performance Studies* 32.1 (1988): 140.

20 Jean Baudrillard, "Fetishism and Ideology: The Semiological Reduction," in *For a Critique of the Political Economy of the Sign*, trans. Charles Levin (St Louis, Missouri: Telos, 1981) 92.

21 We mostly forget, nor did anyone mention during the Iran-Contra hearings, that it was Kissinger who was charged to do that.

22 Friedrich Nietzsche, "On Truth and Lie in an Extra-Moral Sense," in *The Portable Nietzsche*, trans. Walter Kaufmann (New York: Viking, 1954) 46–7.

23 Richard Nelson, "Non-Profit Theater in America: Where We Are," *Performing Arts Journal* 19 (1983): 87–93; and "Polite Cruelty: The Future of the Non-Profit Theater in American Society," *PAJ* 21 (1983): 49–59.

24 Louis Althusser, "The 'Piccolo Teatro': Bertolazzi and Brecht," in *For Marx*, trans. Ben Brewster (London: NLB/Verso, 1977).

25 August Strindberg, *Five Plays*, trans. and intro. Harry G. Carlson (New York: Signet, 1984) 57.

26 Jean-Pierre Vernant, "Greek Tragedy: Problems of Interpretation," in *The Languages of Criticism and the Sciences of Man*, ed. Richard Macksey and Eugenio Donato (Baltimore, Md.: Johns Hopkins University Press, 1970) 278.

27 Pierre Bourdieu, *Outline of a Theory of Practice*, trans. Richard Nice (Cambridge: Cambridge University Press, 1977) 72.

28 Roland Barthes, *Roland Barthes by Roland Barthes*, trans. Richard Howard (New York: Hill & Wang, 1977) 81.

29 See Bert O. States, *Great Reckonings in Little Rooms: On the Phenomenology of the Theater* (Berkeley, CA: University of California Press, 1985) chapter 1.

3 THE SURPASSING BODY

1 Leon Trotsky, *Literature and Revolution*, trans. Rose Strunsky (Ann Arbor, Mich.: University of Michigan Press, 1960) 159; this volume will be abbreviated hereafter as *L&R*.

2 The term is used by Foucault in his essay "Theatrum Philosophicum" to describe "the absence of God and the epidermic play of perversity" in the metaphysics of Deleuze (Michel Foucault, *Language, Counter-Memory, Practice: Selected Essays and Interviews*, ed. Donald F. Bouchard, trans. Donald F. Bouchard and Sherry Simon (Ithaca, N.Y.: Cornell University Press, 1977) 171–2; abbreviated hereafter as *LCP*). Since it concerns itself with phantasms it is a metaphysics that is, like the operations of the unconscious, theatrical.

3 Étienne Balibar, "The Vacillation of Ideology," *Marxism and the Interpretation of Culture*, ed. and intro. Cary Nelson and Lawrence Grossberg (Urbana, Ill.: University of Illinois Press, 1988) 188.

4 Jean Genet, *The Balcony*, trans. Bernard Frechtman (New York: Grove, 1960) 59.

5 Jean Baudrillard, *In the Shadow of the Silent Majorities . . . or the End of the Social*, trans. Paul Foss, Paul Patton, and John Johnston (New York: Semiotext[e], 1983) 98; abbreviated hereafter as *SM*.

6 Sam Shepard, *The Tooth of Crime and Geography of a Horse Dreamer* (New York: Grove, 1974) 16.

7 See, e.g., Andrew Ross, "The Rock 'n' Roll Ghost," *October* 50 (1989): 108–17.

8 Vaclav Havel, quoted in *The New York Times* 29 November 1989: 1.

9 See Gilles Deleuze and Félix Guattari, *Anti-Oedipus: Capitalism and Schizophrenia*, trans. Robert Hurley, Mark Seem, and Helen R. Lane (New York: Viking, 1977) 19.

10 See Gilles Deleuze and Félix Guattari, *A Thousand Plateaus: Capitalism and Schizophrenia*, trans. and foreword Brian Massumi (Minneapolis, Minn.: University of Minnesota Press, 1987); abbreviated hereafter as *Plateaus*.

11 Jean-Paul Sartre, *Being and Nothingness: An Essay on Phenomenological Ontology*, trans. Hazel E. Barnes (New York: Philosophical Library, 1956) 326.

12 Roland Barthes, *The Grain of the Voice: Interviews 1962–80*, trans. Linda Coverdale (New York: Hill & Wang, 1985) 365.

13 Mikhail Bakhtin, *Rabelais and His World*, trans. Helene Iswolsky (Cambridge, Mass.: MIT Press, 1968) 26.

14 See Jean-Pierre Vernant, "Dim Body, Dazzling Body," *Fragments for a History of the Human Body: Part 1*, ed. Michel Feher, Ramona Naddoff, and Nadia Tazi, in *Zone* 3 (1989): 21.

15 Heiner Müller, *Hamletmachine and Other Texts for the Stage*, ed. and trans. Carl

Weber (New York: PAJ Publications, 1984) 53; abbreviated hereafter as *Hamlet-machine*. Further references to Müller's plays will be from this volume.

16 Julia Kristeva, *Powers of Horror: An Essay on Abjection*, trans. Leon S. Roudiez (New York: Columbia University Press, 1982) 3; abbreviated hereafter as *Powers*.

17 Bertolt Brecht, *Baal*, trans. William E. Smith and Ralph Mannheim, vol. 1 of *Collected Plays* (New York: Vintage, 1971) 57.

18 Bertolt Brecht, *In the Jungle of Cities*, trans. Gerhard Nellhaus, vol. 1, *Plays* 130.

19 Quoted by Carl Weber in the prefatory note to *Quartet*, in *Hamletmachine* 105.

20 Josette Féral, "Performance and Theatricality: The Subject Demystified," trans. Terese Lyons, *Modern Drama* 25.1 (1982): 172–3.

21 Whether conceptual or expressive, in body art the concealed mechanism of previous art – the muscular output or labor that produces the work – moved to the forefront. With the body as ground upon which meaning is declared, what was the hidden instrument of art became the acknowledged object, acting and being acted upon. The artist's body is a palimpsest: in a more or less erotic register, it records the material force of the artistic act. If there were psychic and even moral complexities that had to do with self-inflicted pain, it was also possible to see it in another dimension: imagine the explosive calligraphy of an action painting inscribed in the human organism or, as if reversed on film, sucked up into the body – sometimes with such intensity as to dissever the body parts. More on body art later in this chapter.

22 Michel Foucault, *History of Sexuality: An Introduction*, trans. David Hurley (New York: Pantheon, 1976) 157.

23 National Endowment for the Arts.

24 See Sue-Ellen Case, "Towards a Butch-Femme Aesthetic," in *Discourse* 11.1 (1988/9): 55–73; for commentary on a specific lesbian theater event, see Kate Davy, "Reading Past the Heterosexual Imperative: *Dress Suits to Hire*," *The Drama Review* 33.1 (1989): 153–70.

25 It was more the literalization of a transformative desire than a totally sympathetic response to this condition that caused Vito Acconci, in a year's interval during the early seventies, to abuse himself in an experiment with gender called *Conversions*. What he did was to burn the hair from his chest, squeeze his nipples so that they would appear to be female, and hide his penis between his legs while training his body to carry out familiar activities. When he finally conceded his failure, it was with a reversion rather than a last conversion, a reassertion of phallic authority, in which he made his penis disappear into the mouth of a young woman kneeling below the space in which he "performed."

26 Holly Hughes, "Dress Suits to Hire," in *The Drama Review* 33.1 (1989): 133.

27 Annie Sprinkle, interviewed by Linda Montano, "Summer Saint Camp 1987: With Annie Sprinkle and Veronica Vera," *The Drama Review* 33.1 (1989): 98.

28 Heinrich von Kleist, "On the Puppet Theater," *An Abyss Deep Enough: Letters with a Selection of Essays and Anecdotes*, ed. and trans. Philip B. Miller (New York: Dutton, 1982) 214.

29 See Nina Auerbach, *Ellen Terry: Player in Her Time* (New York: Norton, 1987).

30 Tadeusz Kantor, "The Theater of Death (1975)," *The Drama Review* 30.3 (1986): 137–8.

31 In a book in progress, *Feminist Stagings*, Elin Diamond suggests that in picking up the language and medical models of the female hysteric, realism catches her disease.

32 William Butler Yeats, *The Collected Plays of W. B. Yeats* (New York: Macmillan, 1953) 439.

33 Jean Genet, *The Screens*, trans. Bernard Frechtman (New York: Grove, 1962) 18.

34 Roland Barthes, *The Pleasure of the Text*, trans. Richard Miller (New York: Hill & Wang, 1975) 29.

35 Quoted by Jacques Derrida, "La parole soufflée," *Writing and Difference*, trans. and intro. Alan Bass (Chicago: University of Chicago Press, 1978) 180; abbreviated as *W&D*.

36 Samuel Beckett, *Not I*, in *Collected Shorter Plays* (London: Faber & Faber, 1984) 222; abbreviated as *Shorter Plays*.

37 Franz Kafka, *In the Penal Colony*, in *The Penal Colony: Stories and Short Pieces*, trans. Willa and Edwin Muir (New York: Schocken, 1976) 200; emphasis mine.

38 See Beckett's *Footfalls*, in *Shorter Plays*.

39 See Michael Gill, *Images of the Body* (London: Bodley Head, 1989).

40 See George Lichtheim, *The Concept of Ideology and Other Essays* (New York: Vintage, 1967) 7–8.

41 Georg Büchner, *Complete Plays and Prose*, trans. and intro. Carl Richard Mueller (New York: Hill & Wang, 1963) 47: act 3, scene 3 (no line numbers).

42 See *The Audience* (Baltimore, Md.: Johns Hopkins University Press, 1990) 280–8.

43 Jane Comfort, quoted in Deborah Jowitt, "Talk to Me," *Village Voice* 19 April 1989, Dance Special: 9.

44 Paul de Man, *Allegories of Reading: Figural Language in Rousseau, Nietzsche, Rilke, and Proust* (New Haven, Conn.: Yale University Press, 1979) 11–12.

45 Roland Barthes, *Roland Barthes by Roland Barthes*, trans. Richard Howard (New York: Hill & Wang, 1977) 60–1.

46 Francis Barker, *The Tremulous Private Body: Essays in Subjection* (London: Methuen, 1984) 12.

47 Valie Export, "The Real and Its Double: The Body," *Discourse* 11.1 (1988/9): 5.

48 The latter resemble the French theorists whose "tropes of proximity" have been looked at askance by American feminists (see, e.g., Mary Ann Doane, *The Desire to Desire: The Woman's Film of the 1940s* (Bloomington, Ind.: Indiana University Press, 1987) 12). The masquerading body is something else again, with variations in the repertoire not at all denying itself access to the symbolic.

49 Luce Irigaray, *Speculum of the Other Woman*, trans. Gillian C. Gill (Ithaca, N.Y.: Cornell University Press, 1985) 247.

50 Hélène Cixous, "Aller à la mer," trans. Barbara Kerslake, *Modern Drama* 27.4 (1984): 546.

51 Jean-François Lyotard, "The Tooth, the Palm," *Sub-Stance* 15 (1977): 105.

52 Jerzy Grotowski, *Towards a Poor Theater*, trans. T. K. Wiewloroski (Holstebro, Denmark: Odin Teatrets Forlag, 1968) 16.

53 Samuel Beckett, *Worstward Ho* (New York: Grove, 1983) 7.

54 Michel Foucault, *The Foucault Reader*, ed. Paul Rabinow (New York: Pantheon, 1988) 173.

55 Roland Barthes, "Lesson in Writing," in *Image-Music-Text*, trans. Stephen Heath (New York: Hill & Wang, 1977) 171; abbreviated as *I-M-T*.

56 Laurie Anderson, "From *Americans on the Move*," *October* 8 (1979): 54–5.

57 Charles Olson, *Additional Prose: A Bibliography on America, Proprioception, and Other Notes and Essays*, ed. George F. Butterick (Bolinas, CA: Four Seasons, 1974) 17.

58 For an intelligently skeptical view of various aspects of body art, from its ephemerality to its morality, particularly that of Chris Burden, see Max Kozloff, "Pygmalion Reversed," *Artforum* 14 (1975): 30–7.

59 Bertolt Brecht, "On the Formalistic Character of the Theory of Realism," in

Aesthetics and Politics, ed. Ronald Taylor (London: NLB/Verso, 1977) 73; abbreviated hereafter as *A&P*.

4 DISTRESSED EMOTION

1 See *Meyerhold on Theater*, trans. and ed. Edward Braun (New York: Hill & Wang, 1969) 170; this volume will be abbreviated hereafter as *Meyerhold*.

2 In describing the condition indispensable to the binary organization of the sign, Foucault writes: "An idea can be the sign of another, not only because a bond of representation can be established between them, but also because this representation can always be represented within the idea that is representing. Or again, because representation in its peculiar essence is always perpendicular to itself: it is at the same time *indication* and *appearance*; a relation to an object and a manifestation of itself" (The *Order of Things: An Archaeology of the Human Sciences* (New York: Vintage, 1973) 65).

3 While I am emphasizing here the sort of intuitional acting that seems to bypass technique in favor of experience – or improvisational access to emotional depth – this is not to underestimate the degree to which it may also come from an experienced relation to technique itself. This can use further comment. An experienced actor knows there are misguided notions about improvisation, where what appears to be open-ended is very much overdetermined and the effects of spontaneity arise more often than not from the exhaustion of cliché. Not only are there different kinds of improvisation, but so far as there is anything like a politics in improvisational technique, it is more like the practice of Derridean "reinscription." Meanwhile, what we often tend to discount, in the desire for spontaneity, is the accretion of experience which is the *worldliness* of the actor. By this I do not mean a mere sophistication of behavior, but rather the actor's being in the world, the actual presence of a historical creature, bringing to any occasion of performance, with or without narrative, the considered substance of a particular life.

4 Samuel Beckett, *The Lost Ones* (New York: Grove, 1972) 30.

5 Radically in Artaud – and later Grotowski and the Living Theater – we are made aware of the affinity between acting technique and spiritual disciplines, but we tend to forget that the masters of psychological realism were also attentive to those disciplines, their psychophysical exercises and meditative states. They may have been put off at some apotheosis of ablution by the burning away of affections and the organic impediment of the body itself, but both Stanislavski and Michael Chekov studied yoga, and those who have any experience with devotional techniques, from the exercises of St Ignatius to certain martial arts, will have found cognates there to the sense and emotional memory of naturalistic acting.

6 Karl Marx, *The Early Texts*, ed. David McLellan (London: Oxford University Press, 1971) 152.

7 Maurice Merleau-Ponty, *The Phenomenology of Perception*, trans. Colin Smith (London: Routledge & Kegan Paul, 1965) 27.

8 See Allen Weiss, *The Aesthetics of Excess* (Albany, N.Y.: SUNY Press, 1989) xi.

9 Antonio Gramsci, *Avanti* 3 October 1917, in *Selections from Cultural Writings*, ed. David Forgacs and Geoffrey Nowell-Smith, trans. William Boelhower (Cambridge, Mass.: Harvard University Press, 1985) 67–8.

10 Sigmund Freud, "The Psychogenesis of a Case of Homosexuality in a Woman," *The Standard Edition of the Complete Psychological Works of Sigmund Freud*, ed. and

trans. James Strachey, 24 vols (London: Hogarth & Institute of Psychoanalysis, 1953–74) vol. 18: 160.

11 On this recycling process, see Philip Auslander, "Going with the Flow: Performance Art and Mass Culture," *The Drama Review* 33.2 (1989): 119–36.

12 Another point of corrosive concord: in the *Communist Manifesto* and other writings Marx rejects any millennial socialist schemes or communist utopias as mere dogmatic abstraction; while there are visionary aspects to the drama of Ibsen, one can hardly dream of his buying into any kind of utopian scheme.

13 This is precisely what troubled Peter Szondi: the truth of interiority whose traumatic effect was to divest Ibsen's drama of the presence that, according to Szondi's strict definition, the form requires. He sees the analytical technique as a necessity for material that in its estranging depths is more appropriate to the novel, without acknowledging in the accuracy of his description a far more critical and radical form than his own epistemology could support. See Peter Szondi, *Theory of the Modern Drama*, ed. and trans. Michael Hays, foreword Jochen Schulte-Sasse (Minneapolis, Minn.: University of Minnesota Press, 1987) 16.

14 Here there may still be, more than residually, a desire for the unmediated, with the self shadowing itself in the breach between being and becoming, where an identity is hollowed out in the procession of empty signifiers, aspiring to an imaginary unity that, as it is made of disappearance, performance invariably denies. In that regard, the self *is* transformation, a processual manifestation vanishing into itself. The risk is narcissism, which is, however, a potential reservoir of social energy when it sees itself in the other across the alienating difference that appears to be a void. If the actor is the embodiment of the nothing that is by virtue of what it is not, there is in the acting which is sufficiently *felt* – asserting the semblance of an identity across manifest division – something like the empathic duplicity of a metaphoric leap.

15 Stephen Greenblatt, *Renaissance Self-Fashioning: From More to Shakespeare* (Chicago: University of Chicago Press, 1980) 227.

16 In the sphere of moral sentiments, as defined by Adam Smith, sympathy is also more complicated than we might think: it does not merely enter consciousness, but imagining itself there, experiences the sentiments of another, as an actor does with character, but also with the spectator. As Jean-Pierre Dupuy has remarked, "He imagines himself in the place of the spectator imagining *himself* in his own place.... Sympathy is in the end a form of imitation or contagion of sentiments, but contrary to what the theatrical metaphor suggests, it is not the spectator who imitates the actor, but the actor who imitates the spectator" ("Deconstruction and the Liberal Order," trans. Mark Anspach, *Sub-Stance* 62/3 (1990): 116–17). What this suggests, in short, is that sympathy requires a double act of imagination.

17 Patrice Pavis, *Languages of the Stage: Essays in the Semiology of the Theater* (New York: PAJ Publications, 1982) 86.

18 On the first page of Adam Smith's *The Theory of Moral Sentiments* there is, as David Marshall has pointed out, a realization that, since we have no immediate experience of what others feel, no less their sentiments in a seizure of pain, "acts of sympathy are structured by theatrical dynamics that . . . depend on people's ability to represent themselves as tableaux, spectacles, and texts before others" (*The Surprising Effects of Sympathy: Marivaux, Diderot, Rousseau, and Mary Shelley* (Chicago: University of Chicago Press, 1988) 5). The importance of the tableau moves, as we know, in a continuum of theatrical consciousness up through Meyerhold and Eisenstein to Brecht, who in 1937 had the idea of

founding a society named after Diderot (see Roland Barthes, *Image-Music-Text*, trans. Stephen Heath (New York: Hill & Wang, 1977) 78; abbreviated as *I-M-T*). There is, to be sure, evidence in Diderot, and even in Marivaux, that the notion of sympathy was at times invested with the power to annul both distance and difference, but the conditions and effects of sympathy are throughout the century the object of both dramatic and philosophical investigation.

19 Jean Genet, *The Blacks: A Clown Show*, trans. Bernard Frechtman (New York: Grove, 1960) 18.

20 Roland Barthes, *Camera Lucida: Reflections on Photography*, trans. Richard Howard (New York: Hill & Wang, 1981) 8; abbreviated hereafter as *CL*.

21 Among the few exceptions is Johannes Birringer, in an essay focused on Heiner Müller, but taking up the collaborations with Wilson, " 'Medea' – Landscapes Beyond History," *New German Critique* 50 (1990): 85–112.

22 The production of *Ulrike Meinhof* that I saw was done at the Berlin Festival just about a month and a half after the collapse of the Wall. With the swift passage of history the ideological passion of the Baader–Meinhof group was hardly a matter of legendary urgency to the audience, mostly young, media-struck, indifferent to history, and mostly caught up, it seemed to me, in the profuse theatricality of the staging, its visual sensation, breathless energy, robotic images, and mass cultural elements, like the choreographed gorging of fast food at the opening, and the frenzy of its vomiting.

23 For the war machine, see Gilles Deleuze and Félix Guattari, *A Thousand Plateaus: Capitalism and Schizophrenia*, trans. and foreward Brian Massumi (Minneapolis, Minn.: University of Minnesota Press, 1987) 400; abbreviated as *Plateaus*. This notion seems to have been developed, by the way, in a sort of postMarxist counterpoint to the European Economic Community as a "deterritorialized" form of alternative politics.

24 "The Thought of Performance: Value, Vanishing, Dream, and Brain Damage," *Blooded Thought* (New York: PAJ Publications, 1982) 43–6.

25 Françoise Bataillon, intro. to *Françoise Quardon*, trans. Anne-Yvonne Le Guillon (Paris: Galerie Praz/Delavallade, 1990) n.p.

26 This was, of course, doubly interesting at the time because of *Crooked Eclipses*, the work I had developed with the KRAKEN group some years before (see Herbert Blau, *Take Up the Bodies*: *Theater at the Vanishing Point* (Urbana, Ill.: University of Illinois Press, 1982) 90–1).

5 THE STRUGGLE TO APPEAR

1 Fredric Jameson, *Signatures of the Visible* (New York/London: Routledge, 1990) 1.

2 James Joyce, *Finnegans Wake* (New York: Viking, 1955) 3. The circulatory process in Wilson is something else again, however, from the visceral economy of Joyce and, as we see it in the opening of *Ulysses*, its intestinal materiality.

3 Ernesto Laclau and Chantal Mouffe, *Hegemony and Socialist Strategy: Toward a Radical Democratic Politics* (London: Verso, 1985) 3; this will be abbreviated hereafter as *Hegemony*.

4 Fredric Jameson, "Postmodernism, or the Cultural Logic of Late Capitalism," *New Left Review* 146 (1984): 60.

5 Alain Robbe-Grillet, *For a New Novel: Essays on Fiction* (New York: Grove, 1965) 18–19; abbreviated hereafter as *New Novel*.

6 Virginia Woolf, *The Waves* (London: Hogarth, 1963) 112.

7 Robert Smithson, *The Writings of Robert Smithson*, ed. Nancy Holt, intro. Philip

Leider (New York: New York University Press, 1979) 96; abbreviated hereafter as *Writings*.

8 Andrzej Wajda, quoted in *International Herald-Tribune* 3 May 1989: 8.

9 *The Choephoroe* ("Libation Bearers") was eventually added to the other plays, but the point being made here is unchanged: the sacrifice of Iphigeneia, merely narrated by Aeschylus but dramatized by Euripides, is the datum. The full body of pathos is required.

10 Here an important distinction might be made – as we think of emotions conflated with signs, as with no other life but its outward show – between the mere vertiginous replication of the visual, that is the ven(ere)al image which is the spectacle, and the discrete substance of the image which even as a vortex is not a passing fancy; and even in its passing is not a simulation, fetish of the lost object that, in Baudrillard's terms, becomes the hyperreal.

11 But what, one imagines, if there were no heat anymore? This is essentially what Robert Smithson was imagining as a preface to minimalism, whose structures had some influence upon or affinities with Wilson's. Smithson points out how the urban sprawl and architecture of entropy have brought about a renewal of Malevich's non-objective world, where likenesses of reality or idealized images have disappeared, however, into an industrial waste land, or into cities whose null structures and surfaces perform no natural function. With perception deprived of action and reaction, it's as if the conditions for classical dramaturgy have been extruded. On devastated ground, there is one saving grace: "the clarity of surface-structures increases. This is evident in art when all representations pass into oblivion." Into oblivion they have not entirely passed, nor has minimalism passed from the scene. We have had a return in art to a new figuration and representational images, though the question is whether, as with Wilson's stagings of dramatic texts, these are more than surfaces as conceived in the ethos above. As Smithson is rehearsing the crystalline structures and surfaces of minimalist art, he realizes that its reductions are not escape hatches, and that "beyond the barrier, there are only more barriers: Insley's 'Night Wall' is both a grid and a blockade; . . . Flavin's fluorescent lights all but prevent prolonged viewing; ultimately, there is nothing to see. Judd turns the logic of set theory into block-like facades. These facades hide nothing but the wall they hang on" (*Writings* 12–13). There is something prophetic here, given our recent political experience of the apparent collapse or opening of walls. It is, in any event, the wall they hang on (to) that is the unabolishable subject of the drama, and hovering about that wall is, if not the ghost of depth, a tremulous shadow, the shadow of a shadow, whose name is *ideology*.

12 Christine Dakin, quoted in *The New York Times* 21 October 1989: 13.

13 William Carlos Williams, *Paterson* (New York: New Directions, 1963) 11.

14 Spalding Gray, "About *3 Places in Rhode Island*," *The Drama Review* 23.1 (1979): 32; abbreviated hereafter as "3 Places."

15 Along with the collective impetus, all of this was designed to prevail not only against the ego but the fallacy of the actor's "presence" (further mystified by Stanislavski in its fusion with "charm," a property just about as elusive in the actor as it became with particles in subatomic physics). There might be a certain force or energy in the performer, but the expectation of presence was an impediment to the purely structured reality being claimed for the other arts. Where it didn't move in a mystical direction, acting came under the spell of the same phenomenological impulse that moved through minimalist art, which had to begin with a more intimate relation with dance. Within this dispensation of thought, there was a certain protocol for the actor, with a critique of the

psychologized theater: the actor does not reenact events, s/he does tasks; the actor does not perform symbolic acts, s/he does things with things. S/he does not question things because things do not and cannot answer. Properly considered, the actor is no more than a thing among things, as s/he appeared to be in a Foreman play. Once the idea of the signification of things is abandoned, along with the bourgeois pathos over "man's" distance from things – which is what we mean by alienation – the abyss disappears, communion disappears, and tragedy disappears, along with its false conquest of the illusory abyss. The abyss has been rejected, as Benjamin did on behalf of Brecht in his description of epic theater – though unlike minimalism, he puts a dais in its place, so that the theater can be a tribunal.

16 There is also the relation between the photograph and the ritual feast that became, in its prosaic debasement, what Brecht called the culinary – an idea anticipated by Ibsen in the minor characters at Werle's party in the first act of *The Wild Duck*. They are not only a surrogate chorus of inadequate elders but a projection on stage of that aspect of the bourgeois audience which, in the age of photography, was soon to consume and deaden experience. "It's so good for the digestion," says the Fat Guest, "to sit and look at pictures." To which the Bald-Headed Guest responds: "And then it always adds a morsel to the entertainment, you know." By this time they are already sated with Werle's food. "Where the larder's superior," says the Fat Guest, "*that* is pure joy" (Henrik Ibsen, *Four Major Plays*, trans. and foreword Rolf Fjelde (New York: NAL/Signet, 1965) 126-7). Which, to be sure, is not Barthes' *jouissance*.

Index

214